Sei Solo: Symbolum?

Sei Solo: Symbolum?

The Theology of J. S. Bach's Solo Violin Works

Benjamin Shute

PICKWICK *Publications* • Eugene, Oregon

SEI SOLO: SYMBOLUM?
The Theology of J. S. Bach's Solo Violin Works

Pickwick Publications
An Imprint of Wipf and Stock Publishers
199 W. 8th Ave., Suite 3
Eugene, OR 97401

www.wipfandstock.com

PAPERBACK ISBN: 978-1-4982-3941-7
HARDCOVER ISBN: 978-1-4982-3943-1
EBOOK ISBN: 978-1-4982-3942-4

Cataloguing-in-Publication data:

Names: Shute, Benjamin.

Title: Sei Solo : Symbolum? : the theology of J. S. Bach's solo violin works / Benjamin Shute.

Description: Eugene, OR: Pickwick Publications | Includes bibliographical references and indexes.

Identifiers: ISBN 978-1-4982-3941-7 (PAPERBACK) | ISBN 978-1-4982-3943-1 (HARDCOVER) | 978-1-4982-3942-4 (EBOOK)

Subjects: LCSH: Bach, Johann Sebastian, 1685–1750—Criticism and interpretation. | Bach, Johann Sebastian, 1685–1750—Religion.

Classification: LCC ML410 B1 S 2016 (PRINT) | LCC ML410 (EBOOK)

Manufactured in the U.S.A. 06/14/16

Sei Solo à Violino senza Basso accompagnato
Libro Primo
da Joh. Seb. Bach
ao. 1720

BWV 1001: Sonata 1ma (G minor)

1. Adagio
2. Fuga
3. Siciliana
4. Presto

BWV 1002: Partia 1ma (B minor)

1. Allemanda—Double
2. Corrente—Double
3. Sarabande—Double
4. Tempo di Borea—Double

BWV 1003: Sonata 2da (A minor)

1. Grave
2. Fuga
3. Andante
4. Allegro

BWV 1004: Partia 2da (D minor)

1. Allemanda
2. Corrente
3. Sarabanda
4. Giga
5. Ciaccona

BWV 1005: Sonata 3za (C major)

1. Adagio
2. Fuga
3. Largo
4. Allegro aßai

BWV 1006: Partia 3za (E major)

1. Preludio
2. Loure
3. Gavotte en Rondeaux
4. Menuet 1re & Menuet 2de
5. Bourée
6. Gigue

Contents

Preface

In the context of the music of J. S. Bach, the Latin word *symbolum* carries two principal meanings. First, it can mean a symbol or representation, as in two of Bach's canons that bear the inscriptions "*Symbolum.* Christus Coronabit Crucigeros" ("Symbol: Christ will crown those who carry the cross") and "*Symbolum.* Omnia tunc bona, clausula quando bona est" ("Symbol: All is then well that ends well").[1] The second meaning of *symbolum* is "creed," as in the *Symbolum Nicenum* or Nicene Creed. The title of this study refers to its central question: Is it possible that Bach uses musical devices in his collection of unaccompanied violin works, the *Sei Solo,* to symbolize his devoutly held Lutheran faith, thus making it something of a confession or creed in tones?

This study will propose that Bach's solo violin works do indeed contain a theological dimension that unfolds according to the Biblical Christ-narrative. And I should be very clear from the outset that this idea is not new; neither are several elements of the basic outline I will propose, namely, that the nativity of Christ is represented in first sonata in G minor while the juxtaposed D-minor partia and C-major sonata are the locus of passion-resurrection imagery. These ideas have long been hovering, so to speak, in the collective musical consciousness, and variants of them have been prominently articulated in recent years by musicians including Paul Galbraith and Helga Thoene. What has not yet appeared, however, is a defensible demonstration of the likelihood that Bach did (or did not) conceive the *Sei Solo* to contain this hypothesized dimension of theological allegory. For instance, most arguments proposing the theological dimension have fallen into one of two categories: on one hand, those that use logically or musicologically indefensible methods, often numerological (see Appendix A); and on the other hand, those that rest primarily on interpretation of the music's emotional content, which may be valid but which nonetheless falls outside the more "scientific" sphere of musicology. Consequently, the idea of the Christ-story embedded in the *Sei Solo* has assumed the quality

1. The former is BWV 1077, and the music of the latter is lost.

of a myth that can be neither confirmed nor dispelled, being just plausible enough to seem credible but not concrete enough to be demonstrated in any meaningful way.

For this reason, I have been inclined to approach the idea of spiritual signification in Bach's solo violin works with a degree of skepticism, and indeed it is not without considerable self-consciousness that I publish my observations on a subject that many have already (and, I submit, prematurely) relegated to the sphere of musicological pulp fiction. I must clearly emphasize that my starting point for the present study has not been a desire to seek the rumored spiritual symbolism of Bach's violin works, much less a resolve to discover it. After all, it is easy enough to discover evidence for a foregone conclusion—and in most cases to persuade a few others along the way. Rather, as a violinist regularly engaging these works over a number of years, I began noticing that prominent or unusual musical elements within the six solos create complex yet elegant parallels with the theological views we know Bach held, by means of methods resembling those abundantly found in his vocal works. Pursuing this further led me to an understanding of Bach's solo violin works as containing a degree of theological representation that I have not commonly observed in his other instrumental music, which is to say, if my methodology could detect the same significances in any work or collection to which I turned my gaze, I would have to be most suspicious of it.

Presenting the results of my inquiry into Bach's violin works has been the reason for this study, and therefore I must emphasize that it is primarily a work of musicology, not of theology. In other words, my intent has been to reference the theological considerations that appear relevant to Bach's solo violin works, not to use Bach's violin works as a springboard for a comprehensive and systematic study of his theological milieu. Naturally, the broader subject matter of the present study could furnish material for a volume far more substantial than this; but my goal has been to streamline the discussion as much as possible without compromising the depth necessary to lay as solid a foundation as I am able for my premise.

A few brief comments may be in order about some of my material and its presentation. It is, of course, essential that any proposition of theological signification in Bach proceed with an awareness of Bach's own theological outlook, as best it can be determined. But, having situated Bach as an Orthodox Lutheran who appears to have been sympathetic to the devotional emphasis of Pietism,[2] I have not found it necessary for the purposes of this study to dwell on the various and already well-documented sectarian cross-currents of his day. Indeed, the often-striking parallels I observe between

2. See Holborn, "Bach and Pietism"; and Leaver, "Bach and Pietism."

music and theology in Bach's collection of solo violin works pertain considerably to mainstays of historic Christian theology shared not only between Orthodoxy and Pietism but also between Lutheranism and other branches of Reformation theology, even between Protestantism and Roman Catholicism.[3] The reason may simply be that complex ideas relating to the order of salvation, the nature and proper structure of the church, the role of the sacraments, and so forth—that is, the issues separating various branches of Christianity in Bach's day—are generally less amenable to discernable representation in purely instrumental music. In any case, what will be explored in the following study is a Christ-themed allegory that, although interpreted (to the best of my ability) through the lens of Bach's Lutheran theological context, nonetheless evinces something like what Jaroslav Pelikan calls "the evangelical Catholicity that marked his entire life-work,"[4] focusing on the gospel of redemption through the death and resurrection of Christ.[5]

Because this gospel is called the "good news" in Greek (εὐαγγέλιον, *euangélion*), I have approached it as such in the study that follows, seeing no reason either to project a cynical tone or to obscure what eighteenth-century Lutheranism, in common with historic Christianity, understood to be its essential message by dwelling on secondary matters as though they were primary. But I feel constrained to add that my reasons for wanting to accurately convey this gospel (as understood by Lutheranism) in content, emphasis, and tone also prohibit me from wishing to portray any of the persons relevant to this study in a way that is less than historically faithful. I am

3. I say this with no intention of minimizing the very real differences between these various branches of Christianity, nor of implying that these differences were not imbued with a great deal of importance by theologians across the spectrum.

4. Pelikan, *Bach among the Theologians*, 127.

5. Concerning Bach's understanding of the centrality of this essential gospel message, it is notable that he substantively underlines the portion of commentary on Romans 1:7 in his study Bible that reads: " . . . the primary cause of blessedness [used strongly, with overtones of salvation] is God, whose word and power is the gospel, as the means of blessedness. The meritorious cause, however, is Christ; the means on our side is faith, which grasps the righteousness of Christ revealed in the gospel, to which alone faith entitles: the one that will thus be justified is a sinful person who believes on Christ. The form is the righteousness of Christ, which comes through faith alone. The final cause [that is, the purpose] is life and eternal blessedness" ("die Haupt-Ursach der Seligkeit sey Gott/ dessen Wort und Krafft ist das Evangelium/ als das Mittel der Seligkeit. Die verdienstliche Ursache aber ist Christus/ das Mittel auff unser Seiten ist der Glaube/ so die im Evangelio geoffenbahrte Gerechtigkeit Christi ergreifft/ welches allein dem Glauben zustehet: Der so gerechtfertiget wird/ ist ein sündlicher Mensch/ der da gläubet an Christum. Die Form ist die Gerechtigkeit Christi/ so uns durch den Glauben zugeeignet wird. Die Endursach ist das Leben und ewige Seligkeit." CB [see Abbreviations] 6:19.) The markings in Bach's Bible have been made available, with commentary, in Leaver, *J. S. Bach and Scripture* and Cox, *The Calov Bible of J. S. Bach*.

thinking of a certain hagiography or at least idealization that is sometimes to be found in purportedly historical writings on Christian figures that can at times involve a degree of whitewashing that is both out of step with the aims of scholarship and, perhaps more to the point in such cases, ironically at odds with the very worldview they would appear intent on flattering, since "a false balance is an abomination to the LORD, but a just weight is His delight."[6] I mention this in order to emphasize that I do not intend for anything I cite concerning the beliefs or output of Bach, Luther, or anyone else to have any ramifications for their life, character, or psychology; but I specifically want to avoid the implication (and the inference) that their adherence to the message of "the good news" suggests either the state or the status of "saintliness" as it is popularly conceived.

In this connection it is appropriate to recall what is often the elephant in the room of Lutheran theological studies, the virulent anti-Jewish sentiments that Luther expressed particularly in his later years,[7] which I mention for two reasons. First, of course, as someone presenting a study that touches substantially on Luther's teaching, I want to emphasize my own complete repudiation of and repugnance toward this most upsetting of his views, even though one would hope it would go without saying. But second, in light of the many correlations the present study notes between Lutheran theology and Biblical teachings, it seems appropriate here to voice my consternation at how a man who so insightfully exegeted Scripture and so heavily emphasized its sole authority in the formation of belief and practice could hold a view that, as far as I can see, flies so brazenly in the face of the clearest New

6. Prov 11:1.

7. Whereas the 1523 essay "That Jesus Christ was born a Jew" ("Das Jesus Christus ein geborener Jude sei," WA 11:314–36) presents a comparably favorable image of Jews, within two decades Luther had dramatically changed his tone. In the 1543 treatise "Of the Jews and their lies" ("Von den Juden und ihren Lügen," *WA* 53:412–552), Luther chillingly advocates burning their synagogues and schools, destroying their homes, confiscating their possessions, subjecting them to slave labor, and expelling them, even going so far as to write, "Thus it is also our fault that we do not strike them dead" ("So ists auch unser schuld, das wir . . . sie nicht todschlahen"). *WA* 53:522. I must add that the fact that this is enjoined in the name of avenging the innocent blood of Christ and of slain Christians ("das grosse unschüldige Blut . . . unserm Herrn und den Christen bey dreyhundert jaren . . . rechen") makes it not only horrifying but also theologically puzzling: beyond contradicting numerous Biblical statements against judging others and taking vengeance (e.g., Matt 5:38–48, 7:1–5, and 7:12; Rom 2:1 and 12:14–21; 1 Cor 4:5; and Gal 5:14 in light of Luke 10:29–37), it would appear to fly in the face of several prominent Lutheran emphases, including the culpability of all humanity in Christ's death (see ch. 6, n. 42) and, still more, the sovereign will of God in the cross of Christ, which was a central emphasis in Luther's teaching. Eric Gritsch wrestles with this troubling and perplexing inconsistency in *Martin Luther's Anti-Semitism: Against His Better Judgment.*

Testament perspectives on the subject.[8] Although Luther's anti-Jewish views appear to represent a comparatively small portion of his thought-world—a portion that does not pertain to the following study—I nonetheless recognize the disproportionate and profoundly harmful effect these views have subsequently had; and in light of that I have felt it appropriate to mention them here, if only superficially, so that their absence in the following pages will appear neither as a whitewashing of history nor as tacit consent to their equation with New Testament teachings, which in good conscience seems entirely unfounded to me. But here ends my commentary. In the pages that follow, I approach the perspectives of Bach, Luther, and Lutheranism to document rather than to evaluate as I trace the line of reasoning that makes it seem overwhelmingly likely to me that Bach's collection of solo violin works uses musical devices to represent what he appears to have believed about Christ and the hope of redemption.

To conclude, it is my sincere hope that the following study, though necessarily representing my perspective, is nonetheless responsible and credible, and that as such it might be beneficial to performers, music lovers, and students of theology and the arts while also being a constructive contribution to the ongoing scholarly discussion about Bach's processes and priorities in composing instrumental music.

8. See Matt 15:21–28; John 4:22; Rom 2:28–29, 9:1–5, 11:1 and 11–24. In my view, the only comparably strong passage that, decontextualized, could conceivably be used to support Luther's antisemitic view is 1 Thess 2:14–16; but consideration of the generally accepted Pauline authorship of the letter—and of its predating Romans and Galatians, two other generally accepted Pauline epistles in which his continued identification with the Jewish people is clearly articulated—makes an antisemitic reading far less tenable than one that understands Paul's tone as expressing frustration and sadness toward his own "brothers" (Rom 9:3; see Gal 2:15).

Acknowledgments

A project of this nature necessarily draws upon nearly every resource an author has to offer, and therefore the number of people to whom this project is indebted—people who have shaped me personally, musically, and intellectually from my youth—are too many to name and probably more than I even realize. Since this project essentially grew out of long familiarity with Bach's solo violin works as a performer, I owe a great deal to the instructors and mentors who have guided my musical development over the years, from my early studies with Kathleen Hastings, Lotus Cheng, David Brown, and Lee Snyder to the subsequent deep influences of Masuko Ushioda, Rainer Kussmaul, Lucy Chapman, Bernhard Forck, and Robert Hill. More broadly, I might also mention the music history and theory faculty of the New England Conservatory as well as the HIP department of the Hochschule für Musik und Darstellende Kunst Frankfurt am Main. In the sphere of theology, Bo Matthews, Stephen Um, and Brad Shimizu have been especially instrumental in providing a foundation from which I was able to approach this project.

I am unabashedly indebted to the many scholars upon whose research and publications this study draws, who are cited throughout following pages. I am awed and inspired by their contributions to scholarship, individually and collectively, and I hope the present essay will be an appropriate if small contribution to the conversations their work has engendered.

Behind the scenes of any scholarly endeavor are necessarily the libraries and librarians that are custodians of a scarcely imaginable wealth of historical resources. My sincerest thanks to the Bibliothèque nationale de France, the Gesellschaft der Musikfreunde in Wien, and the Stiftelsen Musikkulturens Främjande (Stockholm) for providing me with reproductions of essential source material. I am also deeply grateful to the many institutions that have digitized scores, treatises, and other historical documents for general viewing online. Without resources like Bach Digital, the Petrucci Music Library (IMSLP), Google Books, Archive.org, and the digitized collections of libraries including the Staatsbibliothek zu Berlin and the Universitäts- und Landesbibliothek Sachsen-Anhalt, it would have been prohibitively difficult, in multiple respects, for me to consult the necessary source material for this study.

Among those who contributed directly and personally to this book, I must first name Rebecca Cypess, a mentor, friend, and collaborator who has been a great encouragement over the years. She is the one who recommended I commit my thoughts on Bach's solo violin works to paper and also provided advice and feedback at multiple stages of this project despite an abundance of projects of her own. I am indebted to her as well as to Calvin Stapert, Timothy Smith, and Michael Katz for their generosity in reading and providing insightful comments on the full manuscript in its various stages. Helen Greenwald, from whom I have learned a great deal about musicological research and writing, vetted an early version of the material on BWV 1052 appearing in Appendix B, as did Matthias Truniger. Feedback from an anonymous reviewer prompted me to fully overhaul the presentation of material in this study, to its great benefit. Others who have helped to inform its various ideas include Karl Böhmer and Panagiotis Linakis. I am also grateful to my colleagues and students at Cairn University for two enjoyable years of dialoguing about Bach and theology, which has been the catalyst for several of the arguments presented in the following pages.

While these all contributed invaluably to the final form of this book, nonetheless I should be clear that its essential content, and any shortcoming therein, is entirely my own. This study is of a kind that deals more in interpretation of musical and historical data than in their discovery or compilation; and while the aim of such "interpretation" is to accurately convey the properties of the music and the likely intentions of its composer, nonetheless conclusions are inevitably drawn from the appearance of the data through the lens of my own perception, however objective I have tried to be. And therefore I take full responsibility for the interpretations put forward in this study as well as for its tone and orientation. They should not be taken to reflect those of any I have named above, though I gratefully acknowledge the vast extent to which their own perspectives and insights have helped to enrich, balance, and refine my own.

In the realm of editing and production, Thomas Finnegan provided a thorough, sensitive, and highly informative copy edit of the manuscript, and Lynette Bowring typeset the myriad and not always straightforward musical examples with care, creativity, and a healthy dose of flexibility. Both were truly a pleasure to work with. Special thanks goes also to K. C. Hanson and the wonderful team at Wipf and Stock Publishers for their helpfulness, professionalism, and good-naturedness at every phase of production—in addition, of course, to the obvious fact that this book owes its existence as such to their labors.

Closest to home is the wonderful family that I am blessed to have: my parents, Simon and Jill, whose wise and loving guidance through the years I appreciate more and more the older I become; my brother, Micah, who has helped me in various ways both to refine my own thinking and to remain conscious that the attempt to accurately distill some aspect of reality in an intellectual premise is a process requiring exploration and wrestling, in which we become staid at our own peril; and my mother-in-law ("in-law" being purely nominal), Sarah Teiler, for whose love and encouragement I am deeply grateful, not to mention her understated patience with my work on this book.

But my deepest love and gratitude go to my truly amazing wife, Anna, to whom marriage is a joy that becomes deeper and more wonderful by the day. Not only has she been a model of grace in her support of this project, coming as it did during an already taxing period marked by the exigencies of the adjunct teaching circuit; she also contributed many hours to helping me refine my ideas, providing insightful assistance with translations, and helping me copy musical examples in preparation for typesetting.

Above all, I gratefully attribute any strengths this study may have to the grace of God and only hope that I have been a good steward of his resources by using them honestly and responsibly.

Abbreviations

BD	*Bach-Dokumente*, supplement to the *Neue Bach-Ausgabe.* 7 vols. Kassel: Bärenreiter, 1968–2008
BLC	Rambach, Johann Jacob. *Betrachtung über das ganze Leiden Christi.* Jena: Hartung, 1730
BWV	Bach-Werke-Verzeichnis (List of [J. S.] Bach's Works), compiled by Wolfgang Schmieder
CB	Calov, Abraham, ed. *Die Heilige Bibel nach S. Herrn D. Martini Lutheri.* 6 vols. Wittenberg: Christian Schrödtern, 1681–82
LB	Luther-Bibel (Luther's translation of the Bible), 1545
ML	Walther, Johann Gottfried. *Musicalisches Lexicon.* Leipzig: Wolffgang Deer, 1732
NBA	*Neue Bach-Ausgabe* (New Bach Edition). Properly *Johann Sebastian Bach: Neue Ausgabe Sämtlicher Werke.* 119 vols. Kassel: Bärenreiter, 1954–2007
NBA KB	*Neue Bach-Ausgabe, Kritische Berichte* (*NBA* Critical Notes). 103 vols. Kassel: Bärenreiter, 1955–2008
NBR	Wolff, Christoph, Arthur Mendel, and Hans T. David, eds. *The New Bach Reader: A Life of Johann Sebastian Bach in Letters and Documents.* New York, Norton, 1998
SR	Strunk, Oliver, ed. *Source Readings in Music History.* Rev. ed. Leo Treitler, general ed. New York: Norton, 1998
WA	*Weimarer Ausgabe* (Weimar edition of Luther's works). Properly *D. Martin Luthers Werke: Kritische Gesamtausgabe.* 73 vols. Weimar: Böhlau, 1883–2009
WA BR	*D. Martin Luthers Werke: Kritische Gesamtausgabe. Briefwechsel.* 18 vols. Weimar: Böhlau, 1930–1985

WA TR	*D. Martin Luthers Werke: Kritische Gesamtausgabe. Tischreden.* 6 vols. Weimar: Böhlau, 1912–1921

Scripture abbreviations (sequential):

Gen	Genesis
Exod	Exodus
Lev	Leviticus
Deut	Deuteronomy
Judg	Judges
1–2 Sam	1–2 Samuel
1–2 Kgs	1–2 Kings
Neh	Nehemiah
Ps	Psalm
Prov	Proverbs
Eccl	Ecclesiastes
Isa	Isaiah
Jer	Jeremiah
Lam	Lamentations
Ezek	Ezekiel
Dan	Daniel
Mic	Micah
Nah	Nahum
Zech	Zechariah
Matt	Matthew
Rom	Romans
1–2 Cor	1–2 Corinthians
Gal	Galatians
Eph	Ephesians
Phil	Philippians
Col	Colossians
1–2 Thess	1–2 Thessalonians
1–2 Tim	1–2 Timothy
Heb	Hebrews
Jas	James
1–2 Pet	1–2 Peter
Rev	Revelation

General references: chap(s). = chapter(s); m(m). = measure(s); ms. = manuscript; n(n). = footnote(s); op. = opus; p(p). = page(s); v(v). = verse(s)

Musical instruments: b. c. = basso continuo; bsn. = bassoon; (picc.) vln. = (piccolo) violin; vla. = viola; vne. = violone

Choral parts: S = soprano; A = alto; T = tenor; B = bass

Musical pitches are specified as *C*, *c*, (middle) *c'*, *c''*, *c'''*. Specific pitches appear italicized; plain type refers to notes irrespective of octave. 8va = all'ottava (an octave above); 8vb = all'ottava bassa (an octave below).

Background

Sei Solo, somewhat mangled Italian for "six solos," is the title that Johann Sebastian Bach (1685–1750) gives to his collection of six unaccompanied violin works, consisting of three sonatas *da chiesa* and three partias of dance movements (today often called "partitas"), whose definitive source is an autograph manuscript dated 1720,[1] when Bach was employed as Kapellmeister to Prince Leopold of Anhalt-Cöthen. Little is known of the genesis of these works, and clues are scant. Although as an instrumentalist Bach was (and is) known primarily as an organist, he was also a proficient violinist whose playing from "his youth until well into the approach of old age" was described by his son Carl Philipp Emanuel as "clean" and "penetrating"[2]—though most of all he loved to play the viola, shaping the inner voice of an ensemble texture "with suitable loudness and softness."[3] In any case, it is entirely likely that the violin was in fact Bach's first instrument,[4] being the son of a town piper, Johann Ambrosius Bach, among whose multifarious musical duties playing the violin served a fundamental role. In any case, Bach's first appointment at the age of seventeen (1703), as a Lacquey in the service of Duke Johann Ernst III of Weimar, would have centered on playing the violin in the court capelle. Here and after, he would certainly have come into contact with the rich German tradition of polyphonic violin playing, both with and without basso continuo, much of the latter being improvised.[5] Most notably, he would have encountered Johann Paul von Westhoff (1656–1705), one of the leading German violinists of his day and the composer of six polyphonic suites for unaccompanied violin (published

1. *D-B Mus. ms. Bach P 967*.

2. "In seiner Jugend bis zum ziemlich herannahenden Alter spielte er die Violine rein und durchdringend . . . ." Letter from C. P. E. Bach to J. N. Forkel, December 1774, in BD III, no. 801; NBR, no. 394.

3 "mit angepaßter Stärke und Schwäche." Ibid.

4. Sackmann, "Warum komponierte Bach BWV 1001–1006?" 5.

5. Ibid., 4.

in Dresden, 1696), a likely model for the *Sei Solo*.[6] Though Bach remained in Weimar only six months, he would return in 1708 as court organist, being promoted in 1714 to Konzertmeister, where he would remain through 1717, directing the court capelle from the violin while continuing as organist—and, of course, composing cantatas and a variety of instrumental music.

We do not know exactly when Bach began composing his unaccompanied violin works, but Sackmann suggests they likely developed as material Bach would have used for his own unaccompanied violin performances, an eminently practical purpose that would likely reflect the concerns of his Weimar years.[7] Indeed, several interesting similarities between the Fuga from the G-minor solo violin sonata and another G-minor Fuga for violin and continuo (BWV 1026), surviving in a copy from ca. 1714, suggest that the origins of the two works may lie relatively close chronologically.

Although dating is necessarily speculative, Clemens Fanselau presents compelling evidence for a 1713–1714 origin of the earliest material of the *Sei Solo*—the G-minor sonata (BWV 1001) and the D-minor partia (BWV 1004)[8]—which, according to Sackmann's chronology, would leave a gap of some three years before the completion of the B-minor partia (BWV 1002) and A-minor sonata (BWV 1003) in 1717/1718, judging by stylistic properties commensurate with the time of Bach's transition from Weimar to Cöthen. Next to be completed, according to Rampe, is the E-major partia (BWV 1006), which could not have been written before 1719,[9] while the C-major sonata is, in Sackmann's view, "doubtless" the latest of the six.[10]

Complicating the picture, however, is the 1726 manuscript copied by Johann Peter Kellner,[11] which—aside from a number of evident copying errors—transmits a notably different reading of the collection, rearranging the order of the works (sonatas: g, a, C; partias: E, d), leaving out significant portions of certain movements, and altogether omitting the Allemanda and Corrente of the D-minor partia, the Loure, Menuet 2, Bourée, and Gigue of the E-major partia, and the whole of the B-minor partia. If the manuscript is simply a corrupted copy, as has often been assumed,[12] it is easy to dismiss

6. Wolff, *Bach: The Learned Musician*, 133.

7. Sackmann, "Warum komponierte Bach BWV 1001–1006?" 3, 8.

8. Fanselau, *Mehrstimmigkeit in J. S. Bachs Werken für Melodieinstrument ohne Begleitung*, cited in ibid., 4.

9. Rampe, "Virtuoses, Pädagogisches, Publiziertes: Die Klaviermusik," 761.

10. Sackmann, "Warum komponierte Bach BWV 1001–1006?" 5. He presents an overview of this chronology on pp. 4–5.

11. *D-B Mus. ms. Bach P 804*, fascicle 22.

12. See, for instance, Stinson, "J. P. Kellner's Copy of Bach's Sonatas and Partitas for Violin Solo."

the absence of the B-minor partia; but Ruth Tatlow has recently discovered that its contents exhibit tendencies toward perfect proportions that are characteristic of Bachian collections,[13] seriously raising the question of whether the five works in the Kellner manuscript may reflect an early form of the collection (pre-1720) moving toward proportional unity. If so, the omission of the B-minor partia necessarily raises the question of whether it had not yet been composed—especially since inclusion of a work in B minor would both bring the number of the collection to a "perfect" six and also complete the hexachord implied by the (reordered) pitches g—a—__—C—d—E. But then this raises the complicated question of the missing movements of the other two partias. Alternatively, we may note that the Kellner manuscript contains eighteen movements, while the number of full movements absent (excluding the subsidiary E-major Menuet 2) is half that, nine. Those movements that are included in the Kellner manuscript sometimes contain bizarre features that could suggest he was copying from a score that represented a phase in the construction of the *Sei Solo* in which Bach was in the process adding and subtracting bars to achieve the proportions he desired.[14] In that case, is there any possibility that Kellner might have been copying from a partial manuscript in which Bach had been in the process of working out proportions among eighteen movements or two thirds of the collection, perhaps simultaneously working out proportions among the remaining one-third elsewhere? Of course, this also does not rule out the possibility that Kellner could himself be responsible for some of the more musically puzzling points at which his copy differs from other manuscripts, though the reasons are unclear: the omissions (if they are omissions) do not seem to be made in the interest of technical ease; nor, honestly said, would musical interest or flow appear to be driving concerns; and I am unaware of any evidence that could indicate that Kellner himself might have been interested in the kinds of manipulations by which Bach created proportion within his compositions and collections. It may be that Kellner's manuscript is best explained by a complex combination of copying imprecisely and perhaps at times fancifully from a score that represents the solos in a phase of still-incomplete revision. In any case, until further evidence emerges that can shed further light on Kellner's sources and methods, care must be taken in assessing what implications are drawn from his copy.

This has an important bearing on the present study, which depends significantly upon the sequence of musical events spanning the entirety of the six solos. But as mentioned above, the Kellner manuscript presents the

13. Tatlow, *Bach's Numbers*, 142–45.

14. Ibid., 144.

works in a different order than they appear in the 1720 autograph, such that the observations of the present study could not meaningfully apply to their sequence. As we know nothing of the source from which Kellner was copying, we cannot be sure if or how clearly the materials from which he was working conveyed Bach's intended sequence. This is all the more so to whatever extent Kellner's source(s) might have represented only a portion of the then-current state of the collection. Even if an order were clearly indicated in this earlier source material, it is not unthinkable that Kellner, who is acknowledged to have changed details from the various sources from which he copied,[15] could have altered the sequence of works in order to conform to the way in which such collections would typically be grouped: first the sonatas together, followed by the dance-related works (suites, partitas, sonatas da camera). It would, after all, not be the only instance in which a copy of Bach's solo violin works alters their sequence. A now-inaccessible manuscript formerly recorded in Dresden,[16]which Sackmann hypothesizes might have been copied (or had its copying supervised) by none other than the renowned violinist-composer Johann Georg Pisendel, presented the six solos alternating between genres, as in the manuscript, but beginning with the partias in the following order: B-minor partia, A-minor sonata, D-minor partia, G-minor sonata, E-major partia, C-major sonata.[17]

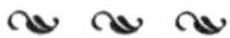

There is one final class of material to be introduced: the several transcriptions of movements of the *Sei Solo* with other instrumentations that are either verifiably by Bach or else could be or have been attributed to him. The Fuga of the G-minor sonata appears in an arrangement intabulated for lute by Johann Christian Weyrauch of Leipzig. Labeled BWV 1000, it transmits a version of the fugue that differs at several points from what is found in the *Sei Solo*. The Fuga also appears transposed in D minor for organ, also with some notable deviations from the violin version. Though labeled BWV 539, it is generally thought not to be by Bach.[18] There are also two clavier (that is,

15. Stinson, *The Bach Manuscripts of Johann Peter Kellner and his Circle*, 65. Zoltán Szabó recognizes Kellner's tampering, at least in keyboard works, even while arguing that Kellner's copies of Bach's solo violin and cello works might have more validity than previously thought ("Remaining Silhouettes of Lost Bach Manuscripts?" 77).

16. Signature *1 R/1* (formerly *Ca5*).

17. NBA KB VI/1:24. For further details on the source history of the solo violin works, see NBA KB VI/1:7–50.

18. See Williams, *The Organ Music of J. S. Bach*, 70–74.

harpsichord or clavichord) transcriptions taken from the solo violin works: the D-minor clavier sonata, BWV 964, is an adaptation of the A-minor solo violin sonata; and the G-major Adagio, BWV 968, is a reworking for keyboard of the opening movement of the C-major violin sonata. Ulrich Bartels notes that the harmonic tendencies of these two transcriptions suggest more the generation of Bach's sons than that of Bach himself, proposing Wilhelm Friedemann Bach as a probable author of both, though it is not certain that both transcriptions are by the same author.[19]

Finally, there exist two transcriptions from the E-major partia. The entire partia appears transcribed in two staves, probably for lute, as BWV 1006a; and the Preludio alone is reworked as an elaborately scored movement for obbligato organ accompanied by an orchestra of trumpets, timpani, oboes, and strings, which served as the opening sinfonia to two non-liturgical cantatas: the partially surviving wedding cantata "Herr Gott, Beherrscher aller Dinge," BWV 120a, probably dating from 1729, and "Wir danken dir, Gott," BWV 29, composed in 1731 to celebrate the inauguration of a new Leipzig city council (*Ratswechsel*).

19. NBA V/12:vii. See Eichberg, "Unechtes unter Johann Sebastian Bachs Klavierwerken," 7–49, 44; Dadelsen, Preface to *J. S. Bach: Suiten, Sonaten, Capriccios und Variationen*.

1

Introduction

It is the glory of God to conceal a matter,
But the glory of kings is to search out a matter.

—Proverbs 25:2

All art is at once surface and symbol.
Those who go beneath the surface do so at their peril.

—Oscar Wilde (Preface to *The Picture of Dorian Gray*)

It is probably safe to say that Johann Sebastian Bach has inspired more scholarship and more poetry, in the broad sense, than any other composer of the Western canon; and scholarship and poetry have each, sometimes loudly, observed the insufficiency of the other to adequately explain the phenomenon of Bach. It is therefore hardly surprising that Bach has likely also generated more musical intrigue than any other Western composer. The sense that the elemental rigors of his counterpoint, harmony, and form yield creations of remarkable scope, freedom, and expressivity has alone generated countless expressions of near-mystical wonder that would require a separate study in Bach reception to document. Undoubtedly adding to this sense of intrigue is Bach's penchant, extensively paralleled in his broader cultural milieu, for complexities beyond what meets the eye.[1]

1. Ruth Tatlow has recently published one of the most important studies to date on this subject, *Bach's Numbers: Compositional Proportion and Significance*, in which she states: "Hybrid parallel forms, including number games, word play and the permutation of numbers, characters, notes and letters, cropped up in every area of daily life in Bach's time and permeated every creative pursuit. Bach would have seen them in the construction and decoration of buildings, in literature, in poetry and imagery, and he

Among myriad examples of this are works whose musical schemas are structured according to interesting and seemingly significant mathematical proportions, collections of works whose tonal sequences create patterns that are both clear and complex, canons written in shorthand whose realization (or realizations) must be sought out by the reader,[2] and so forth. Such things lend to Bach's music the charm of buried treasure. But beyond this, there are numerous indications that Bach conceived of certain elements of a musical text as having the ability to refer to or symbolize an extramusical concept. Among these are his evident fascination with self-reference,[3] his use of various musical devices to allegorize and illustrate ideas in the texts he set, his designation of certain canons as representing ideas or proverbs,[4] and the broader philosophical view that the discipline of music can provide "insight into the depths of the wisdom of the world."[5]

If the concealed depths of Bach's music evoke the allure of buried treasure, then such suggestions of concrete referentiality could perhaps be compared to finding a map that claims to point to the treasure's location. But, as in treasure lore, such "maps" tend to be either vague or merely local, and correct identification of a site—as well as the path to get there—can be fraught with difficulty or danger and can at least be the cause of much wishful thinking. A notable example in Bach scholarship is the twentieth-century fascination with variously finding numerical sums in Bach's music that equal the alphanumeric sums of words or phrases assumed to have had significance to the composer, a practice that takes its starting point in a methodology of Friedrich Smend's that Ruth Tatlow has called into serious question.[6]

---

would have heard them in speeches and music" (36). For a broader study of the roots of signification and mystery in Bach's tradition, see Schiltz, *Music and Riddle Culture in the Renaissance*.

2. One of these, from the *Musical Offering*, bears the almost goading heading *Quaerendo invenietis*: "seek and you shall find."

3. See Tatlow, *Bach's Numbers*, 27–28, 61–72.

4. The only one to survive is BWV 1077, entitled "*Symbolum*. Christus Coronabit Crucigeros" ("Symbol: Christ will crown those who carry the cross"). Another, for which the music is lost, is titled "*Symbolum*. Omnia tunc bona, clausula quando bona est" ("Symbol: All is then well that ends well"), a motto that Bach's tradition connected with dying a "blessed death" (*seliger Lebens-Schluß*) with faith in Christ. For detailed analysis, see Chafe, "Allegorical Music: The 'Symbolism' of Tonality in the Bach Canons."

5. "Einsicht in die Tiefen der Weltweisheit." BD II, no. 441. The statement is from Johann Abraham Birnbaum's defense of Bach against the attack of Johann Adolph Scheibe. Though written by Birnbaum, it is generally agreed that Bach himself played a significant role in its formulation. See Wolff, *Johann Sebastian Bach: The Learned Musician*, 465.

6. Tatlow, *Bach and the Riddle of the Number Alphabet* (see especially her summary

Here it is prudent to address one study that generally follows Smend's methodology because it concerns Bach's solo violin works. Between 2001 and 2008, Helga Thoene published three volumes focusing respectively on the Ciaccona from the D-minor partia and the entirety of the A-minor and C-major sonatas, proposing that Bach gives each of these works definite extramusical meanings through the use of chorale melodies embedded in the musical texture and abstruse correspondences among collections of alphanumeric sums. The Ciaccona, she suggests, is best understood as a tombeau for Bach's deceased wife, Maria Barbara, while the three sonatas of the collection correspond to the three principal feasts of the church year: the first sonata in G minor to Christmas, the second in A minor to Easter, and the third in C major to Pentecost. Thoene's claims have garnered considerable attention but have yet to be substantively addressed, despite the difficulties they present. Because her methodology and conclusions differ considerably from those I will present in this study, I have seen fit to explore them in more detail in Appendix A, where I will explain my reasons for considering that the hidden chorales and numerological correlations she proposes not only are too weak to likely be more than coincidence but are moreover compositionally implausible.

What I submit is not implausible, though, is the idea that an instrumental work or collection of Bach's, like the *Sei Solo*, could contain a referential schema of the scope of what Thoene proposes. However, I suggest the most historically plausible means of creating such a schema is not the collection of alphanumeric sums or the quodlibet-type compiling of melodies with concrete associations, but rather *musical allegory*: crafting various elements of a musical work to parallel or reflect an extramusical idea or narrative, often in ways that can be experienced dynamically to a considerable degree in performance.

Such allegorical signification, even within the context of purely instrumental music, would be a reasonable outgrowth of the thought and values of early eighteenth-century Germany. In contrast to the Romantic philosophy of "art for art's sake," the general belief in Bach's cultural context was that music, by its very being, does and indeed should refer beyond itself. One consequence of this view is that texted music was seen as being superior, even in a moral sense, to untexted instrumental music by virtue of being concretely referential and thus having a greater sense of "purpose."[7] A similar emphasis is evident from the earliest days of what would come to be

on pp. 126–29).

7. See Marissen, *The Social and Religious Designs*, 8, 118–19; Hosler, *Changing Aesthetic Views of Instrumental Music in 18th-Century Germany*; Goehr, *The Imaginary Museum of Musical Works.*

known as the "Baroque" style. In 1607, for instance, Giulio Cesare Monteverdi justifies the new compositional practice (*seconda prattica*) pioneered by his brother Claudio on the grounds that it places music (*harmonia*) at the service of text (*oratio*) rather than vice versa.[8]

What Monteverdi designates the old or "first" practice (*prima prattica*) was an outgrowth of a medieval musical philosophy transmitted from Greek thought to the West by Boethius in the sixth century.[9] According to this view, the significance of music is essentially ontological: pure musical intervals are expressions of pure mathematical ratios believed to have cosmic significance, supposedly corresponding to the proportions of the heavenly bodies ("music of the spheres" or *musica mundana*) as well as those of the human body (*musica humana*). Skillful treatment of these cosmic proportions in music would stir the soul by bringing it, quite literally, into harmony with the music.

With the tide of Renaissance humanism, however, the first half of the sixteenth century saw a notable shift away from this older conception of music as a type of the Aristotelian "unmoved mover" and toward the understanding that the role of music is to "conform to the feelings"[10] and "express the passions of the soul."[11] The center of gravity, so to speak, was shifting away from music, with its intimations of divine wisdom, and toward the human being. This emphasis on the subjective component of music would burgeon throughout the sixteenth century, preeminently in the madrigal tradition, leading to a new valuing of drama and rhetoric that would become a cardinal element of the Baroque musical aesthetic.

But just as strains foreshadowing the new philosophy of music were evident in the "first practice," so elements of the older philosophy remained influential in the second, particularly in Germany, where the dual dimensions of *ratio* (the objective, mathematical component discerned by the intellect) and *sensus* (the sensory, emotional component) remained an important part of musical philosophy through Bach's day, with the supremacy of *ratio*

8. Guilio Cesare Monteverdi, "Explanation of the Letter Printed in the Fifth Book of Madrigals," trans. in *SR*, no. 83. See Dell'Antonio, *Sonatas and Canzonas*, appendix ("*La maniera di sonare con effetti cantabili*: The *Seconda Prattica* and Instrumental Music"); and Cypess, *Curious and Modern Inventions*, chap. 6 ("The *stile moderno* and the Art of History: Artisanship and Historical Consciousness in the Works of Dario Castello").

9. Boethius, *De Institutione musica*.

10. Hans Ott, Introduction to *Secundus tomus novi operis musici* (1538), trans. in Schlagel, "The *Liber selectarum cantionum* and the 'German Josquin Renaissance,'" 591.

11. Glarean, *Dodecachordon* (1547), book 3, chap. 24, trans. in *SR*, no. 70. Burkholder notes the significance of this and the previous quotation in *A History of Western Music*, 203 and 207.

appearing virtually uncontested until the eighteenth century.[12] Through the relationship between these two dimensions, there developed a concern with conveying the intended affective properties of music by concrete, rational means. Thus arose the seventeenth- and early eighteenth-century passion to classify not only affects (that is, emotions that music can convey) but also musical-rhetorical figures that would be understood to conjure more or less concrete extramusical and affective associations.

The confluence of these old and new strains within the musical thought of Bach's culture certainly yields some degree of tension. On one hand, music—especially contrapuntal music—is understood to have inherent significance that is both cosmic and spiritual in nature, reflecting the harmonious order, complexity, and wisdom of God's creation.[13] John Butt therefore goes so far as to describe Bach's worldview as "musico-centric," built on "the view that the very substance of music both reflects and embodies the ultimate reality of God and the Universe."[14] On the other hand, because music must communicate to the senses by means of the rational mind, there is a sense in which music without the concrete function of text could be seen as incapable of attaining the same degree of perfection as texted music. Although the coexistence of these two ideas is necessarily paradoxical, they need not be flatly opposed. Indeed, their possible simultaneity could explain, to a significant degree, why a composer such as Bach might invest himself in the painstaking creation of self-standing instrumental music (rather than simply focusing on texted or functional music) while at the same time crafting that instrumental music so as to contain symbolic or allegorical significances—that is, with a text in the broader sense of the word.[15]

A similar pair of considerations applies at a specifically theological level, bearing in mind that Bach was a devout Christian in the Lutheran

12. See Bartel, *Musica Poetica*, 25–26.

13. See Prov 3:19 and 8:22–23, Jer 10:12, etc. See David Yearsley, *Bach and the Meanings of Counterpoint*, 18–25, in which he draws attention to the numerous illustrations from Bach's day that represent the ordering of heaven and earth in terms of written counterpoint, perhaps most notably the frontispiece of Athanasius Kircher's monumental *Musurgia Universalis* of 1650.

14. Butt, "Bach's Metaphysics of Music," 54.

15. Marissen, *The Social and Religious Designs*, 119.

tradition,[16] as the contents of his personal library attest[17]: in addition to his Calov study Bible, which he annotated,[18] he possessed a number of volumes of theology, including two collections of the complete writings of Martin Luther.[19] One of Luther's prominent emphases is that God has ordained many things for human flourishing that are outside the church and therefore "secular"; yet because they are divinely ordained, they assume a kind of sacred significance. This is perhaps most famously seen in Luther's teachings on vocation, which he calls a "mask of our Lord God" (*unsers herrn Gotts larben*) because he considers every noble vocation—secular as well as ecclesial—to involve God-ordained work by which benefits that have their ultimate source in divine providence are mediated to others.[20] Thus the divide between sacred and secular is eroded because God is sovereign over all, and therefore all things alike—including music, whether with or without text—are to redound to the glory of God.

Perhaps unsurprisingly, therefore, Luther places greater emphasis than many religious figures of his day on the value of music (as opposed to merely the text that music may set).[21] He considers the natural grace of Josquin to be a representation of the gospel through the medium of music[22] and writes

16. Under the broader canopy of Lutheranism, the sometimes-volatile question of Bach's position within the controversy between Orthodoxy and Pietism has been insightfully addressed by Robin Leaver in "Bach and Pietism: Similarities Today." Although the contents of Bach's library suggest Bach sympathized with certain devotional emphases of the Pietists, Leaver places Bach squarely within the realm of Orthodoxy. Even in the case of certain cantatas that "have the appearance of Pietism in imagery and expression," Leaver notes that "the liturgical purpose, the eucharistic context, and the theological content"—to which might be added the elaborate musical style and even the genre of sacred cantata itself—"mark these cantatas as the product of a vibrant and lively Lutheran Orthodoxy" (pp. 17–18).

17. Here I parenthetically note that several statements from the *Generalbaßlehre* of 1738 (such as that "the end and purpose of [all music] should be nothing other than the glorification of God and the recreation of the mind") continue to be popularly cited as evidence of Bach's faith, even though the attribution of the document to Bach is now considered dubious. See Wollny, "Aufzeichnungen zur Generalbaßlehre."

18. Detailed images of these annotations, with commentary, have been made available in Leaver, *J. S. Bach and Scripture*, and Cox, *The Calov Bible of J. S. Bach*.

19. See Cox, *The Calov Bible of J. S. Bach*; Leaver, *Bachs theologische Bibliothek: eine kritische Bibliographie*; Leaver, *J. S. Bach and Scripture: Glosses from the Calov Bible Commentary*.

20. See Luther's commentary on Ps 147 in *WA* 31 I:436. For a detailed treatment of this subject, see Wingren, *Luther on Vocation*.

21. For a more detailed treatment of this subject, see Buszin, "Luther on Music," and Leaver, *Luther's Liturgical Music*, especially chap. 3, "Luther's Theological Understanding of Music," 65–103.

22. *WA TR*, no. 1258.

that "the devil, the author of sad cares and disquieting turmoil, flees at the sound of music almost as at the word of theology."[23] But implied in these and similar comments is the view that even though music (whether sacred or secular) may have intrinsic value, it is not an autonomous value; music does not exist for its own sake but complements theology and the natural world in proclaiming the gospel of Christ and bringing glory to God. Music, in Luther's view, therefore has inescapably didactic qualities.[24]

This view of the didactic properties of music almost necessarily gives rise to the idea of its symbolic or allegorical potential at some level. To be clear, this does not mean that the sequence of musical events in a given composition would have been understood as programmatically presenting a theological concept or narrative, but rather that the building blocks of music within the European compositional practice were understood to embody theological tenets. For instance, the reason Luther views Josquin's music as representing the gospel is that in it he sees a microcosm of grace that supersedes law.[25] Luther takes this idea of the allegorical properties of music still further in describing the solmization syllables *re, mi, fa* as an expression of the Trinity[26] and likening *musica ficta* to the concord-giving freedom of the gospel to which the strict notation (law) is subservient and not vice versa.[27]

A similar vein of thought is evident in various other writers, among them Andreas Werckmeister, an organist, music theorist, composer, and Lutheran minister of the generation before Bach, whose writings are known to have influenced the younger composer.[28] The appendix of Werckmeister's treatise *Musicae Mathematicae Hodegus Curiosus* is entitled "On Allegorical and Moral Music."[29] Eric Chafe has noted that this reference to the allegorical and moral recalls the Medieval *Quadriga* of biblical hermeneutics, which considers Scripture to consist of the literal (somatic), the

23. ". . . diabolus, curarum tristium et turbarum inquietarum autor, ad vocem musicae paene similiter fugit ad verbum theologiae." Martin Luther, letter to Ludwig Senfl, Oct. 4, 1530, *WA BR* 5:639. See Leaver, *Luther's Liturgical Music*, 93. All translations are mine unless otherwise stated.

24. See Bartel, *Musica Poetica*, 6–9 ("Music: A Pedagogical Tool").

25. See *WA TR*, no. 1258.

26. *WA TR*, no. 815; see Leaver, *Luther's Liturgical Music*, 98–99.

27. *WA TR*, no. 816; see Leaver, *Luther's Liturgical Music*, 101 and 388.

28. See, for instance, Williams, "J. S. Bach—Orgelsachverständiger unter dem Einfluss Andreas Werckmeisters?" and "Noch einmal: J. S. Bach—Orgelsachverständiger unter dem Einfluss Andreas Werckmeisters?"

29. "Von der Allegorischen und Moralischen Musik," in Werckmeister, *Musicae Mathematicae Hodegus Curiosus*, 141–54.

allegorical (typological), the moral (tropological), and the eschatological (anagogic),[30] thus drawing a parallel between music and Scripture that suggests, in Werckmeister's words, that "the Almighty has revealed himself to us not only in Holy Scripture but also in nature and arts (Rom. 1:19–20 and Wisdom of Solomon 13)."[31] Especially striking are Werckmeister's two allegorical interpretations of the harmonic series in terms of the days of creation and the epochs of biblical history (see Figs. 1.1 and 1.2 respectively)[32] as well as his comparison of the impossibility of fixed, just intonation to "our mortality and imperfection in this life."[33]

30. Chafe, *Tonal Allegory*, 11. Chafe further makes the connection with Martin Opitz's statement that "poetry . . . originated as nothing other than a hidden theology" ("Die Poeterey . . . ist anfanges nicht anders gewesen als eine verborgene Theologie"). Opitz, *Buch von der Deutschen Poeterey*, 9 (beginning of chap. 2), cited in Chafe, *Tonal Allegory*, 11.

31. "der Allmächtige nicht allein in H. Schrifft/ sondern auch etlicher Massen/ in der Natur und Künsten sich uns offenbaret hat/ Rom. 1. vers. 19.20 und Sapientiae cap 13." Werckmeister, *Musicae Mathematicae*, 141. In the extended title of the *Musicalische Paradoxal-Discourse*, published posthumously in 1707, Werckmeister's stated intention is to show "how music has a high and divine origin" ("wie die Musica einen hohen und göttlichen Uhrsprung habe").

32. Ibid., 142–44, 146–48.

33. Ibid., 145.

Fig. 1.1. Werckmeister: the harmonic series as an allegory of the days of creation (condensed)

Partial	Octave	Significance
[32.] ⋮ 17.	VI.	Day 6: Humanity is created to have dominion over all creatures of the earth, just as the musician is needed to bring order to the intervals already introduced, using "clean" and "unclean" sounds (consonance and dissonance) each according to its proper time and usage, so as to create *Harmonia* that is pleasing to God and man.
16. *c'''* 15. [*b''*]* 14. – 13. – 12. *g''* 11. – 10. *e''* 9. *d''* 8. *c''*	V.	Day 5 (and 6): God creates every manner of animal, some clean and some unclean, usable to man only at certain times. Similarly, this octave yields some well- and some ill-sounding intervals.
7. – 6. *g'* 5. *e'* 4. *c'*	IV.	Day 4: As the greater and lesser lights (sun and moon) are created for signs and seasons, so now two types of third emerge, one greater (major third) and one lesser (minor third). The intervals in this octave also show times and seasons: the dissonant seventh partial signifies that not all seasons are good; dissonance is part of this life. The completion of the triad parallels the completion of the heavens and earth.
3. *g* 2. *c*	III.	Day 3: Vegetation and trees appear, standing between earth and clouds, just as in the third octave *g* appears, standing between the upper and lower C.
	II.	Day 2: The first separation occurs, dividing the waters below the firmament (i.e., on the surface of the earth) from those above (clouds). In the same way, the second octave brings the first separation between *C* below and *c* above.
1. *C*	I.	Day 1: The fundamental *C* exists alone at the beginning of the series and is the source from which all else springs. As such, it is an image of God, the eternal Being and the source of all that is. Because the fundamental is the first pitch that the senses distinguish from chaotic, non-musical sound, it is like light, the first of God's creations, that is clearly separated from confusion.

* Originally *a''*, a typographical error

Fig. 1.2. Werckmeister: the harmonic series as an allegory of Biblical epochs (condensed)

Partial	Octave	Significance
8. *c″* 7. – 6. *g′* 5. *e′* 4. *c′*	III.	The New Testament: In the third octave, the triad (*Drey-Ein-Stimmigkeit*) is revealed, which is one sonority but consists of three parts. So in the New Testament, the Trinity (*Drey-Einigkeit*) is revealed, who is one God but consists of three persons.
3. *g*	II.	The Old Testament: The addition of *g* is a prefigurement of the triad that will be revealed in the third octave, just as the Trinity is prefigured but not revealed in the Old Testament. The second octave adds partials 3 and 4. 3 + 4 = 7, a holy number, signifying that God chose a people to be holy to himself. But just as the fourth between partials 3 and 4 cannot stand on its own (since contrapuntally a fourth is dissonant) but must be grounded in the fundament, so the people of God cannot subsist in their own holiness but must be grounded in the true worship of God.
2. *c* 1. *C*	I.	The beginning: The beginning of the harmonic series with the octave *C–c*, with no tone between, can be likened to God the Father, who dwells in darkness into which none can enter and who existed before anything was created.

Such "exegeses" are very much in keeping with the general allegorical orientation of much religious thought in seventeenth- and eighteenth-century Germany. For example, in his *Betrachtungen über das ganze Leiden Christi* ("Meditations on the full suffering of Christ") of 1730, Johann Jacob Rambach considers that "every fading flower reminds us of our mortality; but also every little blade of grass that dies in winter and rises again in spring foretells the coming resurrection."[34]

34. ". . . ein jedes verwelcktes Blümlein uns unsrer Sterblichkeit erinnert; aber auch ein jedes Gräslein, das im Winter erstirbet, und im Frühling wieder aufstehet, uns die künftige Auferstehung vorprediget." *BLC* 1265. Bach owned several works by Rambach and may have known or even owned this one as well; one of the theological volumes in the itemization of Bach's estate is listed simply as "Rambachi Betrachtung" (Rambach's Reflection), not specifying which of the many works Rambach entitled "Betrachtungen" is meant.

In this light, it is perhaps not surprising to find German Baroque composers, both inside and outside Lutheranism, crafting purely instrumental music that is not merely susceptible to interpolated significance (as all music is) but makes use of musical structures that are intended to correlate with a particular extramusical concept, event, or narrative, in other words, creating distinctly allegorical music. One example from outside the Lutheran tradition is a set of fifteen sonatas for violin and continuo from ca. 1676 by the Bohemian-Austrian Catholic composer Heinrich Ignaz Franz von Biber, popularly called the "Mystery" or "Rosary" Sonatas[35] because in the sole surviving manuscript each sonata is preceded by a copper-plate engraving depicting one of the fifteen mysteries of the Rosary as they represent successive episodes in the lives of Jesus and Mary according to biblical narrative and Catholic tradition.

An example from within the Lutheran context that comes fascinatingly close to Bach is a set of six sonatas entitled "Musical presentation of several Biblical histories" (*Musicalische Vorstellung einiger biblischer Historien*) composed by Johann Kuhnau, Bach's predecessor as Kantor at St. Thomas's in Leipzig and arguably the leading figure in German clavier music before Bach himself. First published by Immanuel Tietzen of Leipzig in 1700, these "Biblical Sonatas" were reissued by Tietzen ten years later, suggesting they were sufficiently popular to warrant reprinting. Bach would later encounter Kuhnau personally when the two, along with Johann Heinrich Rolle, were invited to examine the newly completed organ by Christoph Cuntzius at St. Mary's Church (Liebfrauenkirche) in Halle in 1716, four years before the completion of Bach's collection of six sonatas and partias for solo violin. It also seems likely that Bach visited Kuhnau during his brief trip to Leipzig the following year. These details alone would make it entirely plausible that Bach might have had opportunity to become familiar with the six Biblical Sonatas during the time of the gestation of the *Sei Solo*.[36]

Moreover, David Schulenberg and others have proposed that these Biblical Sonatas were the model for a significant early work of Sebastian Bach that, irrespective of the question of influence, proves that the idea of explicitly allegorical instrumental music was present in his mind from his teenage years.[37] The Capriccio "On the Departure of a Beloved Brother" (*Cappriccio*

35. Because the title page does not survive, we do not know what title Biber gave. The collection concludes with a monumental Passagalia for unaccompanied violin that is the most striking precursor of Bach's similarly monumental Ciaccona. Interestingly, it appears unlikely that Bach was familiar with these sonatas (including the Passagalia), since they were not published until 1905.

36. On the genesis of the *Sei Solo*, see Background.

37. Schulenberg, *The Keyboard Music of J. S. Bach*, 86. See also Chafe, *Analyzing*

sopra la lontananza de il Fratro dilettissimo), BWV 992, composed in 1704, contains six movements with these designations:

Arioso. adagio: Ist eine Schmeichelung der Freunde, um denselben von seiner Reise abzuhalten ("[This] is a coaxing by his friends to convince him to stay back from his journey")

[no title]: Ist eine Vorstellung unterschiedlicher Casuum, die ihm in der Fremde könnten vorfallen ("[This] is a depiction of various misfortunes that could befall him in foreign places")

adagiosissimo: Ist ein allgemeines *Lamento* der Freunde ("[This] is a general lament of the friends")

[no title]: Allhier kommen die Freunde, weil sie doch sehen, dass es anders nicht sein kann, und nehmen Abschied ("The friends gather, since they see it cannot be otherwise, and bid farewell")

allegro poco. Arie de il Postilione ("Coachman's Aria").

Fuga al Imitatione di Posta ("Fugue in imitation of the post[horn]")

Although this demonstrates only that Bach was familiar with the idea of instrumental music designed to illustrate an explicit program or idea, it provides an important context against which to approach the sometimes-volatile question central to this study: Is it conceivable that Bach could have created intentionally allegorical instrumental music *without* stating an explicit program or idea? This would represent some degree of departure from the values expressed by Kuhnau, who felt it necessary that his allegorical Biblical Sonatas should be given an explanation (*Auslegung*) in words; but, without downplaying the vital role of context in the formation of any personality, artistic or otherwise, it is surely an error to confine Bach solely to the specific practices and values of his predecessors and peers.[38] Indeed, several important studies of recent years have addressed the question of the possibility of allegory in certain instrumental works or collections of Bach, with an affirmative answer.[39]

Bach Cantatas, 34.

38. Laurence Dreyfus observes that "there is precious little of either the past or the present that is 'conserved' intact in Bach's works and a great deal that is altered into a nearly unrecognizable shape, the result of an indomitable inventive spirit. Bach is therefore better understood as a critic and interpreter of his age than as an old fogy or sometime panderer to novelty" (*Bach and the Patterns of Invention*, 243).

39. E.g., Marissen, *The Social and Religious Designs*; Marissen, "The Theological Character of J. S. Bach's *Musical Offering*;" Yearsley, *Bach and the Meanings of Counterpoint*; Leahy, "Bach's Prelude, Fugue and Allegro for Lute (BWV 998): A Trinitarian Statement of Faith?"

Nonetheless, the question is a tricky one, because in the absence of concrete documentary evidence of the composer's intentions it can be difficult to ascertain whether any perceived correlation between the music and an extramusical idea represents the composer's intention or merely the analyst's own creative interpolation. And even intentional use of allegory on the part of the composer does not guarantee that it will be decipherable or even detectable to the listener. For example, when listening to Vivaldi's "Four Seasons" and consulting the composer's program, it is easy to hear how he is musically depicting the singing birds, the fury of the north wind, the reeling drunkard, the icy rain drops, and so forth, as specified in the score. Yet if the program had not been transmitted with the score, it would be difficult to defend any suspicion that these first four concertos of Vivaldi's Opus 8 correspond to the four seasons or even, in many cases, that their various representational devices are in fact representational at all. That is to say, more and stronger evidence is needed to argue convincingly for the presence of musical allegory than will necessarily result from the composer's intention; and in cases where this evidence is lacking, the composer's intentions must remain mysterious.

Here it is appropriate to briefly consider the potential goals of musicological investigation into such questions. First, as a scientific pursuit, musicology must eschew premises that originate a priori and then seek to validate themselves with evidence from what Kołakowski has memorably called the "infinite cornucopia" of possible arguments.[40] Similarly, poetic responses to a composer's music, including interpolations of various kinds, can be edifying and profitable but must not be considered musicology, which is necessarily concerned with demonstrating something objective. At the same time, it is important not to assume that the scientific goal of demonstration is limited to conclusive proof alone. It is also possible, for instance, to demonstrate mere possibility; and even though demonstrating mere possibility is often unprofitable for advancing scholarship, it need not always be so, especially in cases where it importantly revises an incorrect assumption of impossibility. But between these two poles—demonstration of proof on one hand and of possibility on the other—lies a third and critically important option: to demonstrate likelihood. In the study of history, including music history, there is much that cannot be absolutely verified but that the body of relevant evidence shows to be sufficiently likely to warrant its adoption as a working theory until such time as evidence is found that could call it into question, in keeping with the methods of science. And since in many cases a question for which there is no absolute proof must inform a

40. Kołakowski, *Religion*, 16.

further conclusion, decision, or investigative direction, a likely premise is often the best or only possible foundation.

Assessment of the likelihood of a premise is necessarily a somewhat subjective matter, since conclusions cannot be neatly labeled "correct" or "incorrect" but must instead be judged within a continuum of relative credibility. Nonetheless there are some relevant, if general, criteria that can be brought to bear. If we are considering the possibility of allegory—that correlations are intended between particular musical features and an extramusical idea or narrative—then the correlations on which the weight of such an argument rests must first of all be strong; every musical gesture or feature can be associated with something, but there must be reasons for believing a proposed association is likely intended. Second, correlations on which the weight of an argument rests must collectively be specific or unique. In other words, the proposed object of allegory must be the only reasonable one. For example, it may be possible that a piece characterized by steady ascent represents the *gradus ad parnassum*, but there are a number of other ideas or narratives that such an ascent could parallel (if the ascent is intended to parallel anything at all); the correlation is therefore not sufficiently unique. Third, the clear presence of established potential signifiers is immensely helpful for building a conclusive argument. Of course, not every established signifier necessarily carries the same significance, or any significance, all the time. But where other factors (including a noteworthy concurrence of other signifiers) indicate the likelihood that an established meaning of a particular signifier is intended, it can lend an otherwise elusive degree of concreteness and direction to an argument. One example that will be relevant to this study is chiastic structure, which, as I will explain in Chapter 2, can (but need not necessarily) serve as a symbol for Christ or the cross. In isolation, a structural chiasm could be nothing more than a symmetrical structure created in the interest of beautiful proportionality; but if it were to occur, for instance, in the context of a direct quotation of a passion chorale, there could be good reason to see it as an emblem of the cross of Christ. Fourth, correlations on which the weight of any claim of musical allegory rests should be elegant. As a general principle, the weaker the argument, the further afield it must range in an attempt to appear viable. And finally, the methods by which the supposed allegory is detected should not indiscriminately yield (or be able to yield) the same results irrespective of subject matter. The premise that a hypothetical piece by Ives might contain allusions to Emerson would never appear more suspicious than if identical methods could detect the same correlations in Handel.

In the study that follows, I will use the criteria above to propose the likelihood that Bach's collection of *Sei Solo* for violin contains a dimension of allegory, specifically, theological allegory. I will confine my argument to:

- Striking and unusual features that correspond with other similarly striking and unusual features so as to strongly or uniquely correlate with an extramusical idea, event, or narrative;
- Somewhat less striking features that agree with or enhance the correlation suggested by concurrences among more striking musical features;
- Significances that, from a historical and cultural standpoint, Bach could plausibly have conceived or recognized (bearing in mind that the creative act may often generate a significance that the author might immediately recognize but that was nonetheless not the driving force in creating the structure from which it arises);
- Significances to which identical methods applied to other musical elements would not yield contradictory conclusions; and
- Significances that could arise from a plausible compositional process within the finite medium of the (eighteenth-century German) musical vocabulary.

The study will proceed not in musical order but according to the sequence of reasoning by which an allegorical reading of the *Sei Solo* appears credible.

Any evaluation of what significances Bach plausibly could have conceived, recognized, or embraced must of course be situated within an understanding of his intellectual and religious context—and, of course, the thought-world of Bach himself, to whatever extent it can be surmised. In this connection, it will be noted that my citations concerning the theological context of an early eighteenth-century composer, J. S. Bach, consist substantially of the writings of Martin Luther two hundred years earlier, as well as of the writings of the Bible from centuries earlier still. The reason for this is that Lutheranism placed a great deal of emphasis on the Bible as the only revealed Word of God, and Luther's exegeses were considered authoritative, so much so that since his death he was equated with the angel in Revelation 14:6–7 who proclaims an "eternal Gospel."[41] For instance, the extensive

41. In his funeral sermon for Luther, Johan Bugenhagen states, "He was without doubt the angel of whom it is written in Revelation 14 that he flew in the midst of the heavens and had an eternal Gospel" ("Denn er war one zweiffel der Engel/ davon in Apocalypsi xiiij. cap. stehet/ der da geflogen hat/ mitten durch den Himel/ und hatte ein ewig Evangelium"); and again, "This angel who says, 'Fear God and give him honor,' was Dr. Martin Luther" ("Dieser Engel/ der da saget/ fürchtet Gott/ und gebet ihm die Ehre/ war D. Martinus Luther"). Bugenhagen, *Eine Christliche Predigt*, 5, 6.

commentary in Bach's Calov study Bible (1681–82), which cites the sermon equating Luther with the angel of Revelation 14,[42] draws almost entirely from the writings of Luther a century and a half earlier. Robin Leaver moreover notes that the inventory of Bach's own theological library references no fewer than twenty-one "fat folio volumes" dedicated to Luther's writings,[43] a costly investment that would seem to reflect something of what Bach valued.

Here I should clarify my purposes in citing the theological sources from Bach's own library. It is not possible to date most of his theological acquisitions, but his Calov study Bible—a very important theological source for the present study by virtue of containing Bach's personal annotations—has the date 1733 penned in the lower-right corner of the title page, together with Bach's monogram. The *Sei Solo* were completed thirteen years earlier, in 1720. Therefore I must be very clear that in citing sources contained in Bach's library, especially the Calov Bible, my intent is not to imply that Bach was necessarily familiar with their specific content by the time of the composition of the *Sei Solo*. Rather, my purpose is simply to point to the ideas that made up the theological landscape of Bach's immediate context, ideas with which Bach would probably have been familiar and with which his (past or future) purchase of books that propound them would seem likely to indicate a significant level of agreement. Regarding the annotations in his Calov study Bible, they can of course demonstrate only what was on Bach's mind thirteen years and more following the completion of the *Sei Solo*. But given the considerable continuity in what can be discerned of Bach's religious outlook throughout his life, it may not be misguided to think the annotations of an older Bach could potentially relate to the reflections of his younger years to some degree.

Finally, I recognize that any premise of signification within a beloved collection of instrumental music, such as what I will propose in this study, might understandably be met with a degree of reticence on the grounds that any well-written music can be amply enjoyed without knowledge of a referential schema, even if it were to represent the composer's designs. And that is very true. Even from the perspective of Luther, who considered music to be an essentially allegorical medium, music cannot be understood as reducible to a cold proposition; if so, it could scarcely be seen as the vital, affecting force that moved him so deeply, and it would be the proposition, not the music, that contained the affecting power. It follows, therefore, that music

42. CB 6:1433.

43. Leaver, *J. S. Bach and Scripture*, 25. For a detailed discussion of the theological contents of Bach's library, see Leaver, *Bachs theologische Bibliothek*. A summary of Bach's theological library appears in the itemized list of his estate following his passing, reprinted in BD II, no. 626; NBR, no. 279.

transcends its immediate associations. Indeed, the history of the very idea of "classical" music is in many ways the story of the viability and adaptability of music beyond the immediate context of its genesis, whether the work in question be Bach's St. Matthew Passion, Beethoven's Ninth Symphony, or Wagner's *Meistersinger*. But to the extent that we recognize this transcendent capacity in music, we must similarly recognize the redundancy of the concern that acknowledging patterns of allegory will result in a constriction of the music or the musical experience. The present study is undertaken in the hopes that the signification it uncovers might instead contribute to the inevitably multivalent web of associations on which we may draw in encountering and interpreting Bach's solo violin works.

2

Issues of Structure and Style in the Ciaccona

The Ciaccona that concludes the D-minor partia is exceptional in many respects. It is the most towering single movement for unaccompanied violin of its day and perhaps of all time, dwarfing the four movements that precede it in terms of both breadth of invention and sheer size; in fact, its duration is similar to that of all four of the preceding movements combined. This—coupled with its dynamic-static tension of seemingly infinite variety over an incessant ostinato pattern[1] and of course its brooding D minor punctuated in the middle by glorious D major—made the Ciaccona a natural candidate for reinterpretation and adoption by the Romantic era and its progeny as both a stand-alone concert piece[2] and the subject of imaginative recasting by composers from Ferruccio Busoni to Leopold Stokowski to Anne Dudley. Since its revival in the time of Joseph Joachim, it has seemed to many to whisper of profound meaning just beyond the horizon of concrete comprehension, which doubtless accounts for the many attempts to exegete and expound on this elusive meaning that is so clearly felt. But because any such "whispers" of meaning, at least in the way we are prone to interpret them, are far from certain to originate with the Bach, the only fitting point of entry for the present study, which seeks to explore Bach's possible designs, is one that does not concern itself at all with questions of meaning.

1. From here onward I use the term *ostinato* to designate not a specific set of pitches that are repeated verbatim but any manifestation of the four-measure progression from D to A on whose successive (and varied) repetitions the Ciaccona is based.

2. Spitta, for instance, writes that, since the Ciaccona "is longer than all other parts of the partia taken together, it therefore cannot count as the last movement of it, but only as an appended piece: the actual suite is ended with the gigue" ("Sie ist länger als alle übrigen Theile der Partie zusammengenommen, kann daher nicht als letzter Satz derselben, sondern nur als angehängtes Stück gelten: die eigentliche Suite ist mit der Gigue beendigt"). Spitta, *Johann Sebastian Bach*, 703. In fact, it was not unusual for French suites to conclude with a substantial chaconne or passecaille, if not quite of the proportions of the Bach's violin Ciaccona. See "The Ciaccona in Context" below regarding its relationship to the remainder of the partia.

The Problem of Structure in the Ciaccona

Of all the complexities of the Ciaccona that have invited scholarly investigation, one of the most persistently troublesome is its structure. The relationship among its three parts—thirty-three four-measure ostinato statements in D minor, followed by nineteen ostinato statements in D major, concluding with twelve ostinato statements in D minor—comes tantalizingly close to being uniformly structured according to the Golden Ratio or Golden Section, whereby the ratio of a smaller value (*a*) to a larger (*b*) is equivalent to the ratio of a larger value to the sum of the two values ($a + b$), shown below[3]:

$$\frac{a}{b} = \frac{b}{a+b} \qquad \frac{a}{b} = \frac{\sqrt{5}-1}{2} \qquad \frac{b}{a} = \frac{\sqrt{5}+1}{2}$$

Indeed, given twelve as the smallest unit, nineteen is the whole number that most nearly approximates the Golden Ratio, so the proportion applies to the second and third sections. What is tantalizing is that the first section comes frustratingly close to maintaining the proportion but deviates sufficiently that it is difficult to view it as "close enough"; whereas thirty-one statements

3. Tatlow states in *Bach's Numbers* that there "have been several attempts in recent years to demonstrate Bach's use of [the Golden Section], but historical evidence undermines the results" (105). A 2006 article by Tatlow clarifies the nature of this historical evidence: "no-one has yet found a single musical treatise from Bach's time or earlier that encourages a composer to emulate the divine proportion [that is, the Golden Section] in composition," and there is an "ominous" paucity of references to the proportion within the broader literature of Bach's day ("The Use and Abuse of Fibonacci Numbers and the Golden Section in Musicology Today," 81). Tatlow's observations are a welcome corrective to an obsession with finding Golden Section relationships that has undoubtedly overstepped its bounds. At the same time, Tatlow recognizes that Bach would likely have been familiar with the proportion through Mersenne, and it seems likely to me that the fascinating properties of this proportion (particularly its capacity for fractal-like perpetuation, especially evident in the Ciaccona) would not have been lost on the perceptive Bach. Once one is familiar with the concept of the Golden Section, deriving specific numerical relationships from the formula above requires no mathematical knowledge and skill that Bach would not certainly have had. This being the case, the precise and elegant occurrences of the Golden Section that I will observe in connection with the Ciaccona beg the question of how plausible it is that these relationships could be mere coincidence. In Appendix B, I will note other precise occurrences of the Golden Section in the D-minor harpsichord concerto, BWV 1052, and the "Domine Deus" of the Mass in B Minor that appear similarly intentional. With respect and admiration for Tatlow's research, therefore, I wonder whether such pronounced and elegant appearances of the Golden Section in certain works of Bach, coupled with Bach's likely familiarity with the ratio, might perhaps indicate that Bach did at times decide to employ this proportion in musical composition in ways that his contemporaries may not have had interest in doing.

of the ostinato in the first section would most nearly approximate the Golden Ratio, in actuality it contains thirty-three.

Joel Lester suggests that the movement be understood in terms of the structure that unfolds *after* the first two statements of the ostinato, in which the thematic profile of the dance is presented. This reading yields a structure of thirty-one, nineteen, and twelve statements of the ostinato (after the initial two).[4] The difficulty with this approach, however, is that it cannot answer why we should exclude the eight-bar thematic phrase that opens the movement but not the two varied recurrences of that material that conclude both the first section as well as the third and final section. Doing so would yield a structure of 29:19:10, even further from the Golden Section relationship than the straightforward, unadulterated structure of 33:19:12. Ledbetter simply concludes that "proportions do not work out exactly" and that the 33:19:12 ratio is best understood as a rough approximation of the harmonic proportions 3:2:1.[5]

I suggest, however, that there may indeed be something more than rough approximation at play in the proportions of the Ciaccona, and I think Lester has hit on a critical point in looking to the eight-measure thematic phrase that opens the movement for the solution to its structure. The precise placement of its three (varied) iterations throughout the movement is revealing: the first begins the movement, the third concludes it, and the second is situated exactly in the middle such that its first four measures conclude the first thirty-two statements of the ostinato while its second four measures begin the second group of thirty-two. After this are nineteen ostinato statements in D major and the final twelve in minor, yielding a total of thirty-one. Before the second of the three thematic phrases are also thirty-one statements. After the first twelve of these (that is, at m. 49) the bass, and with it the harmonic profile, undergoes a noticeable change. First, the bass, which has thus far always been at least somewhat chromatic, becomes entirely diatonic. Second, for the first time the harmonic rhythm moves away from emphasizing the first and second beats of the measure (although statements 9 and 10 have, from a harmonic perspective, more or less equally emphasized all three beats) and for the first time emphasizes the first and third beats, an effect heightened by the new treatment of the second beat as a point of stasis (see Ex. 2.1a). It may not be coincidence that this new bass motif, which begins at measure 49 (or 7 times 7), remains in force for seven

4. Lester, *Bach's Works for Solo Violin*, 155.

5. Ledbetter, *Unaccompanied Bach*, 144. In acoustics, the ratio 3:2 is that of a perfect fifth, and 2:1 an octave. For the role of harmonic ratios in the philosophy and cosmology of the day, see my Chap. 1.

measures, which is longer than any other single bass motif, not to mention harmonic structure, anywhere else in the movement.[6]

This point of articulation at measure 49 divides the first minor section into two groups consisting of twelve and nineteen ostinato statements, the latter section beginning with the seven statements of the new bass line just discussed. It is interesting, then, that this new bass line that begins the nineteen ostinato statements occurring before the (varied) return of the eight-bar theme in the middle of the movement bears very close resemblance to the bass motif that opens the second group of nineteen immediately following this theme. Both are marked by the pattern of a falling third and rising second. The crucial difference between the two is that the latter is the rhythmic inverse of the former, just as it has undergone an inversion of mode from minor to major (Ex. 2.1).

Ex. 2.1

a. Ciaccona, BWV 1004/5, mm. 49–52 with implied bass line indicated below*

b. Ciaccona, mm. 133–36

* Here and elsewhere, note stem directions are modified for practicality in print.

6. In Bach's context, following biblical usage, the number seven was associated with perfection or completeness (e.g., Gen 2:1–3, 42:1; Ex 24:1; Lev 25:4, 25:10; Judg 16:13; Dan 9:24–27; Matt 18:21–22; note also the sevenfold structure of the book of Revelation and its seven churches, seven spirits of God, seven seals, seven trumpets, seven bowls, etc.). See also Riederer, *Gründliche Untersuchung der Zahl Sieben*; Werckmeister, *Paradoxal-Discourse*, 96. On the association of the number 6 with perfection, see my Chap. 4.

The structure of the movement is therefore as shown in Figure 2.1.

Fig. 2.1. The structure of the Ciaccona

- m. 1: twelve four-bar statements beginning with the eight-measure thematic phrase
  - m. 49: nineteen statements beginning with bass corresponding to m. 133
    - m. 125: two statements comprising the eight-measure thematic phrase (varied)
  - m. 133: nineteen statements in minor
- m. 209: twelve statements in minor concluding with the eight-measure thematic phrase (varied)

This simple structure is notable in two respects. First, it is built on clear Golden Section relationships that require no manipulation of numbers. Fascinatingly, then, the Ciaccona is the seventeenth of twenty-seven total movements of the *Sei Solo*; that is, it falls at the Golden Section of the entire collection.[7] Second, the structure of the movement is elegantly symmetrical.

Structural symmetry in Bach raises an issue that is both important and volatile in the sense of being prone to abuse. The chiasmus or chiasm is an ancient literary device featuring symmetry of ideas or phrases in the shape A, B, (. . .) B' A'. The name refers to its resemblance to the Greek letter *chi* (*X*) when diagramed as shown in Figure 2.2.

Fig. 2.2. Symmetrical structure as *X*-shape

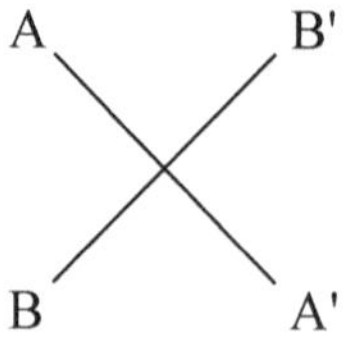

7. This count considers that the *doubles* of the B-minor partia are not independent movements, as they are sometimes curiously viewed, but rather that each belongs to the dance movement preceding it: the B-minor partia properly has four movements, not eight.

Because the letter *X* is not only cross-shaped but also the first letter of the Greek Χριστός (*Chrístos*, or Christ), it had in Bach's day become a well-established symbol for both Christ and the cross. In fact, in his autograph manuscripts Bach occasionally replaces both words with the symbol *X*.[8]

It seems clear, too, that these associations in Bach's mind extended to chiastic structure, not only the letter *X* itself. In the *Actus Tragicus* (BWV 106) of 1707–1708, Christ is explicitly mentioned twice. The first mention occurs at the joint midpoint of the cantata's chiastic structural and tonal schemes, which diverge somewhat from each other but coincide at their centers.[9] The second mention occurs in the final chorus, where the words "durch Jesum Christum, Amen" are set to the chiastic fugue subject shown in Example 2.2.

Ex. 2.2. *Actus Tragicus*, BWV 106: chiastic subject of the final fugue

The heart of the chiasm—which, in the literary tradition, is where the heart of the content is found—coincides with the first syllable of "Christum," where the letter *X* would occur in Greek.

A second notable example is the chiastic Credo of the Mass in B Minor, whose shape parallels the Christocentrism of Lutheran theology by casting the entire creed in the form of the Christ symbol (Fig. 2.3).[10]

8. See Smend, "Luther und Bach," 168; Chafe, *J. S. Bach's Johannine Theology*, 371.

9. See Chafe, *Tonal Allegory*, 109.

10. Stauffer notes this structure in *Bach, The Mass in B Minor*, 142.

Fig. 2.3. Chiastic structure of the Credo from the Mass in B Minor, BWV 232

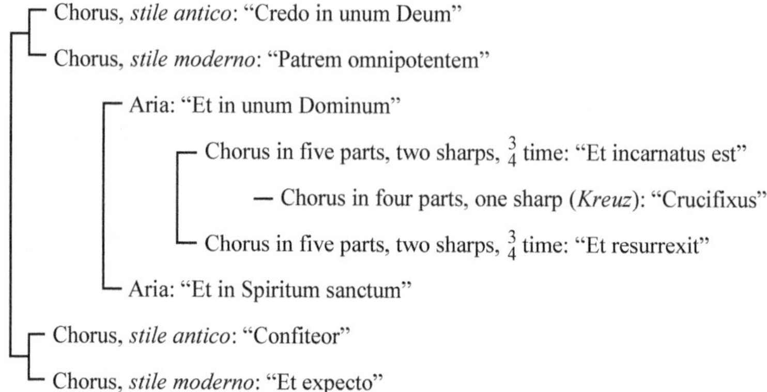

The heart—or, one might almost say, the crux—of this chiastic shape is the "Crucifixus," just as the cross is the crux of Lutheran theology.[11]

At the same time, Alfred Dürr is certainly correct to warn that "it is misguided to treat Bach's symmetrical forms as if they were the most important feature of the music, in the light of which all the other formal categories fade into insignificance."[12] Indeed, it is only by understanding how chiastic structures interface with the other elements of a musical composition that we can responsibly assess whether they can credibly be interpreted as symbolic, and if so, what their specific significance might be. At the same time, in light of Bach's penchant for comprehensiveness, his devout Lutheran faith, and his conviction that music provides insight into the mysteries of creation (and, by extension, its Creator),[13] it is probably not possible to assert with

11. Central to Lutheran thought is the idea of the theology of the cross (*theologia crucis*), which recognizes that true glory comes only through the cross, as opposed to the theology of glory (*theologia gloriae*), which falsely seeks glory apart from the cross. Luther goes so far as to state, "The cross alone is our theology" ("CRUX sola est nostra Theologia"). *WA* 5:176. See 1 Cor 1:23, 2:12.

12. Alfred Dürr, *Bach's St. John Passion*, 126.

13. Bach believed that music provides "insight into the depths of the wisdom of the world" or "Weltweisheit" (see Chap. 1 n. 5). The word *Weltweisheit* had more specific associations than readily translate into English, as the term *Weltweiser* was used to refer to "natural philosophers" such as Newton, with whom Bach began to be compared immediately following his death (BD II, no. 620 and III, no. 903; NBR, nos. 349 and 366). It is important to remember that pre-Enlightenment natural philosophy considered natural discoveries as a revelation of divine activity, which Bacon called "the book of God's works" (*The Advancement of Learning*, 10). Therefore the realms of theology and natural philosophy would be understood to be compatible and indeed interrelated,

any degree of certainty that Bach sometimes used chiastic structure with no thought to the theological dimension. But what can certainly be said is that the presence of chiasm need not necessarily indicate a theological program or anything beyond a simple invocation of Christ, as when Bach writes "SDG" ("Soli Deo gloria," or "to God alone be glory") or "JJ" ("Jesu, Juva," or "Jesus, help") in his scores.

Chaconne or Ciaccona?

Despite Bach's Italianate title Ciaccona, the movement remains popularly known by the French title Chaconne and is even referred to as such in some scholarly studies. At one level, of course, Bach's clear designation of the movement as a ciaccona is or presumably should be definitive, especially in light of the considerable difference of stylistic associations between the French and Italian titles. We would probably not, for instance, refer to Mozart's beloved E♭-major work for violin, viola, and orchestra as a *Doppelkonzert* when he has given the title *Sinfonia Concertante*, and it strikes me as somewhat peculiar that we would think otherwise of Bach.

At the same time, however, the persistence of the French moniker is understandable, as the movement does indeed have many characteristically French traits, including its beginning on the second beat with sarabandelike rhythm and its middle section in the parallel (in this case, parallel major) key. Although the virtuosity of much of its figuration is straightforwardly Italianate, its slowly moving bass and the resulting stately character resemble less the originally vivacious Italian ciaccona than the French chaconne. It is important to note, however, that by the generation of Buxtehude, German composers in particular were writing slower, stately ciacconas incorporating elements reminiscent of the generally more solemn passacaglia. Notable among these elements, found in both ciacconas and chaconnes, was the structuring of the basso ostinato around a descending tetrachord, or a stepwise descent of four notes. In its minor-mode form, the descending tetrachord was also known as a "Phrygian tetrachord" on account of its resemblance to the first (and second) four degrees of the Phrygian scale (Ex. 2.3), and this had become a prominent emblem of tragedy and lament.[14]

with music as a means of insight into both.

14. See Rosand, "The Descending Tetrachord: An Emblem of Lament"; Bartel, *Musica Poetica*, 214–15 (s.v. "Catabasis").

Ex. 2.3. Interval structure of the Phrygian scale

Of course, this does not mean that every ciaccona, passacaglia, or other work in which the Phrygian tetrachord is prominent is conceived as a lament or symbolizes something tragic. To illustrate, a descent that is mostly or fully chromatic, called the *passus duriusculus*,[15] is often used as a variant of the Phrygian tetrachord and has associations with lament that are at least as strong as those of its diatonic cousin[16]; and although its inclusion in overtly lament-oriented music of the Baroque era is so standard as to be almost expected, in other cases its use appears substantially unrelated to semiotics—especially in instrumental music of the period, for example, it seems frequently to be a by-product of exploration of chromatic harmony. Nevertheless, even in such cases it is almost certainly untrue to say that the associations with tragedy and lament have receded entirely. Thus even though the vast majority of ciacconas and passacaglias built on a descending tetrachord have no "deeper meaning" related to lament or tragedy, the lament motif can nonetheless lend the work a quality that is quite appropriately heard as tragic grandeur.

In terms of such tragic grandeur, Bach's violin Ciaccona is exemplary: its uncommon size alone lends a monumental quality to the unfolding repetitions of an essential four-bar ostinato (basically, a progression from D to A) that is given various realizations throughout the movement, the most prominent of which are motifs that are notably associated with lament. The foregoing associations with the descending tetrachord and *passus duriusculus*, well represented in the Ciaccona, are often observed; but the associations with the initial bass motif that recurs throughout the Ciaccona and is prefigured at the beginning of each previous movement of the partia are not commonly discussed. Interestingly, although Bach's incorporation of a number of variants of an essential ostinato recalls French practice, the one that begins the movement is essentially an augmentation of the ostinato pattern typical of older and more rapid Italian ciacconas (Ex. 2.4).

15. This term comes from Christoph Bernhard's *Tractatus compositionis augmentatus* (ca. 1657).

16. See Bartel, *Musica Poetica*, 357–58 (s.v. "Passus duriusculus").

Ex. 2.4

a. Merula: Chiacona, op. 12/20 (1637), ostinato

b. Bach: Ciaccona, BWV 1004/5 (bass stems modified to face downward for clarity)

This augmented variant of the old ciaccona pattern is crafted in such a way as to recall what appears to be a stock gesture in Bach's tradition that frequently occurs in the context of death or lament.

Could solemn reinterpretation of the vivacious and preeminently circular Italianate ciaccona be connected at times with reflection on our mortality (*memento mori*) as dust returning to dust, according to Gen 3:19? It is interesting that in the *Actus Tragicus* a very similar bass ostinato occurs in exactly this context, setting the text "O Lord, teach us to consider that we must die" ("Ach, Herr, lehre uns bedenken, daß wir sterben müssen"), shown in Example 2.5a. It is often observed that the *Actus Tragicus* is Buxtehudian in style,[17] and thus it is interesting that in Buxtehude's passion cycle *Membra Jesu Nostri* a similar bass pattern recurs both as a head motif and as an ostinato in the final chorus (Ex. 2.5b), first appearing in concert with the words "Salve caput cruentatum, totum spinis coronatum" ("Hail, bloody head, all thorn-crowned"), describing Jesus' taking our death upon himself.

17. See, for instance, Wolff, "Johann Adam Reinken and Johann Sebastian Bach," 65.

Ex. 2.5

a. Ostinato pattern from Bach's *Actus Tragicus*

Ex. 2.5 (cont.)

b. Ostinato pattern from Buxtehude's *Membra Jesu Nostri*, BuxWV 75

Ex. 2.5 (cont.)

A still more striking example of the association of a ciaccona-bass variant with lament, although this time not in the context of death, comes from the third movement of Bach's Capriccio "On the Departure of a Beloved Brother," BWV 992 (1704), which is the one movement in the entirety of his surviving oeuvre that he designates as a lament (*Lamento*). The movement follows a pattern strikingly similar the Ciaccona, consisting of varied repetitions of a four-bar minor-mode bass ostinato progressing from scale degree $\hat{1}$ to $\hat{5}$. Its opening bass gesture closely resembles that which opens the Ciaccona (Ex. 2.5c), of course also resembling the foregoing ostinatos in the *Actus Tragicus* and *Membra Jesu Nostri* that accompany references to death and crucifixion respectively. After accompanying the upper voice for the duration of two statements of the ostinato, the bass morphs into the *passus duriusculus*, exactly as in the Ciaccona. If Chafe is correct that the tone of the Capriccio is "tongue-in-cheek,"[18] it would indicate all the more strongly that Bach was using devices of representation that would have been generally and immediately recognizable, and it is reasonable that this would apply to more than just the elements that might appear tongue-in-cheek (such as the extensive sigh motifs with which the right hand enters in the *Lamento*). The fact that the violin Ciaccona shares considerable essential similarities with a movement intended to epitomize lament would seem to suggest that the Ciaccona was almost certainly intended to evoke a sorrowful affect in more than merely subjective terms.

18. Chafe, *Analyzing Bach Cantatas*, 36.

It is also interesting to consider that Bach appears to have generally associated the genre of ciaccona with lament.[19] Apart from the outstanding example for violin, the only surviving movement designated a ciaccona by Bach is the chorus "Meine Tage in den Leiden" ("My days of suffering") from Cantata 150, ca. 1704–1707. Two other examples deserve mention, which are ciacconas in all but name. The opening chorus of "Jesu, der du meine Seele," BWV 78 (1724), speaks of Jesus' "bitter death" (*bittern Tod*), which has rescued the soul from "the devil's dark pit" (*des Teufels, finstern Höhle*, with an evident play on *Hölle* or "hell"). Though the text points forward to redemption, the ensuing aria and recitative make plain that, in the dynamic flow of the cantata, relief from the anguish of the fallen state has not yet been experienced and will not be until the blood of Christ is introduced in the fourth-movement tenor aria ("Das Blut, so meine Schuld durchstreicht").[20] A final example is the chorus "Weinen, Klagen, Sorgen, Zagen" ("Weeping, lamentation, trouble, apprehension") from Cantata 12 (1714), which sets its remarkably dark text in the uncommonly dark key of F minor, the same key as the *Lamento* from BWV 992. In the last decade of his life, as Bach was assembling the Mass in B Minor, he would choose this movement to recast as his only setting of the "Crucifixus" from the Nicene Creed, transposing it down a half step to E minor, whose key signature has a single sharp (*Kreuz*, literally "cross").

In light of all these considerations, it is worth briefly noting the work that appears likely to be the most influential precursor of Bach's violin Ciaccona, composed by Johann Christoph Bach (1642–1703), Sebastian's first cousin once removed and the most outstanding composer of the Bach family before Sebastian, whom the younger man evidently admired deeply, singling him out in his 1735 genealogy as "a profound composer."[21] The second movement of Johann Christoph's 1676 wedding cantata "Meine Freundin, du bist schön" is a long, aching Ciacona in G minor that features a virtuosic solo violin part. This movement, like the entire cantata, uses lament *topoi* in connection with love poetry from the Song of Solomon in a rich tapestry of meanings and associations. Most immediately, the presence of lament *topoi* illustrate the lovesickness of the bride and

19. Ledbetter notes that the seventeenth-century ciaccona could have one of two contrasting associations: "individual, solo, personally anguished operatic lament; or the suave, rounded, courtly social dance" (*Unaccompanied Bach*, 137).

20. The dialectic tension between law/fallenness/suffering yielding to grace/redemption/consolation is common in Bach's cantatas. See Leaver, "Bach and Pietism," 17. In multiple studies Chafe argues that Bach frequently represents this dynamic both tonally and structurally; see especially *J. S. Bach's Johannine Theology*, 84–94.

21. "ein profunder Componist." BD I, no. 184; NBR, no. 302.

groom for each other, which the composer emphasizes with repetitions of the text "for I am sick with love" ("Denn ich bin kranck, bin kranck, bin kranck, ich bin kranck vor Liebe, ich bin, bin kranck, ich bin kranck"). More deeply, however, associations between love and death were deeply embedded in seventeenth-century culture from the Petrarchian tradition, which Lutheranism maintained, reinforced by two theological understandings: first, marital love is a microcosm of the self-sacrificial love of Christ for his bride, the church, as described in Ephesians 5:25; and second, the full joys of union with Christ, the ultimate love to which marriage points, are realized only when death has delivered the believer from this sin-marred life into the arms of the Beloved, which is why wedding imagery is frequently found in Lutheran funeral sermons.[22]

The Ciaccona in Context

The D-minor partia comes closest of any of the *Sei Solo* to an older usage of the word *partia* to mean a set of variations. Bach himself used the term this way in several works, including *Partite diverse sopra "Christ, der du bist der helle Tag"* (BWV 766), *Partite diverse sopra "O Gott, du frommer Gott"* (BWV 767), and *Partite diverse sopra "Sei gegrüßet, Jesu gütig"* (BWV 768). If the *Sarabande con partitis* (BWV 990) is correctly attributed to Bach, it would be still another example.

The D-minor violin partia is not strictly a set of variations, but it does create a sense of variation. Every movement opens with a closely related bass gesture that finally becomes crystalized into a variant of the old ciaccona bass, which initiates the Ciaccona's massive ostinato structure (Ex. 2.6).

22. For a detailed study of this subject, see van Elferen, *Mystical Love*.

Ex. 2.6. Essential bass motion in the D-minor partia*

1. Allemanda

2. Corrente

3. Sarabanda

4. Giga

5. Ciaccona

* While representing an important subsurface motion connected with the bass, I am not proposing that the circled tones represent a concrete bass line, and they should certainly not be assumed to literally define the harmonic rhythm, though in many cases they do.

** The suspension necessarily implies resolution on the downbeat and therefore hemiola. This strenthening of the third beat and weakening of the downbeat reinforces the essential bass figure shared with the other movements. In tension with this, and secondary to it, is the falling diminished fifth in the bass in m. 4, recalling the falling (perfect) fifths in the treble in mm. 1–2.

In this sense the Ciaccona brings into focus a motif that was implied at the start of each preceding movement. But the adumbration arguably extends further back than the D-minor partia. The opening bass gesture of the B-minor partia, for instance, strongly recalls the motif that begins all five movements of the D-minor partia (Ex. 2.7).

Ex. 2.7. BWV 1002/1, mm. 1–3

And although the Ciaccona creates a sense of bringing this motif into focus through repetition, it is in reality only one of the means that the Ciaccona explores of traversing the distance from A to D during a four-bar period. As implied above, the essential ostinato of the Ciaccona is therefore better understood as this tetrachordal space rather than any specific realization of how to traverse that space. In this sense, the Ciaccona can also feel as if it is encompassing and bringing into focus the A-minor sonata's nearly obsessive emphasis on the descending tetrachord, which we will observe later and which seems to go beyond the inevitability of such figures to arise in some form, as a comparison with other works and collections will demonstrate.[23] In fact, beginning with the general descending pull of the Adagio and Fuga of the first sonata, proceeding to the single adumbration in the B-minor partia, continuing to the tetrachord-saturated A-minor sonata, and finally arriving at the D-minor partia, where the head motif of the Ciaccona appears at the beginning of every movement, it is possible to feel the Ciaccona as the destination of a process of clarification throughout the *Sei Solo* thus far. But even if we dismiss that as coincidental and look only at the D-minor partia, the Ciaccona nonetheless epitomizes the idea of coming into focus. Is it accidental that the movement in which this occurs is placed at the Golden Section of the entire collection of *Sei Solo*? Could this be Bach's creating in music something aesthetically akin to perspective in painting?

23. cf. Ledbetter, *Unaccompanied Bach*, 138.

In any case, it is interesting that three particularly noteworthy features of the Ciaccona are its elegant chiastic form, its bringing into focus a lament topic, and the sheer magnitude of the structure in which this lament topic is variously realized. This is interesting because it bears a striking resemblance to a crucial Lutheran (and historic Christian) understanding of Christ and of the cross, both of which can traditionally be represented by the chiasm: namely, that Christ, and especially his atoning death on the cross, is the focal point of redemptive history, the antitype to which all previous biblical prophesies,[24] laws,[25] histories,[26] artifacts,[27] and persons[28] ultimately point.[29] Christ's incomparable sufferings on the cross therefore also represent the focal point of humanity's woes, since the man Jesus Christ, as the "second Adam,"[30] ultimately bears the curse for sin, with all its sorrows, that fell upon humanity through the rebellion of the first Adam.[31] And it is precisely because the plight of all humanity comes into focus in the cross of Christ that

24. The majority of New Testament documents, by diverse writers, quote Jewish Scriptures in reference to Christ. For instance, the Gospel of John, after quoting Isaiah, strikingly states, "These things Isaiah said because he saw [Jesus'] glory, and he spoke of Him" (John 12:41). See also Matt 26:42; Luke 24:27, 44–49.

25. See 1 Cor 9:9–10; Gal 4:24–26; Col 2:16–17; Heb 8:5; 9:22–24; 10:1.

26. See John 3:14; 1 Cor 10:1–11; Heb 3:16—4:10 (esp. 4:8); 1 Pet 3:20–21.

27. See John 2:21; Heb 9:24.

28. See Rom 5:14; Gal 4:22–31; Heb 7. Typical of both Catholic and Protestant thought in the seventeenth and early eighteenth centuries is Johann Arndt's description of Christ as "der himmlische (that is, heavenly) Isaac, der himmlische Jacob, der himmlische Joseph, der himmlische David" (*Gecreutzigter und wieder auferstandener Christus*, 67). Elsewhere in the same volume Arndt refers to Christ as the heavenly Moses (304, 993), Noah (558), Daniel (821), Jonah (906), Samson (621), Adam (1017, 1023), and Joshua (1061). Bach was evidently familiar with Arndt's theology and personally owned at least one of his works, the five-volume *Wahres Christenthum* (*True Christianity*).

29. This idea is central to Lutheranism, permeating the writings of Luther and his followers. Luther himself famously states that "there is therefore in all of scripture nothing other than Christ, either in open or concealed words" ("Sic in tota scriptura nihil aliud est quam Christus vel apertis verbis vel eingewickelten worten"). *WA* 11:223. See "Luther and the Christ-Centeredness of Scripture" in Wood, *Captive to the Word*, 169–78.

30. 1 Cor 15:21–22, 45–49; see Rom 5:12–21. The role of Christ as the second Adam and corporate representative of humanity is central to Lutheran thought and permeates its theological writings.

31. Gen 3:16–19. Luther's understanding of the fall of man is a central element of his theology whose importance is difficult to overstate. Bach himself appears to have been a careful student of the theology of the fall. See Leaver, *J. S. Bach and Scripture*, 33, 57.

he can be the savior of the entire world.[32] This alone would suggest the incomparable scope of Christ's sufferings, but a more direct expression of this idea comes from application of Lamentations 1:12 to Christ, notably in the text "O vos omnes,"[33] originally a Catholic responsory for Holy Week that was set in motet form by both Catholic and Lutheran composers. Among the former is Alessandro Grandi, who composed a setting contained in the library of St. Michael's School (St. Michaelisschule) in Lüneburg, where Bach studied as a teenager[34]; among the latter is Hieronymus Praetorius, organist in nearby Hamburg around the turn of the seventeenth century.

In short, then, the Ciaccona's bringing a lament motif into focus within a massive movement with clear chiastic structure strongly and uniquely recalls the heart of Bach's faith.[35] It is not unthinkable that this parallel, striking as it is, could be the product of coincidence. It is also not improbable that the sonata following the dark and solemn D-minor partia[36] would be brighter in tone, as indeed is true of the C-major sonata. That is why it would be premature to assume, on the basis of this brighter tonality, that the C-major sonata probably represents resurrection. To be sure, a Lutheran of Bach's time might well have consciously perceived the progression from the dark solemnity of the D-minor partia to the brighter tonality of the C-major sonata as a *type* of the resurrection, in the sense of pointing toward or representing it at some level, just as Rambach encourages his readers to view the death of vegetation in winter and its rebirth in the spring as prefiguring the resurrection.[37] But the near-universal applicability of such an approach

32. John 1:29; 3:16–17; 4:42; Rom 8:20–21; 2 Cor 5:14; Col 1:20; 1 John 2:2; and 4:14. Christ's role as savior of the entire world is a recurring topic in Rambach's *BLC*. He emphasizes, for instance, that the site of the crucifixion outside the city walls was fitting for a universal sacrifice (*allgemeinen Opfer*) for the sins of the whole world (947).

33. "O vos omnes qui transistis per viam, attendite et videte: Si est dolor similis sicut dolor meus. Attendite, universi populi, et videte dolore meum. Si est dolor similis sicut dolor meus." ("O all you that pass by the way, attend and see whether there is any sorrow like unto my sorrow. Attend, all people, and see my sorrow, whether there is any sorrow like unto my sorrow.")

34. Seiffert, "Die Chorbibliothek der St. Michaelisschule," 606.

35. It appears that the idea of Christ's atoning death as the fulfillment of Scripture was particularly important to Bach. In the substantial commentary on John 19:30 given in his Calov study Bible, the one clause Bach underlines states "that Christ's suffering [on the cross] is the fulfillment of Scripture and the accomplishment of the redemption of the human race" ("daß CHristus Leiden der Schrifft Erfüllung/ und der Erlösung des Menschlischen Geschlechts Vollbringung ist"). CB 5:947.

36. In describing the "solemnity" of D minor, I am not so much making a subjective aesthetic judgment as reiterating a historical perspective. On aesthetic associations with the key of D minor, see Chap. 6 n. 104.

37. See Chap. 1 n. 34.

is exactly what makes it unsuitable to determine whether any given descent-ascent pattern in art has primarily theological intentions, and, if so, what those specific intentions are. For example, Eric Chafe notes that many Bach cantatas follow a descent-ascent pattern, since it is in many ways the deeper shape of Scripture, in whole and in many of its parts, as well as of important parts of the liturgical year; and because this fundamental shape of Scripture and the liturgy molded believers' perceptions of their own experience, musical structures with this same basic shape have enabled believers to identify with them and (in the case of texted sacred music) with the message they convey.[38] Although typifying the pattern of death and resurrection, the specific representation of death and resurrection per se need not be the primary impetus behind the creation of such descent-ascent structures.

That said, the C-major sonata that follows the D-minor partia contains multiple, strong, and straightforward correlations to a theology of the resurrection—comparable to those in the D-minor partia paralleling the passion of Christ—which would seem to suggest that the correlations evident in both works might be better attributed to design than to chance.

38. See Chafe, *Analyzing Bach Cantatas*, 10.

3

"Al riverso": Resurrection Imagery in the C-major Fuga

In Scripture and Lutheran theology, the redeeming work of Christ on the cross is repeatedly described in terms of cleansing,[1] an image closely related to the gospel message of forgiveness of sins (a particularly strong Lukan emphasis) and justification (a particularly strong Pauline emphasis) as well as to its basis, the vindication of the sin-bearing Christ by his resurrection from the dead.[2] Therefore it is noteworthy that the tonality of the work immediately following the passion-evoking Ciaccona should be C major, a key associated with purity not only because of its lack of diatonic sharps or flats but also because of the related fact that in historical temperaments C major is generally the most purely tuned.[3] In light of the possibility this raises of the theological allegory continuing into the C-major sonata, what is immediately interesting is that the subject of the second-movement Fuga has long been regarded as a chorale quotation, although there has been disagreement as to which chorale it actually quotes, since it resembles two distinct but similar chorale melodies: "An Wasserflüssen Babylon" ("By the waters of Babylon") and "Komm, heiliger Geist" ("Come, Holy Spirit"), shown in comparison in Examples 3.6–7.[4]

1. John 13:8; 1 Cor 6:11; Eph 5:25–26; Heb 9:13–14; 1 John 1:7 and 9. Rambach associates the cleansing fountain of Zech 13:1 with the blood of Christ (*BLC*, 1181), whereas Luther's commentary reprinted in Bach's study Bible associates it with Christian baptism (CB 4:647–48). The two interpretations are similar, since the purification that baptism represents (1 Pet 3:21) is rooted in identification with the death and resurrection of Christ (Rom 6:4, Col 2:12; see Mark 10:38; Luke 12:50) through his cleansing blood (1 John 1:7).

2. Rom 4:25; 1 Cor 15:17; 1 Tim 3:16; see Luke 24:46; Acts 2:29–36; and 13:35–39.

3. In connection with Bach's *Trias harmonica* canon, BWV 1072, Wolff notes that the C-major triad is "the acoustically purest of all triads, which represents the natural, God-given, most perfect harmonic sound." Wolff, *Bach: The Learned Musician*, 336.

4. Among recent studies, Joel Lester connects the subject with "An Wasserflüssen Babylon" (*Bach's Works for Solo Violin*, 85–86), whereas Helga Thoene connects it with "Komm, heiliger Geist" (*Bach: Sonata C-Dur*).

It is unwise to assume that a melodic resemblance to a chorale alone must indicate that the composer intended the association, as evidenced in Thoene's problematic attempts to find supposedly "hidden" chorales in Bach's solo violin works.[5] Nor must a certifiable chorale citation indicate the presence of a schema of signification beyond itself. In what follows, therefore, I will address the questions of whether a chorale citation might plausibly be intended; if so, which one; and, finally, what the implications of the treatment of that chorale throughout the fugue would be.

The supposition that the subject of the C-major fugue might cite a chorale, as well as the confusion over which chorale might be in view, arises from considerations that I will now flesh out in some detail. The C-major sonata appears to have been the most recently written of the *Sei Solo* when Bach completed the definitive copy of the collection in 1720, presumably around midyear.[6] In November of the same year, Bach auditioned for the post of organist at St. James's Church (Sankt-Jacobi-Kirche) in Hamburg, reported in Bach's obituary as follows:

> During this time, around the year 1722 [sic], he made a trip to Hamburg and was heard before the Magistrate and many other upstanding persons of the city on the beautiful organ of St. Catharine's Church, to general astonishment, for more than two hours. The old organist of this church, Johann Adam Reinken, . . . listened to him with particular enjoyment. Especially concerning the chorale "An Wasserflüssen Babylon"—upon which, at the request of those present, our Bach improvised extensively, for almost half an hour, in diverse ways—[Reinken] paid him the following compliment: "I thought this art was dead, but I see that in you it still lives." This pronouncement from Reinken was all the more unexpected, as years ago he had set this chorale himself, after the manner described above; this, and also that he had always been a bit envious, was not unknown to our Bach.[7]

5. See Appendix A.

6. The autograph of the *Sei Solo* bears a watermark, unique among Bach's manuscripts, indicating it was from a mill in Joachimsthal near the spa town of Karlsbad, where from May to July 1720 Bach was accompanying Prince Leopold, presumably to represent the musical culture of the Cöthen court before other nobility who would have been present at the spa. See Sackmann, "Warum komponierte Bach BWV 1001–1006?" 8.

7. "Während dieser Zeit, ungefehr im Jahr 1722, that er eine Reise nach Hamburg, und ließ sich daselbst, vor dem Magistrate, und vielen anderen Vornehmen der Stadt, auf der schönen Katharinenkirchen Orgel, mit allgemeiner Bewunderung mehr als 2 Stunden lang hören. Der alte Organist in dieser Kirche, Johann Adam Reinken . . . hörete ihm mit besonderem Vergnügen zu, und machte ihm, absonderlich über den Choral: an Wasserflüssen Babylon, welcher unser Bach auf Verlangen der Anwesenden, aus dem Stehgreife sehr weitläufig, fast eine halbe Stunde lang, auf verschiedene Art . . .

There can be no doubt that Bach's long and varied improvisation on "An Wasserflüssen Babylon" would have included a fugue on the chorale subject. Forkel describes how in improvising on any given theme Bach typically "first used this theme for a prelude and a fugue with full organ. Then his art of registration was displayed in a trio, a quartet, &c. . . . Later followed a chorale . . . Finally, the conclusion was made with full organ by a fugue."[8] Tellingly, he adds, "This is actually the very art of organ playing that old Reinken in Hamburg thought already lost in his time, but which, as he afterward found, not only still lived in Joh. Seb. Bach but through him had reached its highest perfection."[9] Also noteworthy are Mattheson's descriptions of the required components of two organ auditions in Hamburg, in 1725 and 1727, which he records in his *Grossen General-Baß-Schule* of 1731. Although slightly different in their specifics, each audition was to include a modulating prelude, a fugue on an assigned subject, a chorale setting in three-part harmony, a vocal-style aria with basso continuo accompaniment, and a ciaccona or fantasia to conclude.[10]

In sum, then, less than half a year after penning the final copy of a fugue whose subject strongly resembles the opening line of "An Wasserflüssen Babylon"—a fugue that happens also to be one of Bach's grandest and most majestic—Bach was called on to improvise (among other things) a fugue on the same subject for an audition. But it is difficult to imagine that Bach considered this like any other audition when among its attendees was (and was probably certain to be) a now-aged Johann Adam Reinken, the man who, according to Wolff, had been "a major, perhaps even the major

ausführete, folgendes Compliment: Ich dachte, diese Kunst wäre gestorben, ich sehe aber, daß sie in Ihnen noch lebet. Es war dieser Ausspruch von Reinken desto unerwarteter, weil er vor langen Jahren diesen Choral selbst, auf die obengemeldete Weise gesetzet hatte: welches, und daß er sonst immer etwas neidisch gewesen, unserm Bach nicht unbekannt war." Agricola and C. P. E. Bach, "Johann Sebastian Bach," 165. (In BD III, no. 666; NBR, no. 306.) Despite the fact that the year is given as "about . . . 1722," Wolff connects this account with Bach's 1720 audition (*Bach: The Learned Musician*, 212).

8. "Zuerst gebrauchte er dieses Thema zu einem Vorspiel und einer Fuge mit vollem Werk. Sodann erschien seine Kunst des Registrirens für ein Trio, ein Quatuor &c. . . . Ferner folgte ein Choral . . . Endlich wurde der Beschluß mit dem vollen Werke durch eine Fuge gemacht." Forkel, *Bachs Leben, Kunst und Kunstwerke*, 22 (in BD VII, p. 34; NBR, p. 440).

9. "Dies ist eigentlich diejenige Orgelkunst, welche der alte Reinken in Hamburg schon zu seiner Zeit für verloren hielt, die aber, wie er hernach fand, in Joh. Seb. Bach nicht nur noch lebte, sondern durch ihn die höchste Volkommenheit erreicht hatte." Ibid.

10. Mattheson, *Grosse General-Baß-Schule*, 34–37 (§LIX, LXII–LXIV).

figure in young Bach's life."[11] Reinken was himself famous for his rich improvisatory-style setting of "An Wasserflüssen Babylon," the sole surviving copy of which is in the hands of none other than a fifteen-year-old Johann Sebastian Bach. If Bach had reason to believe "An Wasserflüssen Babylon" would likely be requested of him at his Hamburg audition—conceivably by Reinken himself—it seems not unreasonable that he might have prepared his "improvisation" at least to some degree,[12] especially in light of possible indications that throughout his life he could be dissatisfied with the results of his extempore performances, brilliant as they must have been.[13] Wolff, for instance, suggests that Bach's audition may have drawn on his two organ chorale settings of "An Wasserflüssen Babylon," BWV 653a–b.[14] On these grounds alone, it would seem fully plausible that he might also have premeditated the fugue, the most contrapuntally virtuosic element of the improvisation and the best suited to making the deepest impression on the man whose own contrapuntal setting of "An Wasserflüssen Babylon" appears to have so impressed the young Bach. For such a purpose the C-major violin fugue would be without parallel in the surviving Bach oeuvre.

11. Wolff, "Johann Adam Reinken and Johann Sebastian Bach," 57.

12. This in turn would suggest that the account given in Bach's obituary has been slightly romanticized to imply (without actually stating) that Bach's improvisation was unpremeditated. Gardiner has observed that C. P. E. Bach appears to have been willing to romanticize his father's past, often downplaying what he received from others, in order to bolster his image of accomplishment, an objective that seems not incommensurate with the anecdote's focus on Bach's receiving praise from the "envious" Reinken. See Gardiner, *Bach: Music in the Castle of Heaven*, 67. Similar romanticizing is evident in connection with Bach's improvisation before Frederick the Great, for instance. Reading between the lines of Forkel's 1802 biography, we may conjecture that the king requested that Bach improvise a six-voice fugue on the theme the king supplied but that Bach declined and instead improvised in six voices on a subject of his own choosing (Forkel, *Bachs Leben, Kunst und Kunstwerke*, 10; BD VII, p. 23; NBR, p. 430). The obituary, however, soft-pedals this (BD III, no. 666, p. 85; NBR, no. 306, p. 303), and indeed by 1774 Gottfried van Swieten reports that Frederick the Great had told him that Bach's improvisation included fugues in four, five, and eight (!) parts, all on the king's theme (BD III, no. 790; NBR, no. 360).

13. In referring to his improvisation before Frederick the Great in the dedication to the *Musical Offering*, could Bach be going beyond the vague and sometimes wry self-deprecation typical of formal dedications in general when he states that "owing to a lack of necessary preparation, the execution did not come off as well as such a splendid theme demanded" ("wegen Mangels nöthiger Vorbereitung, die Ausführung nicht also gerathen wollte, als es ein so treffliches Thema erforderte")? (In BD I, no. 173; NBR, no. 245). By contrast, in the dedication of the Brandenburg concertos, Bach's speaking of their "imperfections" (BD I, no. 150; NBR, no. 84) must surely assume at least a slightly ironic hue in light of the collection's consisting of a "perfect" six works (Marissen, *The Social and Religious Designs*, 84–85).

14. Wolff, *Bach: The Learned Musician*, 212–13.

What is extremely fascinating, then, is that in his description of the 1727 audition in Hamburg, Mattheson—who was in attendance at Bach's 1720 audition and evidently impressed[15]—writes out the subject on which candidates were expected to improvise their fugue, and it is alarmingly similar to that of Bach's C-major violin fugue, albeit in G major (Ex. 3.1).

Ex. 3.1

a. Mattheson: fugue subject for a 1727 organ audition in Hamburg

b. Bach: subject of the C-major Fuga for solo violin, BWV 1005/2

But it is not only the subject that is similar; so too the stipulations Mattheson gives for developing it. First he puts forward a chromatic countersubject nearly identical to Bach's (Ex. 3.2), which he says should regularly accompany the subject, as indeed it does in Bach's fugue.

15. In 1728, Mattheson recounts that "several years ago a certain great virtuoso—who since, according to his merits, has advanced to a handsome cantorate [certainly referring to Bach's position in Leipzig since 1723]—presented himself for the position of organist in no small city and drew admiration from everyone on account of his skill. There applied at the same time, among other incompetent journeymen, the son of a wealthy artisan [Johann Joachim Heitmann], who could prelude better with thaler [that is, money] than with fingers, and to him fell the position." ("Ich erinnere mich, . . . daß vor einigen Jahren ein gewisser grosser Virtuose, der seitdem, nach Verdienst, zu einem ansehnlichen Cantorat befördert worden, sich in einer nicht kleinen Stadt zum Organisten angab, . . . und eines jeden Bewunderung, seiner Fertigkeit halber, an sich zog; es meldete sich aber auch zugleich, nebst andern untüchtigen Gesellen, eines wolhabenden Handwercks-Mannes Sohn an, der besser mit Thalern, als mit Fingern, praeludiren kunnte, und demselben fiel der Dienst zu . . . .") Mattheson, *Der Musicalische Patriot*, 316. In BD II, no. 253; NBR, no. 82. Heitmann, in the words of Wolff, "demonstrated his gratitude" for winning the position by paying 4,000 marks (Wolff, *Bach: The Learned Musician*, 215).

Ex. 3.2

a. Mattheson: tonal answer and chromatic countersubject (1727)

b. BWV 1005/2: tonal answer and countersubject

Then Mattheson describes inverting the subject, as Bach also does prominently. The next operation stipulated by Mattheson is a three-way combination of the subject (Ex. 3.3a). Although this understandably does not appear in Bach's violin fugue, what does appear is a temporal recombination of the voices—that is, stretto at the half-bar in addition to the bar—on which the viability of the three-way combination depends (Ex. 3.3b–c). It will be observed that in measures 109–11 of the C-major Fuga (Ex. 3.3c), Bach combines the realigned two-voice stretto not with a third voice in stretto but with the chromatic countersubject, yielding a result that is both more playable on the violin and arguably more satisfying musically, at least less academic.

Ex. 3.3

a. Mattheson: threefold stretto involving imitation at one- and two-bar intervals

b. BWV 1005/2: stretto at the bar (the equivalent of two bars in Mattheson's notation)

c. BWV 1005/2: stretto at the half-bar (the equivalent of one bar in Mattheson's notation)

Interestingly, of the various contrapuntal operations Mattheson cites, the only one entirely without parallel in Bach's violin fugue is the simultaneous statement of the subject in both prime and inverted forms (Ex. 3.4), which is not only the least feasible on the violin but also the most musically stagnant.

Ex. 3.4. Mattheson: subject in prime and inverted forms combined

Ledbetter is certainly correct that Mattheson's subject is characteristic of pedagogical *partimento* fugues and therefore ideal material for

improvisation, but the astonishing similarities with the violin fugue Bach penned some half a year before his Hamburg audition cannot be so simply dismissed.[16] The best explanation for these otherwise perplexing coincidences is that Bach's 1720 improvisation on "An Wasserflüssen Babylon" in Hamburg included a G-major organ fugue that substantially resembled the C-major violin fugue he had committed to paper only months earlier; and Mattheson, admiring the potential inherent in Bach's subject as well as his development of it, used the subject, to the best of his recollection, for subsequent auditions.

Two further considerations lend credence to this conjecture. First, the one other organ audition that Mattheson details in the *Grossen General-Baß-Schule*, which took place in 1725, also featured a subject by Bach that is likewise imperfectly recollected: that of the G-minor organ fugue, BWV 542/2 (Ex. 3.5).

Ex. 3.5

a. Mattheson: fugue subject for a 1725 organ audition in Hamburg

b. Bach: subject of the G-minor organ fugue, BWV 542/2

Mattheson gives a characteristically oblique nod to the composer, writing, "I knew well to whom this theme belonged, and who previously worked it out artfully on paper."[17] On the basis of this, Wolff proposes that Mattheson would likely have heard the fugue in recital in the course of Bach's 1720 Hamburg audition,[18] especially as the subject resembles a Dutch folk song ("Ik ben gegroet van") that would have made it especially fitting as a nod to the Dutch-born Reinken. If Bach's Hamburg audition was the source of the fugue subject being used to audition organists in Hamburg in 1725, there is every reason to suppose it would probably also have been the source

16. cf. Ledbetter, *Unaccompanied Bach*, 152.

17. Mattheson, *Grosse General-Baß Schule*, 34.

18. Wolff, Bach: *The Learned Musician*, 213. It is doubtful, though, whether Mattheson ever saw the working-out on paper to which he refers.

of subject used in 1727, especially given its similarities to the already-extant C-major violin fugue.

Second, twice later in the 1730s Mattheson would cite the same essential G-major fugue subject—in *Kern Melodischer Wissenschaft* (1737)[19] and *Der Vollkommene Capellmeister* (1739)[20]—except in these citations the subject conforms to Bach's in details of contour and notation, suggesting that by the late 1730s Mattheson had seen a notated version of the fugue that previously he could only recall by ear.[21] The fact that the subject remains in G major and is first answered, as in 1731, by a lower voice—not a higher voice, as in the C-major violin fugue—seems to suggest that Mattheson is citing not the C-major violin fugue but a keyboard transcription of it. Interestingly, in both *Kern Melodischer Wissenschaft* and *Der Vollkommene Capellmeister*, these quotations are almost immediately followed by the subject of Bach's A-minor solo violin fugue, which Mattheson cites as a model of economy and invention. Although this would presumably indicate the probability that he knew the C-major violin fugue by this point, he curiously continues to cite the G-major keyboard version, perhaps because after hearing Bach perform it in 1720 he most readily associates it with the organ.

If Bach indeed notated a G-major keyboard transcription of his C-major violin fugue reflecting the "improvised" fugue on "An Wasserflüssen Babylon" that he would have performed in Hamburg in 1720, it could explain another musical curiosity. BWV 968 is a G-major clavier adaptation, possibly by Wilhelm Friedemann Bach, of the first movement of the C-major violin sonata alone, despite the fact that its ending on V makes the movement unsuitable as a stand-alone work. If a keyboard version of the following fugue already existed, especially if it were crafted so as to be playable on either clavier or organ—bearing in mind that in Bach's day organ works, like those for other keyboard instruments, were typically notated either in two staves or, somewhat less commonly, in open score—then it is conceivable that BWV 968 might have been adapted as a prelude to this already-existing keyboard fugue.

All of this implies an association of the subject of the C-major violin fugue with "An Wasserflüssen Babylon," and it is in light of this substantial connection that a remark by Mattheson must be viewed. In his stipulations for the 1727 audition, he notes that the given fugue subject, recalling Bach's

19. Johann Mattheson, *Kern Melodischer Wissenschaft*, 146 (chap. 8, §7).

20. P. 368 (part III, chap. 20, §16).

21. This in itself would suggest that the notated version probably did not originate as a writing-down of the improvisation as a subsequent portion of the audition process, like what Mattheson describes in connection with the 1725 audition (though not 1727). Mattheson, *Grosse General-Baß Schule*, 35.

C-major fugue, contains the first eight notes of a chorale melody that is to be the basis for a subsequent improvised chorale setting in three voices. Although the overall structure of the fugue subject most nearly resembles "An Wasserflüssen Babylon" (Ex. 3.6), Mattheson's description arguably applies more neatly to "Komm, heiliger Geist" (Ex. 3.7).

Ex. 3.6

a. "An Wasserflüssen Babylon" (*Teutsch Kirche Ampt*, 1525)

b. "Komm, heiliger Geist" (Erfurt *Enchiridion*, 1524)

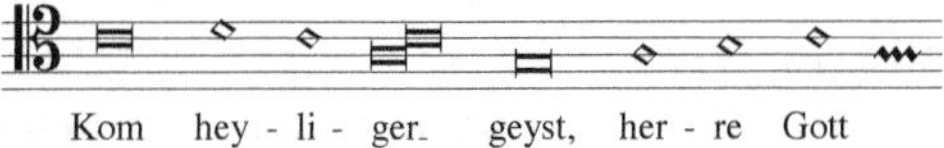

c. Bach: "An Wasserflüssen Babylon," BWV 267, with melodic structure emphasized

d. Bach: chorale, "Komm, heiliger Geist," BWV 59/3, with solmization syllables emphasizing the sequence of intervals that end the phrase

e. Mattheson: fugue subject for the 1727 organ audition. The contour most resembles "An Wasserflüssen Babylon," while the syllables *re, mi, fa* occur in the same place as in "Komm, heiliger Geist."

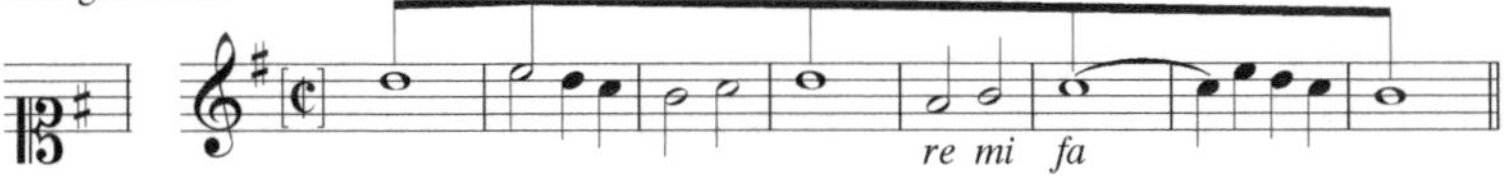

f. BWV 1005/2: subject. In addition to the attributes of Mattheson's subject, Bach's contains a returning-note figure (bracketed) that recalls his treatment of "An Wasserflüssen Babylon" in BWV 267. The extension of the bracket to g' reflects the ornamented presentation of the chorale in BWV 653a and 653b.

Ex. 3.7

a. The first eight notes of "Komm, heiliger Geist" within Mattheson's 1727 fugue subject

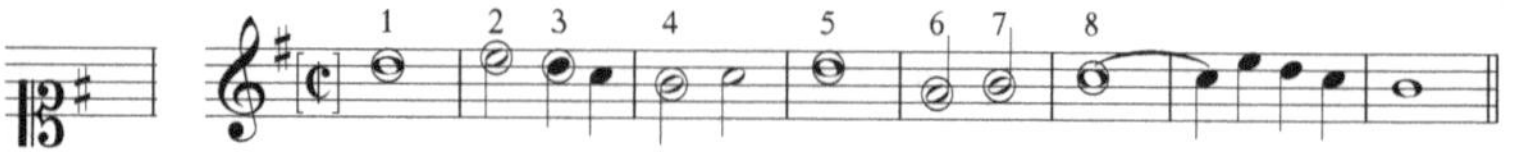

b. The first eight notes of "An Wasserflüssen Babylon" in Mattheson's 1727 fugue subject

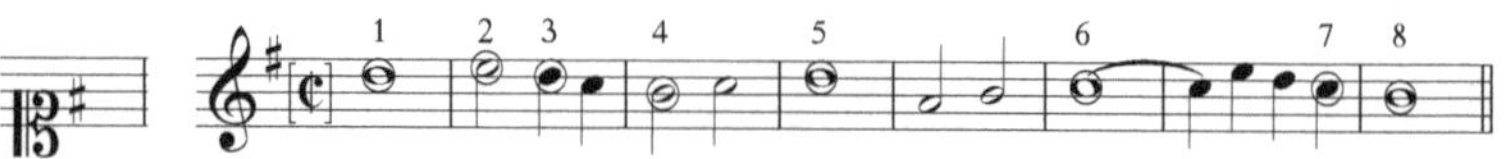

If that association is correct, it is essentially immaterial whether Mattheson had forgotten the association with "An Wasserflüssen Babylon" from seven years earlier or he intentionally changed the association so that, in the chorale setting to follow, candidates would be improvising on a still more commonplace melody.[22] In the final analysis, the crucial link between Bach's C-major Fuga and the subject given in Hamburg in 1727 is Bach's own Hamburg audition in 1720. And that, as reported in Bach's obituary, is precisely what establishes the connection with "An Wasserflüssen Babylon."

Moreover, there are musical reasons to support the association of the C-major fugue subject with "An Wasserflüssen Babylon" rather than "Komm, heiliger Geist." The reason the subject exhibits greater overall correspondence with "An Wasserflüssen Babylon" (Ex. 3.6 compared with 3.7) is because it magnifies the tetrachordal descent inherent in the chorale, such that each successive note of the descent falls on the first beat of a measure. The general association of the tetrachord with lament is reinforced by the still-more-dolorous character of its prevalent chromatically descending countersubject, giving the fugue undertones of mourning that are much less suited to the Pentecost invocation "Komm, Heiliger Geist" than they are to "An Wasserflüssen Babylon," a verse translation of Psalm 137 by Wolfgang Dachstein that describes the weeping of the Israelite captives in exile in a distant and heathen land.

Here it is appropriate to note the similarity of the subject and countersubject of the C-major violin fugue to those of Bach's early keyboard canzona in D minor, BWV 588 (Ex. 3.8).

22. Mattheson seems interested in assigning a chorale that is known to everyone and suitable for daily use ("jedermann bekannten/ und täglich-gebräuchlichen Choral-Gesang"). Ibid., 37.

Ex. 3.8. Canzona in D minor, BWV 588: tonal answer (upper voice) with chromatic countersubject

As the treatment of the chromatic descent and the surrounding counterpoint in both works recalls a common seventeenth-century trope,[23] its appearance in BWV 588—dating from 1705 or earlier and thus clearly a work of Bach's formative years—is far less surprising than in the mature C-major violin fugue.[24] It seems noteworthy, then, that this stylistically anomalous figuration, which can (but need not always) lend itself to signifying lament, occurs within a fugue that can be strongly identified with the lamenting chorale "An Wasserflüssen Babylon." That is to say, there is reason to be open to the possibility that the lament figuration of the C-major Fuga might be more than a by-product of the process of musical invention; it is not unthinkable that Bach found this now-outmoded figuration well suited to signifying lament, commensurate with the associations of "An Wasserflüssen Babylon." If that is so, it is especially appropriate that the fugue on "An Wasserflüssen Babylon" should have originated for violin. Deeply moving statements about music permeate two of the three stanzas of Psalm 137, but the only explicit mention of a musical instrument, in verse 2, describes the desolate exiles' hanging their harps on the willows, unable "to sing the LORD's song in a foreign land." The word translated "harp" (*Harffen* in Luther's translation) is *kinnōr* (כִּנּוֹר), denoting the iconic instrument played by King David that had long since become what Ben-Horin describes as "a

23. Ledbetter gives an illuminating series of examples from Sweelinck, Pachelbel, Westhoff, and the Langloz Manuscript in *Unaccompanied Bach*, 153.

24. Ibid., 152.

central trope of calamity, mourning, and lamentation."[25] It is also the name given to the modern Western violin.[26]

Fascinatingly, there is another text, commonly accompanied by the same melody as "An Wasserflüssen Babylon," that has even deeper undertones of lament and whose possible, if secondary, association with the C-major violin fugue has not, to my knowledge, been considered. That text is Paul Gerhardt's "Ein Lämmlein geht und trägt die Schuld" ("A lamb goes and bears the guilt"), a passion chorale for Good Friday. Though the only text with which this melody is ever explicitly associated in the surviving works of Bach is "An Wasserflüssen Babylon," a number of his contemporaries use the melody to set "Ein Lämmlein geht und trägt die Schuld," including Telemann (Johannes Passion, TWV 5:30/1), Christoph Graupner (GWV 1119/24), Carl Heinrich Graun (GraunWV B:VII:4), and Bach's cousin Johann Gottfried Walther. Bach must certainly have been aware of this association, especially since "Ein Lämmlein geht und trägt die Schuld" appears in *Schuldiges Lob Gottes*, the Weimar hymnal that Bach would have used while employed there, with the indication that the hymn is to be sung to the melody of "An Wasserflüssen Babylon."[27] This raises a small but important point. Whereas the hymnbook contains the instruction that "Ein Lämmlein geht und trägt die Schuld" is to be sung to the melody of "An Wasserflüssen Babylon," the converse is not true; there is no indication that "An Wasserflüssen Babylon" is to be sung to the melody of "Ein Lämmlein geht und trägt die Schuld,"[28] which would seem to indicate that "An Wasserflüssen Babylon" is the primary textual association with the melody. The fact that Bach only explicitly connects this melody with "An Wasserflüssen Babylon," even in the instrumental genre of the organ chorale, suggests the primacy of this association in his mind as well.

This is not to imply that any secondary association with "Ein Lämmlein geht und trägt die Schuld" would therefore be out of place. Indeed, a theological affinity that might speculatively account for use of the same melody for both texts could also make the passion associations of "Ein Lämmlein geht und trägt die Schuld" a welcome undertone for the quotation of what is probably intended as "An Wasserflüssen Babylon" in the C-major violin fugue. Within the context of Lutheran thought and practice, "An Wasserflüssen Babylon" can itself have notable associations with Christ's sufferings at three levels.

25. Ben-Horin, "The Secular and Its Dissonances," 123.

26. See Olearius, *Biblische Erklärung* 1:69.

27. *Schuldiges Lob Gottes*, 122–25.

28. Ibid., 265, 356.

First and most generally, the entire Christ story can be likened to a tale of exile, since its context is Jesus' having come from heaven to earth, where he is rejected by men[29]; and this is especially true of his crucifixion, when, assuming the sins of the world,[30] Jesus experiences what Luther describes as "Verlassung GOTTES"—forsakenness by God—and endures "hellish anguish on account of the turning away of [God's] divinely favorable gaze."[31] Indeed, Jesus' condescension to earth and to the cross is strongly connected with the idea of exile in Bach's 1714 cantata "Himmelskönig, sei willkommen" ("King of heaven, be welcome"—that is, on earth), setting a text by Salomon Franck: the fourth movement (Aria) reads in translation, "Mighty love, that drove you, great Son of God, from the throne of your glory, that you offered yourself as a sacrifice for the world, that you committed yourself with blood"[32]; and in movements 6 and 8, the believer identifies his or her own life's journey with Christ's, who "goes before and opens the way."[33]

Second and more specifically, historic Christianity has understood Israel's exile and longing for restoration to be a type, in the technical sense, of all humanity in its fallen state, expelled from Eden, and longing for redemption. In Luke's account of the transfiguration, Moses and Elijah appear and speak to Jesus about his "departure, which He was about to accomplish in Jerusalem."[34] The Greek word translated as "departure" is ἔξοδον, from which comes the word *exodus*,[35] drawing an obvious connection between Jesus' redeeming work on the cross and the Exodus of Moses (with whom Jesus is speaking), by which he led the Israelites out of their captivity in Egypt. By likening Jesus' redeeming work to the Exodus, the Gospel of Luke is necessarily likening that from which Jesus redeems the world to Israel's captivity in a foreign land.

Third, Jesus' death brings salvation because it is substitutionary; Jesus, the spotless lamb of God, dies on behalf and instead of sinful man. This

29. See, for instance, John 1:14; Matt 2:23, Mark 8:31, Luke 9:22, John 1:11 and 6:38.

30. "Da Er für uns zum Fluch worden ist für GOTT Gal. III. 13. wie Er den für uns war zur Sünde gemacht/ weiwol er von keiner Sünde wuste 2. Cor. V. 21" ("He became for us a curse before God, as He was made sin for us, though he knew no sin"). CB 5:291–92.

31. "höllische Pein/ wegen Abwendung seines Göttlichen Gnaden-Anblicks." Ibid., 291.

32. "Starkes Lieben, das dich, großer Gottessohn, von dem Thron deiner Herrlichkeit getrieben, daß du dich zum Heil der Welt als ein Opfer vorgestellt, daß du dich mit Blut verschrieben."

33. "Er gehet voran und öffnet die Bahn." See Mic 2:13.

34. Luke 9:31. The LB reads: "Ausgang, welchen er sollte erfüllen zu Jerusalem."

35. This is noted in Olearius, *Biblische Erklärung* 5:453, which Bach owned.

means that Jesus' identification with humanity in our "exile" is crucial to the Christian understanding of his atoning death. Accordingly, several episodes in the life of Jesus seem intended to draw parallels to the captivity of Israel in Egypt and the subsequent forty years of wandering in the desert.[36]

It is therefore unsurprising that within Bach's tradition Psalm 137 was read typologically so as to have a direct bearing on the redemptive work of Christ. In his lecture on this psalm, for instance, Luther likens Babylonian tyranny to what the believer faces from "the world, the flesh, and the devil," over which Christ has decisively triumphed on the cross.[37] Johann Arndt, with whose writings Bach was familiar, goes a step further in his sermon on Psalm 137, speaking of "the fleshly and spiritual Babylon" and likening the psalmist's longing for earthly Jerusalem to our "heartfelt, ardent longing for God and his kingdom," the "heavenly Jerusalem,"[38] into which Christ alone delivers us. A similar line of thought is evident in the hymn "An Wasserflüssen Babylon" itself.[39] As it appears in the Weimar hymnal *Schuldiges Lob Gottes*, it consists of six stanzas; the first five paraphrase the psalm, and the sixth and final stanza presents an application to the contemporary believer that likens the Hebrew captivity to our present state in the "vale of tears" (*Jammerthal*) that is this life, while the believer's hope is directed toward the "new way" (*neuer Art*) that is in Christ.[40]

In light of these theological associations, it is interesting to consider some possible implications of how the subject of the C-major Fuga has been altered from the original chorale melody as well as some stronger implications of how this subject is treated within the unfolding structure of the fugue. We have already observed that the subject has been modified away from the original chorale so as to outline a lamenting Phrygian tetrachord, which creates a perceptible connection with the Ciaccona whose possible significance will be discussed below. It is interesting, then, to consider that the three fugues of the *Sei Solo*, of which the C-major is the last, can be seen to represent a progressive intensification of the lament motif. While

36. See Matt 2:15, 4:1–2 (Mark 1:12–13, Luke 4:1–2); John 3:14.

37. *WA* 4:429. A similar analogy is drawn in the title of Luther's treatise *De captivitate Babylonica ecclesiae* ("On the Babylonian Captivity of the Church"), in which Luther uses the Babylonian exile as a metaphor for the prevalence of what he considers false doctrine. *WA* 6:484–573.

38. Arndt, "Der CXXXVII. Psalm in 1. Predigt/ mit seinen Lehr-Puncten," in *Dem ganzen Psalter Davids . . . außgelegt und erklärt*, 297–300.

39. The German text was written by Wolfgang Dachstein, first appearing in the *Teutsch Kirche ampt* of 1525.

40. *Schuldiges Lob Gottes*, 358. See Col 3:10; Eph 4:24; Heb 10:20; Matt 5:21–48; John 13:34.

the subject of the first fugue in G minor suggests an incomplete Phrygian tetrachord, the following A-minor fugue features the *passus duriusculus* prominently, but primarily in an episodic role; and finally in the C-major fugue, a complete Phrygian tetrachord is outlined in the subject while the prominent countersubject starkly presents the *passus duriusculus* (Ex. 3.9).

Ex. 3.9. Progressive clarification of the descending tetrachord in the three fugues of the *Sei Solo*

a. BWV 1001/2

b. BWV 1003/2

c. BWV 1005/2

(N)

Similarly, the subjects of all three fugues not merely contain but fundamentally consist of *X* shapes, and once again an intensification toward the C-major fugue is evident.[41] Whereas the subject of the G-minor fugue contains two crosses somewhat obscured by a single accented passing tone,[42] the subject of the A-minor fugue plainly presents its two crosses, and the C-major subject contains three (Ex. 3.10).

41. The intensification in these two areas parallels a broader pattern of intensification among the three fugues collectively that Wolfgang Ruf has documented in terms of increasing length, contrapuntal complexity, formal strictness, and distinct treatment of voicing ("Polyphonie in Bachs Sonaten für Violine solo").

42. I use the term with regard to its relation to the melodic cross-imagery in the subject. In its various contrapuntal contexts throughout the fugue it does not always function as an accented passing tone.

Ex. 3.10. Intensifying *X*-shapes in the three fugue subjects of the *Sei Solo*

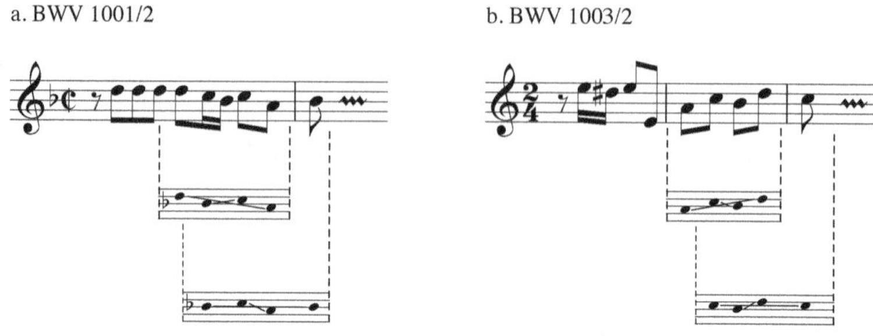

c. BWV 1005/2

It may not be accidental that these three crosses correspond to the number of crosses on Golgotha as Jesus hung crucified and "exiled," as it were, on our behalf; in Chapter 5 we will observe a similar image in the three structural chiasms of the D-minor partia.[43]

Unlike the previous two fugues, the C-major Fuga consists of clearly delineated sections—seven, to be exact[44]—that are alternately fugal and episodic. After the initial exposition of the exile subject and its lamenting countersubject, the bassline of the following episode (mm. 66–92) continues to develop the stepwise diatonic descending motion inherent in the subject—which, parenthetically, has an important implication for performance. It is common to hear the downbeats of measures 73 and 75 emphasized as though they were bass notes—sometimes more than those of measures that precede them. But this yields an incomprehensible bassline, especially in its supposed motion from *g#'* in measure 75 to *e'* (the foundation of a $^6_4$ chord)

43. See "The Number 4 (and 5) in the D-minor Partia, BWV 1004" in Chap. 5.

44. On the associations of the number seven with fullness and completeness, see Chap. 2 n. 6.

in measure 76. Rather, the voice leading should be understood as shown in Example 3.11 and played accordingly.

Ex. 3.11. BWV 1005/2, mm. 72–78 with implied harmony indicated below

After this first episode concludes with a half cadence on E, there begins a second fugal section (mm. 92–165), the longest in the movement, which

develops the subject in stretto, a technique concentrated entirely within this section. Aesthetically, stretto necessarily creates a feeling of intensification on account of increased contrapuntal/textural density, or "vertical" density, which is paralleled by increased density on the horizontal plane as well; that is, for its length, this section has the fewest measures of any in the fugue in which the subject or closely related material is not being developed. Related to this increase in both vertical and horizontal density is the sense that this second section of fugal entries draws out the musical and developmental possibilities inherent within the subject more extensively than anywhere else in the movement. These all combine to create a sense of an intensifying of the lament topic inherent within the subject, which is abetted by the predominance of the minor mode, a feature also unique to this section. Consequently there is a feeling that this section is draining "to the dregs" everything that this lamenting and possibly passion-associated subject has to offer. This is interesting in light of the extent to which Lutheran devotional literature refers to the suffering of Christ using the language of draining the cup of suffering and wrath to its bitter dregs (*bittre Hefen*).[45] At last the section comes to a close on E minor, which, perhaps coincidentally, is a key associated with suffering in Bach's vocal music,[46] especially the suffering of Christ, presumably on account of the single sharp (*Kreuz* or "cross") in its key signature.[47]

After a second episode (mm. 165–201), Bach writes the words "*al riverso*"—the only time, as far as I am aware, that he gives such an indication in the middle of a movement[48]—and what follows is a section of fugal entries

45. See, for instance, *BLC*, 56, 89, 93; Matt 10:22 (Mark 10:38), 26:36–45 (Mark 14:32–42, Luke 22:39–46); John 18:11; Isa 51:17.

46. See Chafe, *Tonal Allegory*, 152, n. 1.

47. It is, for instance, the key with which Bach's St. Matthew Passion opens as well as that of his one setting of the "Crucifixus." The association with E minor appears valid beyond Bach. For instance, in Buxtehude's *Membra Jesu Nostri*, in which multiple references to the wounded body of Christ are to be found, E minor is reserved for the text "Vulnerasti cor meum, soror mea, sponsa" ("You have wounded my heart, my sister, my bride"), which is the one time that the implied voice of Jesus speaks of being wounded. The inclusion of this text within a cycle of passion cantatas is certainly intended to refer to Jesus' being wounded by those he came to redeem and call his bride (Eph 5:25–32; Rev 19:6–9), in keeping with the Lutheran emphasis that "I" bear responsibility for Christ's death (see Chap. 6 n. 42). Thus this sixth of the work's seven cantatas brings the thoroughgoing union of passion imagery with love poetry to new heights of intensity, underscored by the change of accompaniment from violins to viols.

48. If Kellner's manuscript does in fact represent an early version of the violin solos (see Background), it may be telling that this indication appears there as well, as it could indicate that Bach considered it especially important for reasons that, apart from some sort of symbolic or representative significance, would remain unclear to me, as it

in which subject and countersubject are presented exclusively in inversion. The exile theme, with its possible secondary association with the passion, is turned emphatically upside-down as the very material that had previously formed an unequivocal descent (including the variants of the lamenting tetrachord that so prominently contributed to the sorrowing affect of the Ciaccona) is turned on its head to create a similarly unequivocal, glorious ascent (Ex. 3.12).

Ex. 3.12. BWV 1005/2: *al riverso*

It is, I suggest, a stunning and elegant depiction of the resurrection. Nor is it the only time Bach uses such musical imagery in connection with the resurrection. In the Mass in B Minor, the four-measure pulsating chromatic descent that constitutes the ostinato bass of the "Crucifixus" is symbolically reversed in the "Et resurrexit" by the four-measure pulsating chromatic ascent in the bass preceding the four most structurally important cadences (mm. 28–31 preceding the cadence at 34, mm. 60–63 preceding the cadence at 66, mm. 105–8 preceding the cadence at 111, and mm. 125–28 preceding the final cadence at 131).[49]

Several other considerations reinforce the viability of considering the *al riverso* entries in the C-major Fuga as an image of the resurrection. If the C-major Fuga represents the next episode in the Christ story following the crucifixion that is represented in the Ciaccona, then in light of the fact that the Fuga does not follow immediately after the Ciaccona (there is one intervening movement), it is especially relevant that there are strong links between the Ciaccona and the C-major Fuga at multiple levels. We have already observed the motivic connection between the variously realized tetrachordal ostinato of the Ciaccona and the reemergence of two of its principal manifestations—the diatonic tetrachordal descent and the chromatic *passus duriusculus*—in the subject and countersubject of the C-major Fuga,

is not an important performance indication.

49. I am grateful to Calvin Stapert for bringing this to my attention.

by virtue of which the inversion beginning at measure 201 of the fugue has such a striking impact. Second, the clearly delineated seven-part structure of the fugue yields an elegant seven-part chiasm, as seen in Figure 3.1.

Fig. 3.1. Structure of BWV 1005/2

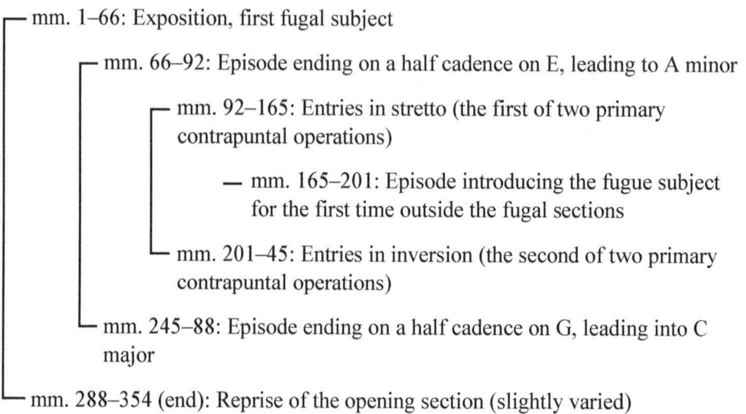

mm. 1–66: Exposition, first fugal subject
mm. 66–92: Episode ending on a half cadence on E, leading to A minor
mm. 92–165: Entries in stretto (the first of two primary contrapuntal operations)
mm. 165–201: Episode introducing the fugue subject for the first time outside the fugal sections
mm. 201–45: Entries in inversion (the second of two primary contrapuntal operations)
mm. 245–88: Episode ending on a half cadence on G, leading into C major
mm. 288–354 (end): Reprise of the opening section (slightly varied)

This places the C-major Fuga together with the Ciaccona as the only two movements of the *Sei Solo* to exhibit clear and comprehensive chiastic structure. These two movements are also the most massive of the collection, their individual measure counts surpassing that of the entirety of the remainder of the sonata or partia in which each is situated. There is actually one other movement in the collection to which the same applies, the Fuga of the A-minor sonata. Ruth Tatlow has observed that these three musical monoliths—the Ciaccona and the fugues in A minor and C major—together add up to a round 900 measures.[50] This is all to say, given the strong connections between the Ciaccona and the C-major Fuga, it is unsurprising that the theological representation evident in the Ciaccona should continue in the C-major Fuga; the fact that there should be an intervening movement between the representation of the passion in the Ciaccona and the next episode of the Christ story, the resurrection, in the C-major Fuga seems not at all problematic.

Indeed, it is possible that the presence of an intervening movement between the Ciaccona and C-major Fuga could correspond to the intervening day between the crucifixion and resurrection according to the historically understood chronology: Christ is crucified on Friday and raised Sunday,

50. Tatlow, *Bach's Numbers*, 141–42. She notes that such sums are frequently found in finished collections of Bach.

on the third day—that is, after two days. In this light, it is interesting that within the C-major Fuga the *al riverso* entries, which I suggest represent the resurrection, begin in measure 201, which is after exactly two hundred measures. Tatlow has noted that significant numbers in Bach's collections frequently appear in multiples of ten or hundred.[51] Could this introduction of resurrection imagery after exactly two hundred measures be a second representation of Christ's being raised after two days? It seems not implausible given the similar numerical-structural planning in the G-minor Fuga that we will observe in Example 6.6.

The following episode (mm. 245–88) perpetuates the *al riverso* principle by beginning with an approximate inversion of the material that began the previous episode (Ex. 3.13), soaring upward in measure 263 to *g'''*, the highest note of the *Sei Solo*, which is heard nowhere else in the C-major Fuga and only twice else in the entire collection: two movements earlier in the Ciaccona of the D-minor partia, and two movements later in the final Allegro aßai of the C-major sonata, thus framing the C-major Fuga. Within the Fuga itself, a symmetrical pair of events similarly frames the *al riverso* entries. The surrounding episodic sections—whose significantly developed head motifs, as noted, are approximate inverses of each other—both conclude with substantially identical fantasialike material based on the fugue subject; though the first (beginning in m. 186) is in G major and the second (m. 273) is in C major, both cadence on a G-major chord. Heightening the sense of symmetry between these passages is that the ascent to the high point of this bariolage figuration (mm. 194 and 281) is more chromatic in the second occurrence, whereas the descent from the high point is more chromatic in the first (Ex. 3.14).

Ex. 3.13. BWV 1005/2: beginnings of the episodes framing the *al riverso* entries

51. Ibid., 28 (see also 26).

Ex. 3.14. BWV 1005/2: endings of the episodes framing the *al riverso* entries

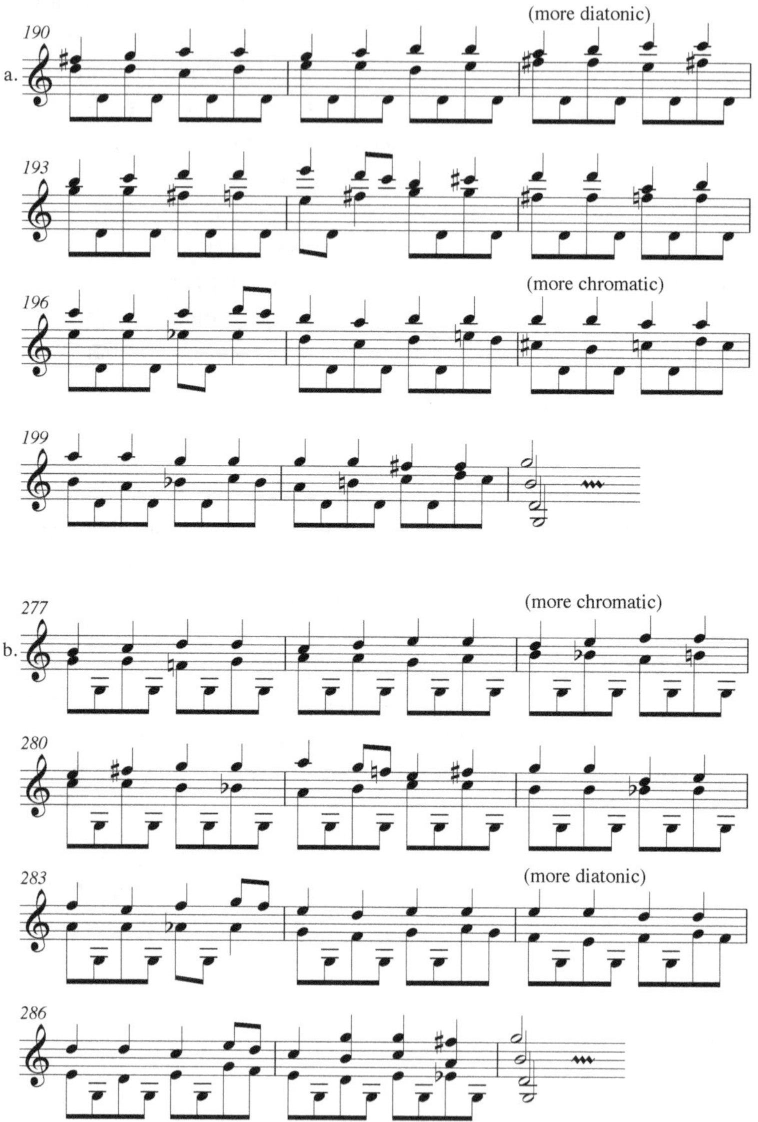

Such aurally perceptible framing of the *al riverso* entries structurally underscores them in the listener's mind, as if perhaps to emphasize their significance, an important historical purpose of such structural "framing."[52]

52. See, for instance, Davidson, "The Structure of Lassus' Motets a 2 (1577)." More generally, the idea of "framing" is essential to chiastic structure, which Bach knew and

Two observations are in order about these rhapsodic presentations of the subject *en bariolage*. First, they represent the sole exception to the general noninclusion of the subject in the clearly delineated episodic sections of the fugue (remembering the clear delineation of the C-major Fuga into seven sections alternating between fugal and episodic). Preceding the first of these bariolage passages are motivic hints of the subject that begin subtly but finally yield to the overt statement of the subject in measure 186. The way in which this virtuosic manifestation of the exile/passion theme breaks into new musical territory can recall the ever-expanding kingdom of the once-exiled and crucified King according to the language of Isa 9:6–7, which historic Christianity has universally understood as a reference to Christ.[53] It seems telling that immediately following this is the inversion that I suggest represents the resurrection, which is to say, the point at which the immortal new creation secured by Jesus on the cross breaks into the halls of mortal earth.

Second, the fact that the fantasialike presentation of the subject *en bariolage* appears again following the *al riverso* entries means that the prime (i.e., untransposed) form of the lamenting exile theme is heard again after it has been decisively inverted in a way that would seem to evoke the resurrection. All the more puzzling, then, is that immediately following this episode the fugue concludes with a near-verbatim reprise of the exposition with which it began (mm. 288–354), presenting the exile theme and its lamenting countersubject in prime form with no further trace of inversion. But if that is perplexing in light of the fact that the resurrection has already supposedly been represented, then I suggest it is perplexing in a way that confirms rather than undermines the validity of understanding the *al riverso* entries as an image of the resurrection, because it is exactly the perplexity that Jesus' disciples reportedly felt following his resurrection. Among the various eschatological expectations of first-century Judaism, it was commonly anticipated that the coming of the Davidic Messiah would herald the consolation of Israel with the defeat of his enemies—namely, in this context, Rome—ushering in the kingdom of God with the resurrection of the dead,

used, in which the structural midpoint frequently expresses the core or essence of the idea being conveyed. Though of course Bach's intentions in this instance remain a matter of speculation, the concept of framing as a means of highlighting something of significance was certainly not alien to him.

53. "For a child will be born to us, a son will be given to us;/ And the government will rest on His shoulders;/ And His name will be called Wonderful Counselor, Mighty God, Eternal Father, Prince of Peace./ There will be no end to the increase of his government or of peace,/ On the throne of David and over his kingdom,/ To establish it and to uphold it with justice and righteousness/ From then on and forevermore./ The zeal of the LORD of hosts will accomplish this."

the judgment, and the establishment of eternal justice and peace. Jesus, the touted Messiah, has been raised from the dead, yet "all continues just as it was from the beginning of creation"[54]; the present age continues, suffering and death endure, Roman oppression persists. And then Jesus prepares to depart, prompting his disciples to ask with consternation, "Lord, is it at this time You are restoring the kingdom to Israel?"[55]

But just as the reprise of the initial exposition at the end of the C-major Fuga, with its lament and exile associations, is not quite verbatim—something has changed—so too, according to Christian understanding, the continuation of the sorrows and evils of the world may persist for a time following the resurrection of Christ, but nonetheless something has quietly changed: Christ has triumphed. In Luther's words: "It is finished: the lamb of God has been slaughtered and offered up for the sins of the world, the true high priest has brought his offering to completion, the Son of God has given and offered up his body and life as payment for sin; sin is obliterated, God's wrath propitiated, death overcome, the kingdom purchased and heaven opened. All is fulfilled and completed and no one may contest, as if there were something yet to fulfill and accomplish."[56] And thus there stands the hope of the promise that the full implications of Jesus' redemptive victory will be consummated when he returns in glory at the end of the age.[57]

54. 2 Pet 3:4.

55. Acts 1:6.

56. "Es ist volbracht/ Gottes Lamm ist für der Welt Sünde geschlachtet und geopffert. Der rechte HohePriester hat sein Opffer vollendet/ Gottes Son hat sein Leib und Leben zur Bezahlung für die Sünde dahin gegeben und aufgeopffert/ die Sünde ist getilget/ Gottes zorn versühnet/ der Tod überwunden/ das Himmelreich erworben/ und der Himmel aufgeschlossen. Es ist alles erfüllet und vollendet/ und darff niemand disputieren/ als sey noch etwas dahinden zu erfüllen und zu vollbringen." CB 5:947, *WA* 28:406. It is worth noting parenthetically that this statement starkly juxtaposes language reflecting what have become categorized as two separate theories of the atonement that are sometimes felt to be in tension with each other: on the one hand is substitution theory, describing Christ's substituting himself for sinful man on the cross, so that the cross is God's absorbing and thus propitiating—as a man—his own wrath against sinful man; and on the other hand is what Aulén in his eponymous book has called the *Christus Victor* theory, emphasizing Christ's triumph over the powers of evil. For Luther, these two mechanisms and purposes of the atonement existed side by side and would continue to do so in the Lutheranism of the seventeenth and early eighteenth centuries. See Althaus, *The Theology of Martin Luther*, 202–11.

57. See, for instance, Rom 8:18–25; 1 Cor 15:20–27; 1 Thess 1:10; Heb 9:28; 2 Pet 3:3–13; 1 John 3:2. In Christian theology, the *eschaton* (ἔσχατον) is the culmination of history connected with the return of Christ, the coming of the kingdom of God, the resurrection of the dead, the final judgment, the institution of the glorified new heavens and new earth, and the inauguration of what Luke (18:30, 20:35) describes as the "age to come."

Historic Christianity has therefore understood the interval between the resurrection of Christ and his promised return in glory at the end of the age as a time in which two ages exist in parallel: the new creation, associated with the age to come, has already been inaugurated through Christ's redemptive work,[58] but at the same time "this present evil age" continues,[59] and with it the assaults (*Anfechtung*) of "the devil, the world, and our flesh."[60] Luther understands this period as one in which the blessings Christ purchased for us by his death and resurrection are both "already" and "not yet."[61] In describing the symbolism of the so-called Luther Rose, which would become the preeminent symbol of Lutheranism, Luther explains that the white rose represents the "joy, comfort, and peace" (*Freude, Trost und Friede*) that come through "faith in the crucified one" (*fide crucifixi*), and that this white rose is set against a sky-blue field (*im himmelfarben Felde*)[62] because "such joy in spirit and faith is a beginning of the heavenly joy to come, now indeed already comprehended within and clung to in hope, though not yet revealed."[63]

The return of the exile-themed subject with its lamenting countersubject at the end of the C-major Fuga recalls ideas that reflect this duality. We groan, writes Paul, and all creation with us, not only because of the continuing reality of evil but because we long for the promised redemption,[64] living as exiles sojourning through this world toward our heavenly home.[65] Even the passion overtones by association with "Ein Lämmlein geht und trägt die

58. 2 Cor 5:17; Heb 6:5.

59. Gal 1:4.

60. "desz teuffels der welt und unsers fleyschs." *Der Kleine Katechismus* (*Smaller Catechism*), *WA* 30 I:252. The struggle between the two "ages" is reflected in Paul's lament that "I joyfully concur with the law of God in the inner man, but I see a different law in the members of my body, . . . the law of sin" (Rom 7:22–23), which in turn contributes significantly to Luther's understanding of the believer in Christ as *simul justus et peccator*, simultaneously righteous and sinner. That is, although the believer is never free from sinning in this life, he or she is nonetheless in another sense already righteous, justified before God through the imputation of Christ's own righteousness (what Luther calls "alien" righteousness) through faith in him. See Althaus, *The Theology of Martin Luther*, 243–45.

61. See ibid., 236–37.

62. In German, "Himmel" refers to both sky and heaven, as with the Latin "caelum," the Greek οὐρανός (*ouranos*), and the Hebrew שמים (*shamayim*).

63. " . . . daß solche Freude im Geist und Glauben ein Anfang ist der himmlischen Freude zukunftig, itzt wohl schon drinnen begriffen und durch Hoffnung gefasset, aber noch nicht offenbar." *WA BR* 5:445. Althaus elaborates on Luther's understanding of this idea in *The Theology of Martin Luther*, 236–37.

64. Rom 8:22–23.

65. Heb 11:13; 1 Pet 2:11 (1:17); see 1 Cor 7:29–31; Phil 3:20.

Schuld" are not inappropriate; not only is the Christian hope affixed solely on Christ crucified,[66] but throughout life in this broken and sinful world the believer is "always carrying about in the body the dying of Jesus, so that the life of Jesus may be manifested in our body."[67] But just as "the sufferings of this present time are not worthy to be compared with the glory that is to be revealed to us,"[68] so the C-major Fuga, despite its inescapable evocations of lament, progresses with a sense of assurance and an unsurpassed majesty toward its glorious conclusion on a C-major chord that, for sheer brightness and resonance on the violin, adds the fifth (*g*") like an overtone above the melodic cadence on *c*".

Similarly, as if to address the concern that the return of the lamenting subject and countersubject indicates something has not gone according to plan or the work is left incomplete, the end of the Fuga reveals—as only an ending can—that the clearly delineated alternations between fugal and episodic sections, by which the movement's elegant chiastic form is created, add up to seven, a number widely associated not only with perfection and completion but also with the Sabbath, the seventh day of the week, on which God rests from his completed labors.[69] The association of Sabbath rest extends to the triumphant accomplishment of Christ's redemptive work as well, since the work by which Christ inaugurates the new creation is fin-

66. 1 Cor 1:22–24; 2:2. See Chap. 2 n. 11.

67. 2 Cor 4:10. Luther so strongly emphasizes the believer's ongoing identification with the death of Christ in the mortification of the "old man" (i.e., the sinful flesh) that Althaus finds "no statements corresponding to [Paul's affirmation in Col 3:3 that the believer "has died"—as a past event] in Luther" (*The Theology of Martin Luther*, 357). Althaus considers this a "deviation from Paul," but care must be taken; Luther's emphases and concerns may indeed be different from Paul's, as Althaus himself observes (358), but the two perspectives should not be seen as contradictory. The emphasis in Col 3:3 is not only in the past; two verses later, Paul urges his readers "therefore" to put their sinful desires to death. His argument is that the believer is to put the sinful flesh to death in the present *because* he or she has died with Christ (and therefore also died to sin: Rom 6:10) as a past event. This ongoing identification with the death of Christ in mortifying the sinful nature is likely in view in Paul's statement in 1 Cor 15:31 that "I die daily," echoing Jesus' statement that any who would follow him "must deny himself, and take up his cross daily and follow Me" (Luke 9:23). And just as Paul views our participation in the death of Christ as a past event entailing ongoing action, so Luther's emphasis on the believer's present state of justification, even while a sinner, necessarily implies that his or her ongoing participation in the death of Christ is rooted in the fact of already standing forensically dead to sin before God through faith in Christ.

68. Rom 8:18.

69. Various writers on music in Bach's day observed that the seventh partial of the harmonic series does not form a proper pitch of the scale, and therefore the realm of usable tones "rests" from the seventh partial. This they connected with God's resting on the seventh day, earning the number seven the designation "Ruh[e]-Zahl" or "rest number." See Conrad Matthäi, *Modis Musicis*, 15; Werckmeister, *Musica Mathematicae Hodegus Curiosus*, 144 and *Musicalische Paradoxal-Discourse*, 91.

ished, like the first creation, on the sixth day of the week, after which his work is complete and he rests from his labor.[70]

As noted above, it hardly seems coincidental that intimations of Christ's resurrection, with its prominent overtones of cleansing, occur within the broader context of C major, a key associated with purity.[71] At least to that extent, there would appear to be a tonal dimension to the allegory of the C-major sonata.[72] In fact, arguably the two most notable tonal features of the C-major sonata present further correspondences with the triumphant resurrection of Christ and the subsequent persistence of brokenness in the present "already-but-not-yet" age.

Prior to the C-major sonata, the minor mode had dominated the collection, with all of the four previous works and all but two movements being in minor. But coinciding with the resurrection imagery of the C-major sonata is a tonal turning point: not only are the remaining two works in major, but the minor mode never again governs the tonality of a single movement. In fact, the C-major Fuga could be seen as articulating the point at which the latter becomes evident, as the Largo that immediately follows the Fuga is the one movement among the remainder of the collection that would have been most likely to be in minor. Whereas all movements of a Baroque dance suite (such as the E-major partia) are typically in the same key, with the occasional exception of trios or subsidiary dances that shift to the parallel minor or major, the third movement of a sonata da chiesa in Bach's day was typically in a contrasting key, most commonly the relative major or minor, as indeed is the case with the first two sonatas of the *Sei Solo*. If the C-major sonata continued this pattern, its third movement would be in A minor. Instead, it is in F major—a common enough key relationship, to be sure—but thus it becomes the only complete movement of the *Sei Solo* whose key

70. Rambach describes the entombment of Christ as when "the Son of God rests from the work of salvation, which with all validity can be seen part as a fulfillment of the Sabbath of the Old Testament and part as a preparation for the great Sabbath of the New Testament, in which the people of God shall rest from their hard service to the law" ("der Sohn GOttes von dem Werck der Erlösung ruhete, und welches mit allem Recht angesehen werden konte, theils als die Erfüllung der Sabbather des Alten Testamentes, theils also eine Zurüstung zu dem grossen Sabbath des Neuen Testamentes, an welchem das Volck Gottes von dem schweren Dienst des Gesetzes ruhen sollte"). *BLC*, 1241, with reference to Heb 4:9–10. The New Testament repeatedly describes Christ after his ascension as seated at the right hand of God, implying victory and rest (see Matt 26:64, Mark 6:19, Col 3:1, Rev 3:1). This idea is echoed in both the Apostles' Nicene Creeds, and accordingly the idea of the "session" of Christ (that is, his being victoriously seated) has historically been an important concept in Christian theology.

71. See this chap. nn. 1–3.

72. Eric Chafe has extensively documented tonal allegory in Bach's vocal music (see, i.a., *Tonal Allegory in the Vocal Music of J. S. Bach*; *Analyzing Bach Cantatas*; *J. S. Bach's Johannine Theology*; and *Tears into Wine*).

signature differs from the overall key of the work in which it is situated.[73] In short, the technique that maintains the unbroken "reign" of major following the resurrection imagery of the C-major Fuga, although not uncommon, is nonetheless unique to the *Sei Solo*, which heightens the appearance that Bach may have intended the exclusive use of major tonalities following the representation of the passion of Christ, as well as the preponderance of minor keys beforehand, to have symbolic significance.

Although blanket attribution of affective qualities to keys or modes (whether individually or as a class) is at best difficult and necessarily subjective, Zarlino's view that modes with a major third are "cheerful and lively" ("allegri, & vivi") whereas those with a minor third are "melancholy or languid" in character ("mesto, o languido") appears to have been influential within Bach's context.[74] Even Johann Kuhnau, who notes the difficulty of ascribing definite attributes to specific keys, writes in the same essay that keys with a minor third "depict something sad, melancholy, and . . . yearning" ("etwas trauriges, melancholisches, und . . . sehnliches vorstellen") whereas those with a major third depict "something perfect, and merry" ("etwas vollkommenes, und lustiges"),[75] recalling the older association of the major triad with perfection and the minor triad with imperfection.[76]

It is premature to dismiss these associations on the grounds that not all pieces in a major key are intended to be "happy" nor all in a minor key to be "sad." That would be to underestimate the many other aspects of a musical composition that can contribute to its overall affect. In reality, the most enduring musical compositions often exhibit a complexity of expression arising from the interrelation of elements that, in isolation, might lend themselves to divergent affective assocations. For instance, I find "Mache dich, mein Herze, rein" from Bach's St. Matthew Passion to be more, not less, sad for being in a major key—and the reason is because the major mode relates to the text, the broader narrative, the plaintive sound of the oboes d'amore, and the poignant harmonies in such a way as to make the aria not merely sad but bittersweet; the emotion is more complex. Within the *Sei Solo*, a similar observation might be made of the achingly beautiful D-major middle section of the Ciaccona. But the fact that the major mode can be felt to create such complexity within a predominantly sad affect (or, conversely, the minor mode within a predominantly vivacious or elegant affect) would seem to speak *for* rather than against the viability of the general affective

73. The middle section of the Ciaccona moves to D major and so has a different key signature from the remainder of the partia, but the final/tonic of D remains constant.

74. Zarlino, *Le Istitutioni Harmoniche*, 156.

75. Kuhnau, foreword to *Musicalische Vorstellung einiger Biblischer Historien*, xi (numbering from the title page).

76. See Dahlhaus, *Die Termini Dur und Moll*, 294.

associations Zarlino and Kuhnau describe; that is to say, I do not see sufficient grounds for dismissing the relevance of these associations to Bach's thinking on the evidence of his music. Indeed, they might explain why he structured the *Sei Solo* such that the minor mode dominates through the D-minor partia, with its proposed passion symbolism, whereas every movement of the remaining two works is in major.

If the *Sei Solo* could be using minor tonalities, at least representationally, to suggest the sad, imperfect state of humanity and major tonalities to signify restoration through Christ's redemptive work, the question of the two major-mode movements during the "reign of minor" preceding the C-major sonata must be addressed. It is initially tempting to view these two movements—namely, the third movements of the first and second sonatas—as mere exceptions to the overall tonal pattern, perhaps in the interest of musical variety, that cannot be seen as doing any real damage to an allegorical schema that nonetheless might have been even more pronounced had they been in minor. But in fact if the foregoing associations of major and minor within the *Sei Solo* are valid, then the inclusion of these two major-mode movements actually presents a closer parallel to Christian theology than if every single movement prior to the C-major sonata were in minor; historic Christianity, including Lutheranism, has recognized that the grace and providence of God remain evident even amid the brokenness and fallenness of rebellious man,[77] including the time historically prior to Christ's accomplishment of the redeeming work that was the eternal purpose of God.[78] It might also be noteworthy that the D-minor Ciaccona, exhibiting what I propose is crucifixion imagery, contains a middle section in D major,[79] as Luther's theology of the cross is centered on the understanding that it is on the cross that Christ's work is decisively accomplished and redemption won.[80]

The second particularly noteworthy tonal feature of the C-major sonata is that in every movement, the parallel minor mode prominently asserts

77. See, for instance, Matt 5:45; Acts 14:17; 17:24–28; Rom 1:19–20.

78. Rom 3:25; see Althaus, *The Theology of Martin Luther*, 211. On God's eternal purposes in Christ, see Rom 11:32; Gal 3:22; Eph 3:11; 2 Tim 1:9; 1 Pet 1:19–20. For Luther's view of God's sovereignty in man's fall and redemption, see Chap. 6 n. 137.

79. Although the concept of the switch to the parallel key is not unprecedented (it is not uncommon, for instance, for generally lengthier French chaconnes or passecailles in a major key to have a middle section in the parallel minor), the motion from a minor key to the parallel major and back again is more unusual, as is the appearance of this typically French tonal gesture within a movement that is given the Italianate title Ciaccona.

80. See this chap. n. 56 for Luther's commentary on John 19:30, Jesus' declaration from the cross that "It is finished!"

itself in the approach to the final cadence (and sometimes elsewhere), as if threatening to shipwreck the tonality of the movement (Ex. 3.15).

Ex. 3.15. Recurrences of the parallel minor in BWV 1005

The reason the occurrence of the parallel minor is tonally threatening is because, unlike the diatonic minor triads that are frequently tonicized in Bach's harmonic language (ii, iii, and vi), the parallel minor is a fundamentally alien tonality. Johann Georg Ahle, Bach's predecessor in Mühlhausen, relates that "when part of a piece is in C [major] and another in A [minor], the mode alone is changed; but if part is in C major and the other C minor, then the modulatory genus as well as the mode is transformed."[81] And the modulatory genus is transformed by being pulled strongly in the direction of what Heinichen would call the enharmonic end of the harmonic spectrum (i.e., in the direction of increasing flats),[82] which is associated with the concept of *mollis* or "soft," terminology that was originally applied to the "soft" hexachord (*hexachordum molle*) and later adapted in German to describe minor keys (for instance, D minor is d-*Moll*). This dual association of *mollis*—referring to "flat" tonalities on one hand and to keys with a minor third on the other—is evident, for example, in the fact that manuscripts of Bach's day frequently use the soft or "molle" *b* (♭) to indicate not only a flatted pitch, as is typical today, but also a minor key; for instance, a work in D minor might be labeled "D♭" as shorthand for "D-Moll."

That is to say, the C minor that emerges periodically throughout the C-major sonata is *Moll* in two senses: it has a minor third, making it a minor key in the modern sense, but it also lies on the "flats"/enharmonic/*mollis* side of the tonal spectrum. Thus its continuing reemergence after the tonal "tide" of the *Sei Solo* has turned sharply from minor to major conceptually parallels the return of the lamenting prime form of the subject and countersubject of the C-major Fuga following what I propose is the depiction of the resurrection; in context, both features suggest a parallel with the "already-but-not-yet" state in which evil is allowed to endure for a time following Christ's triumphant death and resurrection.

If the alien tonality of the parallel minor within the pure, "redeemed" C major can indeed be associated with the evil that endures in the "already-but-not-yet" age, then the fact that this alien nature is cloaked in a superficial similarity to the redemption-associated tonic key would seem to recall the deceitfulness of the evil that threatens to shipwreck the believer in the

81. "Wän ein teil eines Stükkes aus dem C, und der andere aus dem A geht/ so wird *Modus* allein verändert; gehet aber ein teil aus dem C *natural*iter, und der andere daraus *moll*iter, so wird samt dem Modo auch das Genus modulandi verwandelt." Ahle, *Musicalisches Frühlings-Gespräche*, cited in Chafe, *Tears into Wine*, 408 (translation mine).

82. Present in the first edition of Heinichen's *Anweisung des General-Basses* (1711) but removed in the updated edition of 1728, these terms reflect older paradigms of German theory in which substantial retention of modal and hexachordal thought coincided with development of a harmonic practice that paved the way for modern tonality.

present age.[83] In the same way, the parallel minor, the tonal "wolf in sheep's clothing,"[84] consistently emerges at the approach to the final cadence of every movement as if threatening to shipwreck its tonal structure at the very point of its final arrival on the tonic. But the fact that this deceitful menace never ultimately succeeds in getting the upper hand completes a picture resembling that which Luther famously paints in his hymn "Ein' feste Burg ist unser Gott" ("A Mighty Fortress Is Our God"), which I reproduce here in its entirety to illustrate the extent to which it dwells on the threat of the devil and our deliverance from it:

Ein feste burg ist vnser Gott /	"A mighty fortress is our God,"[85]
ein gute wehr vnd waffen /	a good shield and weapon.
Er hilfft vnns frey aus aller not /	He helps us freely out of all affliction
die vns ytzt hat betroffen /	that presently has affected us.
Der alt böse feind /	The ancient, wicked fiend
mit ernst ers ytzt meint /	with dire severity seeks [our harm];
gros macht vnd viel list /	great might and much deceit
sein grausam rüstung ist /	is his cruel armament;
auff erd ist nicht seins gleichen.	on earth is not his equal.
Mit vnser macht ist nichts gethan /	With our strength is nothing done;
wir sind gar bald verloren /	we would soon be lost.
Es streit fur vns der rechte man /	There fights for us the right man,
den Gott hat selbs erkoren /	whom God himself has chosen.
Fragstu wer der ist /	Do you ask who that is?
er heist Jhesu Christ /	He is called Jesus Christ,
der Herr Zebaoth /	the Lord of Hosts,
vnd ist kein ander Gott /	and there is no other God;
das feld mus er behalten.	he must hold the [battle]field.
Vnd wenn die welt vol Teuffel wehr /	And if this world were full of devils
vnnd wolt vns gar vorschlingen /	and were bent on devouring us,

83. 1 Tim 1:19; see Gen 4:7 and 1 Pet 5:8. The deceitfulness of evil is a consistent theme in New Testament writings (see, for instance, Matt 13:22; Luke 12:19–20; 1 Cor 6:13; 2 Cor 11:3–4; Gal 3:1; Eph 5:6; Heb 3:13; 1 John 3:7) and is perhaps best exemplified in the temptation of Jesus in the wilderness (Matt 4:1–11; Luke 4:1–13), where the devil tempts him using the words of Scripture itself.

84. See Matt 7:15.

85. I begin with the opening line of Frederick Hedge's famous English adaptation (1853), as it is both accurate and iconic.

So fürchten wir vnns nicht zu sehr /	we would not be too afraid;
es sol vns doch gelingen /	even then it should indeed work out for us.
Der Fürst dieser welt /	The prince of this world,
wie sawr er sich stelt /	however sour he appear,
thut er vnns doch nicht /	can still do nothing to us:
das macht er ist gericht /	that is, he is judged;
ein wörtlin kan yhn fellen.	a little word can fell him.
Das wort sie sollen lassen stahn /	That word they shall neglect
und kein danck dazu haben /	and have no thanks for it.
Er ist bey vnns wol auff dem plan /	He stands by us, according to the plan,
mit seinem geist vnd gaben /	with his Spirit and gifts.
Nemen sie den leib /	If they take away the body,
gut eher kind vnnd weib /	goods, honor, children, and wife,
las faren dahin /	let them go;
sie habens kein gewin /	they have not won anything from it:
das reich mus vns doch bleiben.[86]	the kingdom must remain to us.

I conclude with a brief summary of the main observations of the last two chapters. Historic Christian theology has understood Christ's sufferings on the cross to be massive in scope (God suffering for the redemption of the entire world), the focal point of redemptive history, and the antitype of all human suffering. The monumental D-minor Ciaccona, a movement that is exceptional not only within the *Sei Solo* but within the entire Bach oeuvre, closely parallels these distinctive ideas, bringing a substantially adumbrated lament topic into focus within a massive chiastic structure.

And just as Christ is vindicated in his resurrection on the third day after the crucifixion (that is, as we would say, two days later), so two movements after the Ciaccona, the Fuga in the "pure" key of C major features a prominent and decisive inversion of its exile-themed subject and lament-connoting countersubject, atypically emphasized by Bach with the words *al riverso*; and since both subject and countersubject are notably marked by a downward melodic pull, their joint inversion in the third set of fugal entries creates an unmistakable turning of the exile- and lament-associated descent into a glorious ascent. But after this resurrectionlike imagery, the

86. I have used the text as it appears in Joseph Klug's *Geistliche Lieder . . . zu Wittemberg* (1535).

subject and countersubject return in their original forms, just as following the death of Christ the sorrows of the present age continue. Yet something has changed, because now Christ is risen; similarly, the reprise of the opening material that reintroduces the subject and countersubject in prime form is not quite identical to what it was at the beginning.

These ideas are exemplified at a tonal level as well. The Ciaccona marks the end of what was the overwhelming supremacy of the minor mode throughout the collection, as the C-major sonata, containing what I propose is resurrection imagery, ushers in a "reign" of major that is even more dominant than was the former "dominion" of minor. Even though the parallel minor mode reasserts itself in every movement of the C-major sonata, just as evil and sorrow persist for a time following Christ's resurrection, nevertheless the minor mode appears thoroughly "disarmed," unable to regain governance of even a single movement through the end of the *Sei Solo*, even as Christ has disarmed the powers of evil on the cross.[87]

These correlations are sufficiently strong in my mind to advance the theory that they are likely intended by Bach and therefore also that the collection of *Sei Solo* contains a dimension of theological allegory, at least to the extent of the imagery I have just described.

87. Col 2:15.

4

A Broader Theological Schema in the *Sei Solo*?

The question of an appropriate name for Bach's collection of unaccompanied violin works has historically been a matter of some disagreement. Bach's own title, *Sei Solo à Violino senza Basso accompagnato*, which roughly translates "Six solos for violin without accompanying bass," has been used little, perhaps because the designation "solos" leaves genre unspecified.[1] Ferdinand David's 1843 edition refers to the collection as "Six Sonatas"[2]—as does Leopold Auer's 1917 edition—preserving the number six but misrepresenting the genre constituency of the collection. By contrast, Joachim's edition of 1908 refers to the works simply as "Sonatas and Partitas,"[3] accurately reflecting genre but omitting the number. The fact that today the collection is most popularly called "Six sonatas and partitas" is probably because this designation refers to both number and genre, though it is necessarily a bit ambiguous. (Is six the total number? Or are there six sonatas and six partitas, recalling the structure of Corelli's Opus 5?) Perhaps for this reason, Bärenreiter chooses to title the collection "Three sonatas and three partitas."[4] But Bach's including six works in the collection seems not to be arbitrary, and therefore his explicit reference to the number six in the title seems likely to be more than merely descriptive.[5] A cursory examination of Bach's instrumental output clearly indicates the importance to him of collections of six. In addition to the collection of six solo violin works, there are six suites for solo cello, six sonatas for violin and obbligato harpsichord, six keyboard partitas in *Clavier-Übung* I, six "French" suites, six "English"

1. I will return later to the question of the translation of "*Sei solo*" (see "The title of the collection" in Chap. 6). In the discussion here, I will present only a cursory overview of titles historically assigned to the six solos. For a more detailed survey, see Lester, *Bach's Works for Solo Violin*, 19–22.

2. *Sechs Sonaten für Violine allein von Joh. Sebastian Bach.*

3. *Sonaten und Partiten für Violine allein.*

4. *Drei Sonaten und drei Partiten.*

5. See Marissen, *The Social and Religious Designs*, 83.

suites, six trio sonatas for organ, six Schübler chorales, six Brandenburg concertos, and six harpsichord concertos in the surviving complete set. The same affinity for collections of six (or multiples of six, especially twelve) is evident throughout the baroque era, from Uccellini's *Sonate, sinfonie et correnti*, Op. 2, of 1639 to Soler's *Seis conciertos* for two keyboards dating around 1770.

The significance of the number six was deeply entrenched in the tradition Bach inherited, with roots extending back at least to Pythagoras, who considered that six was a "perfect" number by virtue of being the sum of its divisors (6 = 1 x 2 x 3 = 1 + 2 + 3). Augustine would later give theological application to this idea, stating that God created the world "in six days . . . because six is a perfect number. It is not that any interval of time was necessary to God. . . . Rather, the number six is used to signify the perfection of God's works."[6] In the realm of music, six ratios consisting of the first six natural numbers, known as the *senarius*, form the principal consonances of modern Western theory.[7] The system of hexachords described by Guido d'Arezzo in his *Micrologus* (ca. 1026),[8] which continued to be influential in the music theory of Bach's day,[9] is based (as the name suggests) on groups of six notes and was thus associated with perfection.[10] In Part 1 of *Le Institutioni*

6. "Haec autem propter senarii numeri perfectionem eodem die sexiens repetito sex diebus perfecta narrantur, non quia Deo fuerit necessaria mora temporum, . . . sed quia per senarium numerum est operum significata perfectio." Trans. Dyson in Augustine, *The City of God Against the Pagans*, 490 (Book 11, chap. 29).

7. The intervals 1:1, 1:2, 2:3, 3:4, 4:5, and 5:6 create the intervals of a unison, an octave, a perfect fifth, a perfect fourth, a major third, and a minor third respectively.

8. The three positions of hexachord are "soft" (*hexachordum molle*), beginning on F; "natural" (*hexachordum naturale*), beginning on C; and "hard" (*hexachordum durum*), beginning on G. Each proceeds by step with the syllables *ut, re, mi, fa, sol, la*, with a single half-step in the middle, between *mi* and *fa*.

9. Marissen has noted the influence of hexachordal theory on the structure of the Brandenburg Concertos and *Clavier-Übung* as well as Vivaldi's Opus 3, Kuhnau's own *Clavier-Übung*, and Niedt's classification of keys in his *Musicalische Handleitung* (Marissen, *The Social and Religious Designs*, 92–99). By the 1710s a debate was raging on the continued relevance of hexachordal theory to current compositional practice, but Bach appears staunchly in favor of retaining hexachordal associations. As late as 1749, one year before his death, Bach wrote atop the so-called Faber canon (BWV 1078), "Fa Mi, et Mi Fa est tota Musica" (Fa-Mi, and Mi-Fa, is the whole of music). This seems to be a direct allusion to Johann Buttstett's treatise, *Ut, Mi, Sol,/ Re, Fa, La,/ Tota Musica et Harmonia Æterna* (1716), in which he defends traditional solmization practice derived from hexachordal theory against attack by Mattheson in his *Das Neu-Eröffnete Orchestre* (1713). Mattheson promptly responded with *Das Beschützte Orchester* (1717), whose title page refers to hexachordal solmization as "Todte (nicht tota) Musica"—that is, "dead (not complete) music."

10. See Burtius, *Musices opusculum*, C II.

Harmoniche of 1558, Zarlino devotes no fewer than four chapters (13–16) to describing the importance and perfections of the number six in music, citing six species of sound ranging in purity from the unison to intervals outside the scale system,[11] six consonances,[12] six species of *Harmonia*,[13] and six authentic as well as six plagal modes derived from these species of *Harmonia*. Unsurprisingly, then, the perfection of the number six became a recurring topic in musical writings of the German baroque,[14] including the *Synopsis musicae novae* of Johannes Lippius (1612),[15] the *Kurzer, doch ausführlicher Bericht von den Modis Musicis* of Conrad Matthäi (1652),[16] and the *Musicalisches Lexicon* of Bach's cousin Johann Gottfried Walther (1732).[17]

There is a further dimension of unification that the *Sei Solo* shares with many collections by Bach and other composers, namely, an overarching tonal scheme. Although such unifiers should certainly not be taken to imply that the included works are to be understood cyclically, they nonetheless lend some degree of collective identity beyond the mere assemblage of individual works. The respective keys of the six solos (g—b—a—d—C—E) are structured symmetrically or chiastically: from G upward to B is a major third, from B upward to A is a minor seventh, from A to D is a perfect fourth (the midpoint of the relational scheme), from D to C is a minor seventh, and from C to E is a major third. I will continue to emphasize that chiastic structures should not automatically be assumed to be Christ symbols; but it is at least interesting that this potential Christological referent should define the structure of a collection that contains, as I propose, a degree of

11. These are *Vnisone* or unisons; *Equisone*, pitches one or more octaves apart; *Consone*, perfect fourth and fifth relationships irrespective of octave separation; *Emmele*, major and minor thirds and sixths, again irrespective of octave separation; *Dissone* or dissonances, consisting of seconds, sevenths, and tritones; and *Ecmele*, intervals not formed between established musical pitches. Zarlino, *Le Institutioni Harmoniche*, 24 (part 1, chap. 14).

12. These are unison (*Vnisono*), octave (*Diapason*), perfect fifth (*Diapente*), perfect fourth (*Diatesseron*), major third/minor sixth (*Ditono*), and minor third/major sixth (*Semiditono*). Ibid.

13. Dorian, Phrygian, Lydian, Mixolydian/Lochrian, Aeolian, and Iastian/Ionian. Ibid.

14. Klaus-Jürgen Sachs provides a helpful overview of the significance of the number six within Bach's tradition in "Aspekte der numerischen und tonartlichen Disposition instrumentalmusikalischer Zyklen des ausgehenden 17. und beginnenden 18. Jahrhunderts," 243–49. Of course, this significance is not at all diminished by the fact that, on the basis of biblical literature, the number 7 can have similar associations of completeness and perfection. See my Chap. 2 n. 6.

15. Lippius, *Synopsis musicae novae*, A4.

16. Matthäi, *Modis Musicis*, 15.

17. *ML*, s.v. "Numerus perfectus."

Christological allegory. Another important feature of the key scheme of the *Sei Solo* is that it comprises the notes of the "hard" hexachord (*hexachordum durum*) based on G, that is, G—A—B—C—D—E. From this perspective, it seems unlikely to be accidental that the first and last tonic pitches of the six solos, G and E, correspond respectively to the first and last pitches not only of the hard hexachord but also of the entire hexachordal *gamut* that defined the domain of "proper music" or *musica recta*.[18]

But the hexachordal perspective is only one of three from which the keys of the outermost of the six solos can be seen to represent extremity. A second important perspective concerns the concept of harmony that was becoming dominant in Bach's day, one governed less by modality and hexachordal theory and more by fifth-based relationships that, in theory, form a circle incorporating every chromatic pitch, as represented in Heinichen's *musicalischer Circul* of 1711 (Image 4.1).[19]

Image 4.1. Heinichen: *musicalischer Circul*

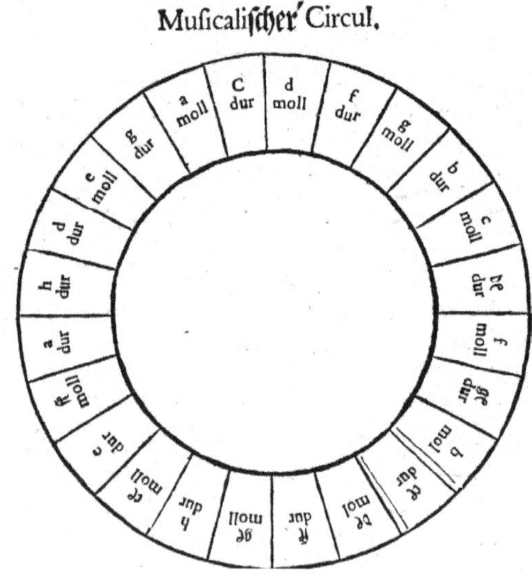

18. The gamut consisted of seven overlapping hexachords extending from G (*Gamma Ut*) upward to e" (*ela*).

19. Johann David Heinichen, *Anweisung des General-Basses*, 261. Joel Lester argues that this type of circular model did not originate with Heinichen but had previously existed as an oral tradition. Lester, *Between Modes and Keys*, 106–10.

According to this model, G minor, the key of the first sonata, and E major, the key of the final partia, represent harmonic antitheses; they are as far removed as possible within the harmonic spectrum, and their modes are opposite. In light of these two more sophisticated representations of extremity, it may not be coincidence that G and E also represent the outermost strings of the violin (*g*, *e*"), for which, of course, the *Sei Solo* are composed.[20] It is possible that Bach could have understood such representations of extremity to connote totality, since that is how they are frequently used in biblical literature and historic Christian liturgy.[21] If the tonal scheme of the *Sei Solo* were intended to symbolize completeness, it would correspond to the representation of completeness or perfection in the collection's containing six works.

All of this means that the allegory of Christ's death and resurrection that I have proposed within the Ciaccona and C-major sonata occurs within the unified, chiastic collection of *Sei solo* at a point corresponding to its place within the biblical narrative: nearer to the end but not at the end, just as in the biblical story Christ's death and resurrection mark the beginning of the "last days"[22] but do not represent the end of the story, which ends looking forward in hope to the return of Christ that has not yet come to pass. Indeed, if the C-major sonata includes a representation of the "already-but-not-yet,"[23] which Bach would have understood to continue into his own time, it might not be irrelevant to consider that the placement of the allegory of the death and resurrection of Christ approximately two-thirds of the way through the *Sei Solo* corresponds roughly with where Bach likely understood the events themselves to have occurred within the span of history.[24] According to the talmudic chronology attributed to Elijah and

20. Later I will explore more extensive antitheses between the G-minor Adagio, the first movement of the first sonata, and the E-major Gigue, the last movement of the final partia. See "Partia in E Major, BWV 1006" in Chap. 6.

21. See, for instance, Gen 8:22; Ps 113:11–12; and Rom 8:38. A well-known liturgical example is "Pleni sunt coeli et terra gloria tua" ("Heaven and earth are full of your glory") from the Sanctus. The opposition of the heights (heaven) with the depths (earth) suggests the totality of what is filled with God's glory.

22. Heb 1:2; see 1 Cor 7:29–31 and 1 John 2:18. On the role of apocalyptic thought in Lutheranism, see Cunningham and Grell, *The Four Horsemen of the Apocalypse*, especially chaps. 1 and 2.

23. See my Chap. 3.

24. Bach appears to have been fascinated by numbers relating to the duration of the world. In his Calov study Bible he places emphasis marks next to the commentary assigning specific dates to the eschatological predictions of Dan 7:25 and recopies in the margins numbers that appear in the text of Dan 12:7–13. See Leaver, *J. S. Bach and Scripture*, 112–13.

reiterated by Luther on the title page of his *Supputatio annorum mundi*, it was widely believed that the world would exist for six thousand years: "two thousand, void; two thousand, law; two thousand, Messiah."[25] Placing the creation of the world at roughly 4000 B.C., as the early Lutheran tradition did,[26] the redeeming work of Christ would occur approximately two-thirds of the way through the course of history.[27]

This invites the question of whether the remainder of the *Sei Solo* might have some role in the Christological schema I am proposing, if only by virtue of creating the temporal space to appropriately situate the crucifixion and resurrection. It is notable, though, that the works immediately surrounding the D-minor partia and C-major sonata—namely, the A-minor sonata and E-major partia—have distinct characteristics closely paralleling the corresponding episodes of the Christ story. These parallels are noteworthy, but I must say in the interest of methodological clarity that in neither the A-minor sonata nor the E-major partia are the potential signifiers as concrete as those of the D-minor partia and the C-major sonata. In isolation from the remainder of the *Sei Solo*, there would be little to compellingly suggest the likelihood (as opposed to the mere possibility) that the A-minor sonata and E-major partia are intended to contain a dimension of Christological allegory. The same can, of course, be said of a *Leitmotif* in Wagnerian music-drama when taken out of context, which is another way of saying that context is an essential consideration in investigations of musical meaning, or any meaning for that matter. And when the A-minor sonata and E-major partia are situated within the context of the *Sei Solo*, they relate importantly to the D-minor partia and C-major sonata, and to the structure of the collection as a whole, so as to suggest meanings appropriate to their respective positioning within the collection, which suggests those meanings might not be accidental. I will first consider apparent significances in the E-major partia, since those will be relevant to the subsequent discussion of the A-minor sonata.

25. "Sex milibus annorum stabit Mundus. Duobus milibus inane. Duobus milibus Lex. Duobus milibus Messiah." *WA* 53:22.

26. Luther places creation at 3961 B.C., that is 5,500 years prior to 1540 A.D. (ibid., 171), whereas the Calov study Bible that Bach would acquire in 1733 places creation squarely at 4000 B.C. The title page is dated "in the year of Christ 1681, which is the 5681st year from the creation of the world" ("Im Jahr Christi cIɔ Iɔc XXCI, welches ist das 5681ste Jahr/ von Erschaffung der Welt").

27. Luther believed this final two-millennium period would be cut short, anticipating in the 1530s and 1540s an imminent end to the world (see Cunningham and Grell, *The Four Horsemen*, 43). Bach's study Bible predicts the end of the world 211 years after its 1679 publication date, that is, in 1890 ("nur noch 211 Jahr übrig von diesen 1679sten Jahr Christi . . . ." CB 3:982).

Partia in E Major, BWV 1006

In light of the apparent significance of the continuing emergence of the parallel minor mode in the C-major sonata, it seems noteworthy that the parallel minor disappears altogether in the ebullient E-major partia, as indeed does every minor tonality except those whose tonic triads occur diatonically within the E-major scale (which therefore do not represent a substantial departure from the governing E-major tonality). This disappearance of the parallel minor seems less likely to be coincidental in view of the conclusion of the final Allegro aßai of the C-major sonata.

Throughout the sonata, the parallel minor has been repeatedly subjugated, so to speak, but not eradicated; it is able to continue returning. I suggest that Bach's treatment of the parallel minor at the end of the Allegro aßai represents this eradication of the parallel minor. At the end of the A-section, having modulated to G major, the parallel minor emerges in measure 37, more serpentine than ever before in the sonata, and it is only overcome with the resolution of the cadence on G major in measure 42 (see Ex. 3.15d). Once again, it has been subjugated but not eradicated and is able to return at the close of the B section at measure 97. By virtue of consistency with measures 37–42, a continuation of the imagery of the minor mode subjugated but not eradicated would involve the parallel minor's having dominance until the resolution of the final cadence at measure 102. But that is not what happens; already at measure 101 the major mode has reemerged, which Bach emphasizes in the autograph manuscript by a bold natural sign before the third note, *e*", even though such gratuitous naturals are not the norm in Bach's notational practice. (With some exceptions, Bach generally considers accidentals to belong only to the note that immediately follows; thus the *c*" that ends m. 79, for instance, is understood to be natural, even though the *c*" last appeared sharped in the same measure.) Bach's natural sign in measure 101 is then all the more emphatic given that no E♭ is heard even in the preceding bar and the recurrence of an unflatted *e*" to begin the third beat would certainly be sufficient to indicate that *e*♮", not *e*♭", is intended throughout the measure. In any case, this early reemergence of the major mode has the effect of cutting short what was already the limited agency of the parallel minor. And thus ends the C-major sonata; never again through the end of the *Sei Solo* does the parallel minor reappear to any degree. If the repeated emergence of the parallel minor in the C-major sonata suggests the persistence of evil during the time between Christ's death and his return, then the final cutting short of the parallel minor at the end of the C-major sonata would most naturally correspond to the cutting short of the tribulations of the present age with the return of Christ[28]; and the "banishment" of the parallel minor from the E-major partia—that is, the remainder of the *Sei Solo*—would most naturally seem to correspond to the return of Christ at the end of the age, when, in the words of Rev 21:4, "He will wipe away every tear from their eyes; and there will no longer be any death; there will no longer be any mourning, or crying, or pain; for the first things have passed away."

The viability of this parallel with Christ's return at the end of the age is further supported by the fact that the E-major partia represents, as I will explain, the culmination of a tonally chiastic collection that I have already suggested might be intended to represent the span of the history of the world. In other words, to the extent that the E-major partia is intended to represent a culmination, it could most naturally be understood to represent the culmination of the Christ (*X*) story as well as of all of history—which, according to Lutheran and historic Christian theology, is the return of Christ.

How this idea of culmination is represented in the E-major partia is quite noteworthy. Most immediately, of course, the E-major partia is the last work of the collection; but it is also the sixth, and therefore readily associable with the perfection and completeness (*Vollkommenheit*) attributed to the number six, as discussed above.

As observed above, the outermost works of the *Sei Solo* represent antithesis with regard to hexachordal theory, harmony based on the circle of fifths, and the open strings of the instrument for which they are written. But in all of these cases, the progression to the E-major sonata represents not merely difference (as in, say, the antithesis of east and west in Ps 103:12) but ascent. In hexachordal theory, *G* (*Gamma Ut*) is the lowest note of the Gamut and *e*" (*ela*) the highest. Similarly, *g* is the lowest open string of the violin while *e*" is the uppermost. In the realm of harmony, the *Sei Solo* progress from G minor, the darkest key of the collection, to E major, the brightest. These associations of darkness and brightness apply at three levels. The first is purely tonal. G minor is what Heinichen would call the most "enharmonic" key of the collection, being the furthest in the direction of increasing flats, while E major is the most "chromatic," being the furthest in the direction of increasing sharps.[29] Second, in the context of violin writing, there is an additional acoustic dimension to the relative darkness and brightness of G minor and E major by virtue of the fact that G minor draws on the resonance of the two

28. See Matt 24:22 (Mark 13:20). On Luther's anticipation of the cutting short of the present age, see previous footnote.

29. See Chap. 3 n. 82.

lowest strings of the violin, whereas E major resonates with the uppermost *e*" string—of which Bach makes extensive use, especially in the E-major Preludio. Third are the aesthetic associations with the two keys evident in Bach's vocal works. G minor tends to set darker texts or ideas—for instance, it famously opens the St. John Passion—whereas E major is, for Bach, typically a joyous key whose principal associations in the cantatas, Chafe notes, include "blessedness," "salvation" and "resurrection."[30]

Similarly to these patterns of ascent, the E-major partia also represents the culmination of a twofold scheme of progressive expansion within the *Sei Solo*. Whereas the three sonatas become progressively larger in measure count and duration, the three partias increase evenly in number of movements.[31] In this context, it is interesting to note that the E-major partia actually has the smallest measure count of any of the partias (and in fact the second smallest of the entire collection, surpassed only by the G-minor sonata).[32] To the extent that the E-major partia can be seen to represent the culmination of history with the return of Christ, it may not be invalid to associate its comparatively diminutive size with Christ's repeated emphasis that "the one who is least . . . is the one who is great"[33] and that in the kingdom of God "the last will be first."[34] In any case, it is interesting that the cantata for which Bach later adapted the E-major Preludio—"Wir danken dir, Gott," BWV 29—describes God's beneficent reign from the heavenly Zion, with distinctly eschatological overtones coming from an allusion to Revelation 19:1 in the third and seventh movements ("Halleluja, Stärk und Macht sei des Allerhöchsten Namen!").

Sonata in A Minor, BWV 1003

The A-minor sonata is permeated throughout by the descending tetrachord that is the most basic form of the ostinato that will come into focus in the Ciaccona. It begins and ends the first movement (Ex. 4.1). It is the basis

30. See Chafe, *Tonal Allegory*, 152 n. 1. On Mattheson's contrasting view of E major, see Chap. 6 n. 135.

31. Marissen observes similar parallel schemes in the six Brandenburg Concertos. See *The Social and Religious Designs*, 86–90, 100–108.

32. Tatlow has demonstrated the importance of measure counts in Bach as the foundation for his use of proportion within and between compositions. See Tatlow, *Bach's Numbers*, 106–29.

33. Luke 9:48.

34. Matt 20:16; see Matt 5:3–5 and 10–12, 18:4, 19:14 (Mark 10:14–15; Luke 18:16–17), 19:30 (Mark 10:31; Luke 13:30), 22:1–10 (Luke 14:16–24); Luke 16:25; see also Isa 11:6.

for the chromatic descent (*passus duriusculus*) that is the principal episodic motif of the following Fuga (Ex. 4.2). A major-mode variant of it begins the following Andante in C major (Ex. 4.3). And in the final Allegro, among numerous four-note stepwise descents (and ascents) at various levels of structure, the proper Phrygian descent is the first bass-harmonic motion to occur in both halves of the movement (Ex. 4.4a–b); it is melodically prominent at the approach to the final cadences of each half (Ex. 4.4c–d); and it additionally articulates modulations to E minor in the first half (Ex. 4.4e) and to C major in the second (Ex. 4.4f).

Ex. 4.1. The descending tetrachord at the beginning and end of BWV 1003/1

Ex. 4.2. The chromatic tetrachord in BWV 1003/2

Ex. 4.3. Major-mode tetrachord beginning BWV 1003/3

Ex. 4.4. Important occurrences of the descending tetrachord in BWV 1003/4

In light of the adumbration of the Ciaccona's falling-fourth bass motif in all previous movements of the D-minor partia, it is at least interesting that the sonata immediately preceding the D-minor partia is permeated by a descending tetrachord, as noted in Chapter 2,[35] which raises the question of whether Bach might also have intended the prominence of the descending tetrachord in the A-minor sonata to adumbrate the Ciaccona. This naturally raises the question of whether this adumbration is purely musical, or whether there is reason to apply the symbolic associations of the lament bass of the Ciaccona to its adumbration as well. Because adumbration is itself an important element in identifying the lament bass of the Ciaccona with the passion of Christ, it seems most natural to hear the adumbration in the A-minor sonata with the same symbolic overtones, that is, as though the latter were referring forward to Christ's sufferings.

Several further considerations from the A-minor Fuga, which dominates the sonata in size, could suggest the viability of hearing the sonata's passion overtones as if referring forward to a future event rather than representing the passion itself. First, as previously noted, Tatlow has observed that the A-minor Fuga, D-minor Ciaccona, and C-major Fuga appear crafted to add up to a round nine hundred measures.[36] Reinforcing the connection among these three movements is the fact that the three adjacent works in which these movements are respectively situated are also the only adjacent works within the *Sei Solo* that are each within the *ambitus* of the others. Though ordered differently by various theorists,[37] the *ambitus* of a particular key refers to the six keys ranging from one step toward the enharmonic or "flat" end of the tonal spectrum to one step away in the chromatic or "sharp" direction. Thus the *ambitus* of the A-minor and C-major sonatas includes not only A minor and C major but also D minor and F major as well as E minor and G major (whose tonics can be rearranged to form the natural hexachord C—d—e—F—G—a).[38] Similarly, the *ambitus* of the D-minor partia includes not only D minor and F major but also G minor and B♭ major as well as A minor and C major; and the tonic pitches of these keys can be rearranged to form the soft hexachord F—g—a—B♭—C—d). The connection among the A-minor Fuga, D-minor Ciaccona, and C-major Fuga in terms of both *ambitus* and collective measure count would seem to support the likelihood that the lamenting tetrachord within the A-minor Fuga, and the sonata as a whole, could be meant to be connected with the

35. See "The Ciaccona in Context."

36. Tatlow, *Bach's Numbers*, 141–42. See my Chap. 3 n. 50.

37. See Chafe, *J. S. Bach's Johannine Theology*, 192 n. 16.

38. Ibid., 193–94.

use of the same device in the Ciaccona and C-major Fuga to represent the death and resurrection of Christ. But to the extent that the connection with these later two works could validate associations with the passion in the A-minor sonata, it would also suggest that the passion imagery is best understood as referring to an earlier point within the narrative sequence than those to which the D-minor partia and C-major sonata correspond; in other words, the A-minor sonata would appear to represent a prefiguring of the passion.

But the fact that the A-minor Fuga is positioned prior to the D-minor partia is not the only reason for hearing it as a meditation on the coming passion of Christ, as opposed to a narration of the event itself. The same conclusion is supported by considering the treatment of the lamenting *passus duriusculus* within the the A-minor fugue, where it appears as the principal episodic motif. Although in its prime form it might lend itself to association with the passion, the *passus duriusculus*, as well as the fugue subject, appears inverted at various points throughout the movement following the rather inconspicuous introduction of the inverted fugue subject in the lower voice at measure 125. As seen in Example 4.5, the fact that the descending motion of the inverted subject is accompanied at measure 125 by chromatic ascent in the upper voice creates a sense of directional ambivalence that is to some degree inherent even in the fugue subject itself.

Ex. 4.5. BWV 1003/2: first statement of the subject in inversion

The subject begins with a returning-note figure, itself a somewhat ambivalent gesture, followed by a downward octave leap that is countered by generally ascending motion in the second measure of the subject; but the scope of this ascent is well within the boundaries of the octave leapt in the first measure, undermining any general sense of direction in the subject as a whole. Even more importantly, the counterpoint accompanying both the prime and the inverted forms of the lamenting *passus duriusculus* throughout the fugue creates a sense of directional ambivalence. Typically the *passus duriusculus* is accompanied by a variant of the fugue subject whose essential motion is contrary to that of the chromatic line (Ex. 4.6a). When the *passus duriusculus* is inverted to an ascending figure, the countermotif based on the fugue subject is inverted to yield primarily descending motion (Ex. 4.6b).

Ex. 4.6. BWV 1003/2: Principal episodic motifs in prime form (a) and inversion (b)

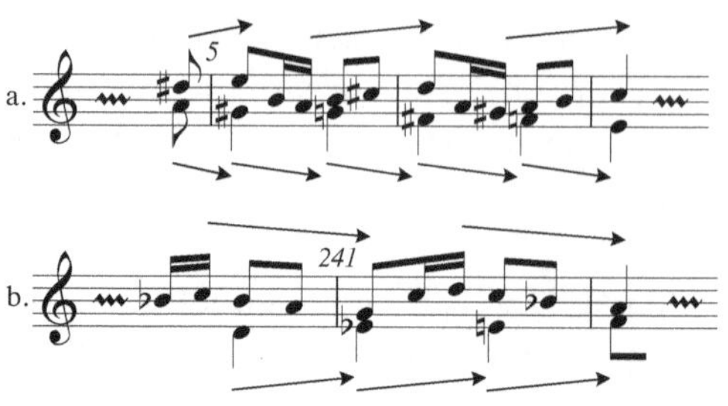

It is important to note that, despite superficial similarities of Ex. 4.6a with the subject and countersubject of the C-major Fuga, the latter—in their most essential motion— descend jointly and markedly; therefore their markedly enunciated and sustained inversion throughout one of seven distinctly delineated sections of the movement contributes to the clarity of what I have proposed is the Fuga's resurrection imagery. By contrast, in the A-minor fugue, the directional ambivalence of both its subject and its typical treatment of the *passus durisculus* means that the effect of each must be equally ambivalent when inverted. This, coupled with the lack of clear sectional delineation in the A-minor fugue, inconspicuous introduction of inversion at measure 125, and free intermingling of prime and inverted statements throughout the remainder of the fugue, prevents the inversion from having an effect comparable to that of the C-major fugue. Whereas the C-major fugue exhibits a linear or "narrative" type of progression, the effect of the A-minor fugue is more kaleidoscopic; therefore to whatever extent the A-minor Fuga's use of inversion (particularly of the *passus duriusculus*) can be likened to the passion and resurrection, the effect is less of a narrative sequence of the events than a simultaneous reflection on the two contrasting but interrelated ideas, perhaps even a reflection on their interrelatedness itself, as expressed succinctly in the lines "Kreuz und Krone sind verbunden, Kampf und Kleinod sind vereint" ("Cross and crown are bound together, struggle and prize are united"), which Bach set in the 1716 cantata "Weinen, Klagen, Sorgen, Zagen," BWV 12. In fact, the virtual (and sometimes actual) juxtaposition of chromatic descent and ascent in the A-minor fugue very much resembles Bach's representation of the motto *Christus Coronabit Crucigeros* ("Christ crowns those who carry the cross") in the canon BWV 1077.

On October 15, 1747, Bach penned this short canon in a notebook belonging to the Leipzig theology student Johann Gottlieb Fulde. Bach had already composed it as the eleventh of fourteen canons (BWV 1087) appended to the *Goldberg Variations* and based on the first eight notes of the bass line of the *Variations*' opening Aria. However, in Fulde's notebook, Bach added the phrase "*Symbolum.* Christus Coronabit Crucigeros." The canon, realized in Example 4.7, represents its motto by means of the reversal of a chromatic descent to form a chromatic ascent (compare to the similar technique in mm. 232–47 of the A-minor violin fugue, Ex. 4.8).

Ex. 4.7. Realization of BWV 1077

Ex. 4.8. Juxtaposed chromatic descent and ascent in BWV 1003/2

The canon's musical representation is apt at several levels. Most immediately, of course, the glory of the crown is the inverse of the suffering and shame of the cross that is represented by the descending *passus duriusculus*. Second, from a structural perspective, a gesture followed by its inverse creates symmetry, which can be associated with chiasm and thus potentially Christ and the cross, as in the subject of the final fugue of the *Actus Tragicus* (see Ex. 2.2). But third and more profoundly, the cross itself is an act of inversion; in what Luther calls the "wondrous exchange" (*admirabili commertio*), Christ bears humanity's sin and shame in our stead in order to present us righteous before God through faith in Christ's atoning work.[39] Rambach comments on a series of ironic reversals emblematic of the very shape of the crucifixion story:

> O what a humiliation this therefore is, that the Lord of glory took upon himself such an ignominious and painful kind of death and was obedient to his Father to the point of death on the cross; that the hands that stretched out the heavens and healed so many sick with their touch become dug through [with nails]; that the feet having the promise that all enemies should be laid in the dust before them become bored through; that he who gives clothing to others hangs without clothing; that he to whom all belongs has nothing of his own; that the king of Israel becomes a horror to all people and a curse before God.[40]

39. *WA* 5:608. See, for instance, 2 Cor 5:21; 1 Pet 3:18; also Rom 3:25.

40. "O welch ein Erniedrigung ist demnach dieses, daß der HErr der Herrlichkeit eine solche schimpfliche und schmerzliche Todes-Art über sich genommen und seinem Vater bis zum Tode des Creuzes gehorsam worden; daß die Hände durchgraben werden, die den Himmel ausgebreitet, und durch ihr Anrühren so viel Krancke geheilet; daß die

Within the Bach canon, this idea of reversal in the cross is evident, for instance, in the chorale "Durch dein Gefängnis, Gottes Sohn, ist uns die Freiheit kommen" ("Through your imprisonment, Son of God, is freedom come to us") from the St. John Passion. Leaver notes that this chorale occurs at the heart of a chiastic structure that is situated at the heart of the Passion,[41] which has twofold significance. First, because chiastic structure is symmetrical about its midpoint, this chorale therefore articulates the point of reversal of the structure in which it is situated. Second, its being situated at the heart of the chiasm emphasizes the centrality of its message, the reversal of the respective lots of Christ and humanity, a centrality that is further underscored by its placement at the heart of the entire passion.

Here two small points may be noted parenthetically. First, concerning the relevance of the motto *Christus Coronabit Crucigeros* to the A-minor Fuga, there is a possibility that Bach's curious penmanship of the title "Ciaccona" in the D-minor partia, in which another *c* appears penned above the two *c*s in the middle of the word, might possibly be intended as an acronym for this motto, which would in any case indicate that the motto was on Bach's mind during the creation of the *Sei Solo* (see Image 6.2).[42] Second, if "Christus Coronabit Crucigeros" is indeed in view in the A-minor Fuga, it is interesting that it is the tenth movement of the *Sei Solo*—represented in Roman numerals by "X"—since "*X*" (understood in Greek rather than Latin, i.e., as the letter *chi*) represents two of the three terms of the motto, "Christus" and "Crucigeros." The association is not as far-fetched as it might initially seem to the modern person and is indeed typical of the subtleties to which Bach's tradition was well accustomed. For instance, it appears not to be accidental that the tenth mystery of the Rosary is the crucifixion and death of Christ; thus in Biber's collection of "Mystery" Sonatas, Sonata X is preceded by a copper engraving of Christ on the cross, and its first melodic gesture is distinctly cross-shaped (Ex. 4.9).

Füsse durchboret werden, welche die Verheissung haben daß alle Feinde vor ihnen in den Staub geleget werden sollen; daß der ohne Kleider hänget, der allen Kleider giebt; daß der nichts eigenes hat, dem all Dinge gehören; daß der König Israel ein Scheusal alles Volcks und GOtt ein Fluch wird." *BLC*, 960.

41. See Leaver, *J. S. Bach and Scripture*, 130–31.

42. This idea was proposed by Heinrich Poos, "J. S. Bachs Chaconne für Violine solo," cited in Randwijck, "Music in Context," 51. See the discussion of the D-minor partia in my Chap. 6.

Ex. 4.9. *X*-shapes in Sonata X (Crucifixion) from Biber's "Mystery" Sonatas

* Notated at sounding pitch

A third feature suggesting that the possible passion imagery of the A-minor Fuga might best be understood as referring to a future event is the most unusual structure of its exposition. But for context we must first examine the exposition of the G-minor Fuga from the first sonata of the *Sei Solo*. In the standard fugal practice of Bach's day, the first voice, *dux*, states the subject in the tonic key and is answered by a second voice, *comes*, at the fifth (or occasionally at the fourth, as the subject demands). This pattern of entries, alternating between *dux* and *comes*, continues until all voices have entered.[43] In the Fuga of the G-minor solo violin sonata, however, there is a most atypical departure from this norm as the voices enter symmetrically in the pattern of *dux—comes—comes—dux*, forming the most straightforward *X* shape possible. Outside the *Sei Solo*, a rare example to follow a similar pattern is the C-major fugue from Book 1 of *The Well-Tempered Clavier*, BWV 846/2. David Ledbetter connects its structure with the older practice among fugal expositions in which adjacent voices (which also tend to enter successively) alternate between authentic and plagal versions of the mode. Therefore he explains the structure of the exposition of BWV 846/2 as being a function of the order in which its voices enter: alto, cantus, tenor, bass.[44]

To the extent that this association explains the chiastic tonal structure of the voice entries in the exposition of BWV 846/2, it actually heightens the uniqueness of the chiasm of the G-minor Fuga. According to the model Ledbetter cites, the final statement of a modally chiastic exposition must be in a different register from the first, which precludes the kind of cross shape that is formed in the G-minor violin fugue by the incipit tones of the successive voice entries (Ex. 4.10).

43. I am here describing common practice for the exposition of a fugue, that is, its beginning as the voices enter for the first time. Subsequent or "middle" entries typically exhibit considerably more flexibility.

44. Ledbetter, *Bach's Well-Tempered Clavier*, 147.

Ex. 4.10. Chiastic exposition of the G-minor Fuga, BWV 1001/2

Moreover, the model by which Ledbetter explains the modal symmetry in the exposition of BWV 846/2 cannot account for that of the G-minor violin fugue. To the extent that the entries of the violin fugue can even be connected to discrete voices, the only plausible succession is the one that Ledbetter himself puts forward: tenor (incipit *d*”), bass (incipit *g*’), cantus (incipit *g*”), alto (incipit *d*”).[45] This, however, means that the cantus enters on *g*”, both the alto and the tenor on *d*”, and the bass on *g*’. In other words, the succession of entries in terms of *dux* and *comes* is chiastic vertically as well as horizontally.

It appears, therefore, that Bach crafted the exposition of the G-minor violin fugue to be symmetrical per se, not as a by-product of another compositional convention like what Ledbetter describes concerning BWV 846/2. It is interesting to note that in neither of the two other transcriptions of the G-minor fugue is the exposition likewise symmetrical. In BWV 1000 for lute, the standard tonal pattern of voice entries alternating between *dux* and *comes* is followed for the four principal statements; and in BWV 539/2 for organ, the first four entries retain the tonal (though not registral) symmetry found in the violin fugue but are followed immediately by other entries not present in the violin version that obscure the symmetry. In other words, it is only in the context of the *Sei Solo*, with its probable dimension of theological allegory, that the G-minor fugue has a patently *X*-shaped exposition.

In this light, it is especially interesting that the Fuga from the A-minor solo violin sonata—the next sonata within the *Sei Solo*—has a similarly chiastic exposition.[46] But the fact of this similarity draws attention to an important difference in its manifestation. Whereas the four entries that

45. Ledbetter, *Unaccompanied* Bach, 101.

46. In the A-minor Fuga, the lower register with which the final entry begins its first full measure suggests that it is intended to be heard as a bass voice. Therefore the entries alternate between *dux* and *comes* registrally but not temporally, as in BWV 846/2, unlike the G-minor Fuga.

form the *X*-shaped exposition of the G-minor fugue occur in close proximity with never more than two beats between the end of one statement and the beginning of the next, in the A-minor fugue the entries stop after the first three—that is, the initial statement of the subject followed by two tonal answers, one below and one above the initial statement—and there follows a thirty-measure episodic passage (in contrast to the eight measures in which the first three entries occur!) before the exposition finally closes with an authentic statement of the subject that fills out the basso register not yet explored in the course of a subject statement. The precedent of a cross-shaped exposition in the G-minor fugue leads the listener to assume the same shape will apply to the exposition of the A-minor fugue once the two tonal answers are heard in immediate succession; therefore, when the ensuing episodic material turns out to be nearly four times the length of the preceding subject entries, the sense (speaking subjectively, of course) is not of having heard a complete if atypically structured three-voice exposition but rather of having heard an abortive exposition that "should" consist of four symmetrically structured entries. Bach confirms this intuition of chiastic structure by including a final authentic statement before the decisive tonic cadence at measure 45; yet the vast stretch of intervening episodic material makes this final statement seem as if tacked onto the end, thus allowing or perhaps encouraging perception of the initial three entries as an incomplete cross.

This image is particularly striking because the work of Christ on the cross is strongly tied to the idea of completion in both the New Testament and Lutheran theology.[47] To this day, Christian traditions consciously rooted in Reformation doctrine and practice speak regularly of "the finished work of Christ" as a cornerstone of their faith.[48] An incomplete cross would therefore not be an arbitrary image; it could tap into an association central to Lutheran understanding in order to convey that the work of the cross, although in view, has not yet been brought to completion in history.[49]

From a tonal perspective, this incomplete cross creates a motion away from the tonic A and toward E, a motion found throughout the sonata and exemplified in the descending Phrygian tetrachord it prominently features.

47. John 19:30. See Chap. 3 n. 56.

48. Luther formulates this idea as "the completion of Christ's work for us" ("opus Christi pro nobis impletum"). *WA* 39 II:188.

49. Naturally such imagery, as any figure, has its limitations. I do not find it sensible, for instance, to consider such an image at odds with the description of the eternal significance of Christ's redemptive work in Rev 13:8, describing him (according to Luther's translation) as the lamb "that was slain from the beginning of the world" ("Das erwütigt ist/ von anfang der Welt").

Indeed, throughout the A-minor sonata the destination of the lamenting tetrachord, E, is given a harmonic significance that at least implicitly supersedes the gravitational pull of A minor and thus seems to transcend its tonal context.

It is not terribly atypical that the Phrygian descent opening the first movement should return at its end such that the movement concludes on E (V); after all, such "Phrygian codettas," as they might be called, are common enough in Baroque slow movements. More striking, though, is the conclusion of the fourth movement, which, unlike the first movement, "must" resolve to A minor; but it does so in the most tenuous way possible. Measure 55 ends—in *forte*—with an arpeggiation of an E-major chord, the dominant to what might be the final chord of the piece. But instead of giving a conclusive tonal resolution to the E-major chord, the following downbeat is suddenly *piano* and arpeggiates an inconclusive A-dominant-7 chord, leaving the E-major chord at the end of measure 55 as the last *forte* chord of the movement. The downbeat of measure 56 begins the *passus duriusculus* in the bass, outlining a falling tetrachord from *a*' to *e*', before the penultimate sonority of the movement, an arpeggiation of an E-major chord ending with the leading tone *g#*", is left melodically unresolved and given only the weakest harmonic resolution by a single low *a* that is nearly two full octaves below the note preceding it. And thus ends the movement, with two successive E-major chords left hanging, so to speak, the latter of which is not only implicitly but explicitly the end of a tetrachordal descent (as seen in Ex. 4.4f).[50]

From a purely structural perspective, it is difficult to disconnect the A-minor sonata's pull beyond its immediate tonality and toward E (major) from the observation that E major is the key of the final partia of the *Sei Solo* and thus, in a teleological reading, the "goal" of the entire collection. This structural feature fits remarkably well with the allegorical schema we have thus far noted. The A-minor sonata, with its intimations of the specter of the cross, features a remarkable tonal pull toward the partia representing the kingdom of heaven precisely because the tonic of the "heaven partia"

50. For this reason, I submit that it is important in performance to maintain the *piano* Bach writes in m. 68 rather than inserting an unsolicited crescendo that would give the movement a more forceful ending. In this regard, I must cordially disagree with Jaap Schröder, who advocates not only making a crescendo to the final note but even, in the repeat, playing the final note two octaves above where it is written for added brilliance (thus also resolving the *g#*"). He bases his decision on the fact that it parallels the ending found in the arrangement of this sonata for clavier, BWV 964 (see Schröder, *Bach's Solo Violin Works*, 112). But not only does BWV 964 not occur in the context of the *Sei Solo*, it is also widely suspected to be the work of a composer other than Sebastian Bach, possibly his son Wilhelm Friedemann. See Background, n. 19.

is the destination of the lamenting tetrachord that permeates the A-minor sonata, just as, in the words of Rambach, the "cross is the ladder on which one ascends to heaven."[51]

Accordingly, the gospels portray Jesus as having a heavenward focus in his approach to the cross.[52] This is perhaps most notably exemplified by the way in which the Gospel of John introduces the evening of Jesus' arrest as "before the Feast of the Passover, Jesus knowing that his hour had come to depart out of this world to the Father."[53] The statement is so striking that the reader almost wants to ask whether the writer has quite forgotten that, before ascending to the Father, Jesus must first be crucified and raised—which, after all, is the centerpiece of the Christ story and of New Testament theology as a whole! But it is precisely because of this that John's statement of Jesus' departure to the Father is all the more striking and theologically important in the context of Jesus' approach to the cross; it emphasizes once again that Jesus' going to the cross is not outside the sovereign plan of the Father but quite the contrary.[54] A reference to Jesus' heavenward trajectory while en route to the cross is therefore not an obscure point of theology but something certain to be part of the theological consciousness of a devoted student of theology like Bach. It is, after all, not unlike the doxology that Bach would set to music only a few years later in the opening chorus of his St. John Passion: "Herr, unser Herrscher . . . Zeig uns durch deine Passion, daß du, . . . auch in der größten Niedrigkeit, Verherrlicht worden bist!" ("Lord, our Ruler . . . Show us through your passion that you, . . . even in the greatest humiliation, have been glorified!")

The association of the A-minor sonata with Christ's approach to the cross would make sense in light of the one previous potential signifier within the *Sei Solo* that could refer to a specific event in the Christ story. Just as the sixth and final work of the *Sei Solo* contains the only nondance movement among the partias (the E-major Preludio), so the first sonata in G minor contains a Siciliana that stands out as the only movement in the

51. "Dieses Creuz ist die Leiter, auf welcher man gen Himmel steiget." *BLC* 963. Similar imagery appears on p. 951, where Rambach describes how the believer's reproach for the sake of Christ becomes transformed into a ladder by which one ascends to the throne of glory ("in eine Leiter verwandelt, auf welcher man auf den Thron der Herrlichkeit steiget"). See Rom 6:5; 2 Cor 1:5; Phil 3:10–11; 1 Pet 4:13.

52. See Matt 24:30–31, 25:31, 26:29, 26:64; Mark 13:26, 14:25, 14:62; Luke 21:27, 22:69, 23:43; John 14:1–6, 14:12, 14:18–20, 14:28, 16:5–11, 16:16, 16:28, 17:4–5, 17:11–13.

53. John 13:1.

54. Acts 2:23. See Chap. 6 n. 137.

sonatas that can be associated with dance to any meaningful degree.[55] In fact, the Siciliana has arguably the most defined associations of any movement type found in the *Sei Solo*. Within Bach's tradition, there are two distinct strains of siciliano: what Ikegami classifies as "the gentle and idyllic major-mode siciliano and the melancholic and sometimes pathetic minor-mode siciliano."[56]

In the surviving works of Bach, this distinction is underscored by the fact that, when genre-specific labels appear at all, the major-mode variety are titled "Siciliana" (BWV 1001/3, 1063/2) and the minor-mode type "Siciliano" (BWV 1017/1, 1031/2, 1035/3, 1053/2).[57] The origins of both strains can be related to the pastoral topic,[58] but in Bach's time the association was particularly strong in the major-mode siciliano.[59] In the case of the B♭-major Siciliana from the first sonata of the *Sei Solo*, the evocation of the pastoral is heightened by frequent use of parallel sixths and thirds, which is frequently found in pastoral-connoting works of Bach's tradition because such parallel intervals recall the paired *auloi*, the quintessential pastoral instrument of classical Greek and Latin literature.[60] One particularly famous example from the Bach oeuvre—not a siciliano but certainly pastoral—is the aria "Schäfe können sicher weiden" from Cantata 208 (with which the Siciliana for solo violin shares the key of B♭ major).

Since the Middle Ages, the pastoral topic was closely associated with the birth of Christ,[61] the "Good Shepherd,"[62] which according to Luke

55. While originating as a vocal genre, the siciliano acquired the status of what Ikegami calls "pseudo-dance" ("Pseudo-Tanztyp") in the early eighteenth century. "Siciliano in der Instrumentalmusik Joseph Haydns und seiner Zeitgenossen," 11.

56. ". . . der sanfte und idyllische Dur-Siciliano und der melancholische und teilweise pathetische Moll-Siciliano." Ibid., 76.

57. Whether this distinction of label is intentional on Bach's part or coincidental cannot be said with certainty—perhaps future discoveries will shed more light on the question—but the pattern is nonetheless interesting. In any case, it should be emphasized that, although the two strains of siciliano appear distinctly as such throughout the period, differentiating between them on the basis of spelling is unique to Bach, as far as I am aware.

58. Ibid., 70–76.

59. For an overview of the history of the signification of the siciliano and its connection to the pastoral, see Raymond Monelle, "The Pastoral Signifier," chap. 13 in *The Musical Topic: Hunt, Military and Pastoral.*

60. See ibid., 207–8. Reinhard Wiesend's habilitation thesis, "Siciliana: Literarische und musikalische Traditionen," unfortunately remains unpublished.

61. See Ikegami, "Siciliano in der Instrumentalmusik Joseph Haydns und seiner Zeitgenossen," 70 n. 109.

62. John 10:11, 14; see 1 Pet 2:25. Similar shepherd imagery forms an important motif of the Hebrew Scriptures, e.g., Ps 23:1–4; Isa 40:11; Ezek 34 and 37:24; Mic 5:4;

2:8–18 was attended by shepherds. And because of the pastoral overtones of the siciliano, the siciliano itself became strongly associated with Christmas.[63] Movements exhibiting the compound duple meter and dotted figures characteristic of the siciliano are frequently to be found in explicitly Christmas-themed works of Bach's era. Well-known examples include the atypical closing movement of Corelli's "Christmas" concerto, Op. 6 no. 8; the instrumental Pifa and the aria "He shall feed His flock like a shepherd" from Handel's *Messiah*; the aria ("Quel pargoletto") that introduces the Christ-child to the warring factions of Peace and Justice in Caldara's Christmas cantata *Vaticini di pace*; various examples from Alessandro Scarlatti's Christmas cantatas, including the closing Pastorale of the *Cantata pastorale per la Natività*; and, perhaps most significantly for the present study, the sole instrumental sinfonia from Bach's Christmas Oratorio, BWV 248, which directly precedes the introduction of the shepherds.

Of course, this is not to say that every major-mode siciliano should be seen as alluding to the nativity of Christ; but it would be a felicitous coincidence that the first sonata of a X-structured collection appearing to contain Christological allegory should contain a movement type that has strong potential associations with the first episode of Christ's earthly life. To the extent that the Siciliana of the first sonata of the *Sei Solo* could indeed be associated with the nativity, it would situate the A-minor sonata between the birth and the crucifixion of Christ, which concurs with the implications of potential signifiers within the A-minor sonata itself.

Zech 11:4–17 and 13:7.

63. See Monelle, *The Musical Topic*, 215–17, 230, 232.

5

Number Correlations in the Partias

The partias of the *Sei Solo* collectively exhibit a particular number correlation not evident among the sonatas. The B-minor partia, the second work of the collection, extensively emphasizes the number 2. The D-minor partia, the fourth work, prominently features the number 4 (interestingly, in conjunction with the number 5). And it seems not to be accidental that the E-major partia, the sixth work of the collection, is the only one to have six movements. Since the numeric connections in both the B-minor and D-minor partias are quite extensive, I will discuss each individually.

The Number 2 in the B-minor Partia, BWV 1002

What is immediately noteworthy about the B-minor partia is that each of the principal dance movements is followed by a *double* or variation, so that the essential form of every movement is heard twice in its entirety. In this respect, the B-minor partia is unique within the entire surviving Bach oeuvre; in no other work by Bach is more than one movement followed by a *double*. Of the six solos, the B-minor partia is the only one in which all the movements are in binary form with repeats, meaning that every movement, along with its *double*, consists of two discrete sections both played twice. Interestingly, the B-minor partia is also the only partia of the three to consist of four principal movements, which can be expressed as 2 + 2, 2 x 2, or 2^2. These four movements can be grouped into twos in every possible combination, each of which I will explain in turn:

1. Allemanda (1) and Tempo di Borea (4), Corrente (2), and Sarabande (3);
2. Allemanda (1) and Sarabande (3), Corrente (2), and Tempo di Borea (4); and

3. Allemanda (1) and Corrente (2), Sarabande (3), and Tempo di Borea (4)

The principal movements of the B-minor partia conform to the most common basic template of the dance suite, except for the last movement, which would typically be a giga (gigue), not a borea (bourrée). Because of this substitution, the outer movements are in simple duple meter while the inner movements are in simple triple meter. A second means by which the movements of the B-minor partia can be grouped is according to the fundamental bass motion that opens each movement, which is arguably at least as definitive of the musical profile of the movements in question as their treble-melodic content. In the first and third movements, the essential stepwise bass gesture that begins the movement is descending, whereas in the second and fourth movements it is ascending (Ex. 5.1).

Ex. 5.1. Inverse bass motion in adjacent movements of BWV 1002

Ex. 5.1 (cont.)

* The curious time signature is given in both the autograph ms. and Anna Magdalena Bach's copy (*D-B Mus. ms. Bach P 268*) not only at the beginning of the Tempo di Borea but again at the beginning of the following Double.

In addition to grouping movement 1 with 3 and 2 with 4, this also creates a parallel between the first and second halves of the partia; each half consists of a movement that opens with a bass descent followed by one that opens with a bass ascent, according to which movement 1 can be grouped with 2 and 3 with 4. In sum, the B-minor partia exhibits a structural emphasis on multiples of two that is arguably unparalleled in its genre.

It would then seem not to be accidental that the B-minor partia is the only one of the six solos to have two *Vorzeichen* (that is, sharps or flats) in the key signature. Interestingly, this trait would not be unique to the B-minor partia if the first sonata in G minor were given the more common key signature of two flats; and indeed there is reason to suppose that at least the first two movements of the G-minor sonata might originally have been notated thus.[1] It is possible that Bach changed the key signature to one flat,

1. Despite the fact that the autograph manuscript of the *Sei Solo* is clearly not a composing score, there are several certainly erroneous omissions of E♭s (e.g., Adagio,

reflecting older (but still current) modal associations,[2] only when including the sonata as the first in a collection of solo violin works. As a result, the first work of the collection, the G-minor sonata, has one *Vorzeichen*, while the second, the B-minor partia, has two.

Similar two-to-one patterns between these first two works are apparent among the various structural levels that Tatlow has extensively documented in researching her theory of proportional parallelism. The ratio of measures between the B-minor partia and G-minor sonata, including repeats—that is, as it would likely be heard in performance—is 2:1.[3] Similarly, the B-minor partia exhibits a 2:1 proportion between the first three movements and the fourth. In fact, it is unique among the *Sei Solo* in containing a 2:1 proportion between any of its constituent movements that remains valid whether or not repeats are taken (that is, in two performance scenarios), whereas the G-minor sonata contains a 1:1 relationship in exactly the same location—between the first three movements and the fourth—but only in one performance scenario, the omission of repeats. But even though the traits of the B-minor partia that form these proportions with the G-minor sonata are unique among the *Sei Solo*, the reverse is not true; the G-minor sonata's key signature of one flat is shared with the D-minor partia, and its 1:1 proportion between movements in one performance scenario is shared with the E-major partia (specifically, between the Preludio, Loure, and Gigue on one hand and the Gavotte en Rondeaux, Menuet 1 & 2, and Bourée on the other). In short, then, whereas the G-minor sonata evinces some degree of emphasis on the number that correlates to its location within the *Sei Solo* (that is, the number 1), the connection is notably weaker than in the partias,

---

m. 3, beat 3; Fuga, m. 2, beat 3) as well as an E♭ mistakenly added to the key signature in the sixth line of the Adagio. Moreover, a key signature of two flats would correspond to those of the only two surviving transcriptions of the Fuga, BWV 539/2 for organ (in D minor, notated with one flat) and BWV 1000 for lute (in G minor, notated with two flats).

2. In the generations before Bach, the minor scale was widely thought to correspond to the Dorian, not the Aeolian, mode (see Lester, *Between Modes and Keys*, 12–13, 100). Thus minor-mode movements were frequently notated with one flat fewer than in modern practice. Though less frequent, examples of the same treatment of major-mode movements (that is, suggesting the Lydian mode) are also to be found. Like the Siciliana of BWV 1001, Corelli's sonata Op. 5 no. 2 is in B♭ major but is notated with only one flat.

3. Tatlow, *Bach's Numbers*, 137, 139. Without repeats the ratio is 2:3. Tatlow notes that this type of proportional planning, using the perfect proportions of *harmonia* (1:1, 1:2, 2:3, 3:4, 4:5, 5:6), is frequently found at multiple levels within authentic Bachian collections. Interestingly, of the many such proportions she documents within the *Sei Solo* at various levels of structure, the present example is the only one that occurs between two complete works within the collection.

to the extent that the correlations in the G-minor sonata between the number 1 and its being the first work of the *Sei Solo* might be attributable to pure coincidence if the same pattern were not evident, in a far more pronounced and unique way, in the partias.

The Number 4 (and 5) in the D-minor Partia, BWV 1004

The D-minor partia, the fourth work of the *Sei Solo*—whose tonic, perhaps coincidentally, is the fourth letter of the alphabet—has five movements. The outer movements, the Allemanda and Ciaccona, emphasize multiples of four amounting to 256, or 4^4. The Allemanda is the only movement of the partia made up primarily of flowing sixteenth notes that divide the beat by four. It consists of two halves of sixteen measures each—that is, two groups of 4 times 4 measures—creating a total count of 256 beats when the indicated repeats are taken. The Ciaccona consists of sixty-four (4 x 4 x 4) statements of a four-measure ostinato, which amounts to 256 measures, excluding the final *d′*.

The three inner movements, by contrast, are built on proportions of four and five. The second-movement Corrente is divided into two parts of twenty-four and thirty measures, which is a ratio of 4:5. When repeats are taken, its fifty-four measures in $\frac{3}{4}$ time yield a total of 324 beats, which is 4(5 + 4)(5 + 4). The first part of the following Sarabanda consists of eight measures (4 + 4), while the measure count of the second part differs on the repeat on account of the second ending; the first iteration of the B section consists of sixteen measures (4 x 4), while the second consists of twenty (4 x 5). The relationship of the first iteration to the second is therefore 4:5. The Giga, the fourth movement, consists straightforwardly of two equal halves of twenty measures (4 x 5); therefore with repeats there are four groups of 4 x 5 measures.

On the basis of these properties, structural similarities between individual movements can be viewed from two perspectives. In terms of how each movement approaches the relationship between 4 and 5, the Allemanda (movement 1) and Ciaccona (movement 5) are constructed entirely with the number 4, making no comparable usage of 5, whereas the Corrente (movement 2) and Giga (movement 4) incorporate 4 and 5 within or between the two sections of their binary form. In the Sarabanda (movement 3) alone does the relationship between 4 and 5 fall only within the B section of the binary form (Fig. 5.1).

Structural similarities can also be viewed among the binary-form movements in terms of how they handle the relationship between the A and B sections. The Allemanda (1) and Giga (4) both feature a 1:1 relationship between their A and B sections. In the Allemanda, each is sixteen measures long; in the Giga, each is twenty. The proportion between these two movements of similar structure is therefore 4:5. By contrast, in the Corrente (2) and Sarabanda (3), the B section is longer than the A section. This reinforces the symmetry that usually, as here, characterizes the standard grouping of Allemanda, Corrente, Sarabanda, Giga; the outer movements are in duple meter (the fourth typically in compound duple) whereas the inner movements are in triple meter (Fig. 5.2).

Fig. 5.1. Relationships in how movements of BWV 1004 treat the numbers 4 and 5

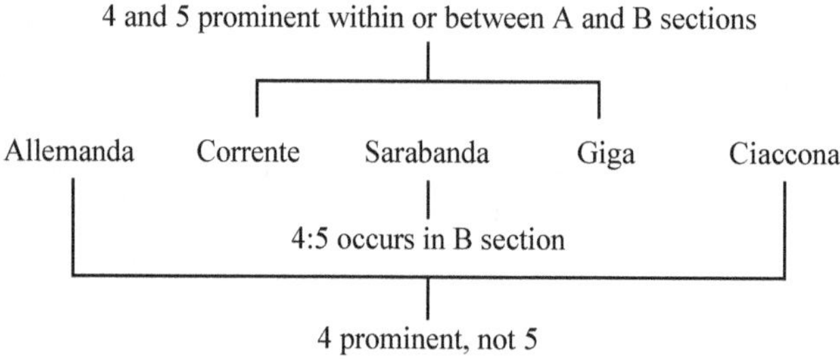

Fig. 5.2. Similarities in relationships between A and B sections among the binary-form movements of BWV 1004

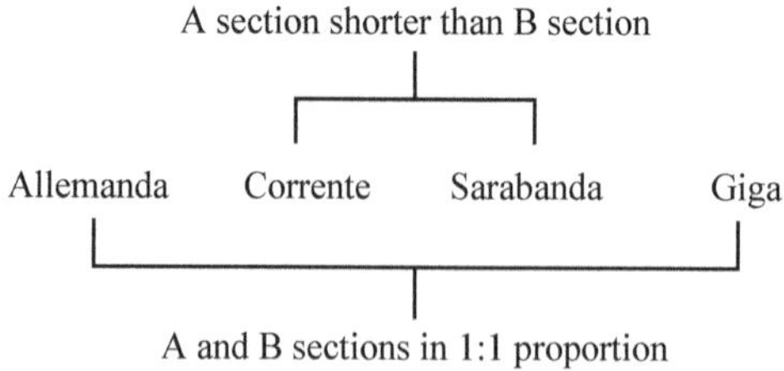

Interestingly, both of these perspectives yield chiastic structures. The first chiasm encompasses the entire partia. The second encompasses only the first four movements, omitting (or, rather, not pertaining to) the Ciaccona; but, as observed in Chapter 2, the Ciaccona has its own chiastic structure, fascinatingly in five parts (Fig. 2.1). If passion imagery were intended in the D-minor partia, could it be coincidence that the partia contains three clear crosses, with two each spanning a half of the partia and a third spanning the entirety of the work? Such imagery bears striking similarity to the three crosses on Golgotha, on one of which hung the one who dies for the entire world.[4]

Possible Implications of Prominent Numbers

The D-minor Partia

Since each of the three partias emphasizes the number that corresponds to its respective location within the *Sei Solo*, it is curious that the D-minor partia, the fourth work, should emphasize the number 5 in addition to the number 4. In light of the fact that this is indeed a curiosity, it is notable that the relationship between the numbers 4 and 5 should be used to create chiastic structures within a work whose use of chiasm appears independently likely to represent the cross of Christ (as discussed in Chapter 2). This appears all the more interesting in view of the fact that 5 is a number particularly associated with the passion of Christ, on account of the traditional understanding of his five wounds: two to the hands, two to the feet, one to the side.[5] The passion chorale, "O Haupt voll Blut und Wunden," for instance, has five stanzas, all five of which Bach includes in his St. Matthew Passion. It is probably not accidental that the cross-shaped Credo from the B-Minor Mass, whose centerpiece is the "Crucifixus," is in five parts. If, as proposed in Chapter 2, the Ciaccona from the D-minor violin partia represents the death of Christ as the focal point of redemptive history, it is appropriate that its chiasm, too, is in five parts.

Moreover, if the considerations discussed in Chapter 4 support the validity of associating the E-major partia with the final consolation—that is, the coming of "the perfect" in the kingdom of heaven[6]—then the E-major partia's prominent display of the "perfect" number 6 (being the sixth work

4. John 3:16–17; 2 Cor 5:15; Col 1:20; 1 Tim 2:6; 1 John 2:2.

5. See Clement, *Der dritte Teil der Clavier-Übung von Johann Sebastian Bach*, 166. Of course, it is not usually possible to establish one-to-one correlations between a number and any potential significance it may have even within the mind of a single writer (Werckmeister is a prime example), not to mention within an entire culture. But it is not necessary to the present argument to do so. What is relevant is that within Bach's culture the number 5 is frequently used to represent the suffering of Christ and that Bach appears to have made use of it in that connection.

6. 1 Cor 13:10. The LB translates the phrase "der volkomen."

and consisting of six movements) is surely noteworthy and might suggest in general that the numbers emphasized prominently within the partias, corresponding to their respective positions within the *Sei Solo*, are intended to convey significances that were well established and understood during Bach's era. In that case, the number 4, prominent in the D-minor partia, might carry its standard association with the world by virtue of association with the four elements, four seasons, four winds, and four points of the compass.[7] The juxtaposition of 5 and 4 within the D-minor partia might then most naturally refer to Christ who suffers and dies for the redemption of the world[8] as its representative head, the second Adam.[9] If Bach were acquainted with the moniker *Sectio Divina* ("Divine Section") that would shortly be used to describe the Golden Ratio in Johann Heinrich Zedler's *Universal Lexicon*,[10] then it is conceivable that the prominence of the Golden Ratio in the Ciaccona[11]—uniquely among the *Sei Solo*—could have a theological dimension by emphasizing that the one who dies for the redemption of the world is none other than God himself.[12]

Finally, since the numbers 2, 4, and 6 respectively emphasized in the B-minor, D-minor, and E-major partias correspond to the position of each work within the collection, it is not inconceivable that the prominence of the number 5 in the D-minor partia, inextricably connected as it is with the number 4, could have been (or become) conceived as a reference to the fifth work of the collection, the C-major sonata, possibly as a reference to the profound interrelatedness of the crucifixion and resurrection, namely, that the cross does not end in despair but must be seen in light of the resurrection[13]; conversely, there is no glorified resurrection without the cross.[14]

7. See, for instance, Werckmeister, *Musicae Mathematicae*, 144 (appendix, chap. 3).

8. See my Chap. 2 n. 32.

9. See my Chap. 2 n. 30.

10. Zedler, *Lexicon*, s.v. "Sectio Divina."

11. See Chap. 2 n. 3.

12. This was an immensely important point for Luther, since only as God himself is Christ able to truly save. See Wood, *Captive to the Word*, 170–71. I will return to this idea shortly.

13. See 1 Cor 15:12–19; Heb 12:2.

14. Rom 6:4; Phil 3:10–11.

The E-major Partia

In this chapter, we have already observed the possible significance of the E-major partia's being the sixth work of the collection and having a "perfect" six movements; and in Chapter 4 we noted that the E-major partia appears to represent a culmination.[15] In this light, it is ironic that the partia's emphasis on 6, the number of perfection, is actually notably weaker than the corresponding associations in the first two partias. If, however, the number 6 is being used to represent not merely perfection in the abstract but specifically the perfections of heaven, as discussed in Chapter 4, then the diminished numerical correlation is not only sensible but might also help to explain another notational curiosity.

Although the Christian tradition, including Lutheranism, has strongly emphasized the perfection of heaven, there is interestingly only one biblical passage that explicitly uses the language of "the perfect" in reference to the age to come, and that is 1 Corinthians 13:10–12[16]: "But when the perfect comes, the partial will be done away . . . . For now we see in a mirror dimly, but then face to face; now I know in part, but then I will know fully just as I also have been fully known."[17] Number symbolism, as with any symbolism, is necessarily a middle point between the thing being represented and the one who is perceiving; in this sense, it is very much like a mirror, and by necessity numbers can actually represent the object of their intended symbolism to only a very limited extent—that is, dimly. If this single biblical passage connecting "the perfect" ("das volkomen") with heaven is in view, the diminishing role of number representation in the E-major partia could possibly signify the disappearance of the "dim mirror" with the coming of the very perfection that the number 6 symbolizes.

15. See "Partia in E Major, BWV 1006" in Chap. 4.

16. Debates about the continuing role of prophecy and tongues (vv. 8–9) have led some to associate these verses with the completion of the New Testament, but the Lutheran tradition clearly associates them with the kingdom of heaven. See the following footnote.

17. "Wenn aber komen wird das volkomen/ so wird das stückwerck auffhören . . . . Wir sehen jtzt durch eine Spiegel in einem tunckeln wort/ Denn aber von angesicht zu angesichte. Jtzt erkenne ichs stücksweise/ Denn aber werde ich erkennen gleich wie ich erkennet bin." Both the CB commentary and that of Olearius connect this verse with the important Lutheran distinction between the realm of belief ("Reich des Glaubens"), in which we presently live, and the realm of seeing ("Reich des Schauens"), which is the heavenly life. CB 6:326; Olearius, *Biblische Erklärung* 5:1227. See also *WA* 34 II:118, 129.

The imagery of this biblical passage might also explain a curiosity of penmanship relating to the E-major partia.[18] Throughout the collection, there is a progression in the way Bach writes the *P* of "Partia": the first is an ordinary *P*, the second includes a stem at the top of its trunk, and the third additionally curves the topmost pen stroke upward (rather than downward, as previously) so as to form the letters *J* and *S*, as shown in Image 5.1.[19]

Image 5.1. Emergence of the letters *J*, *S* in the *P* of "Partia" in the autograph of the *Sei Solo*

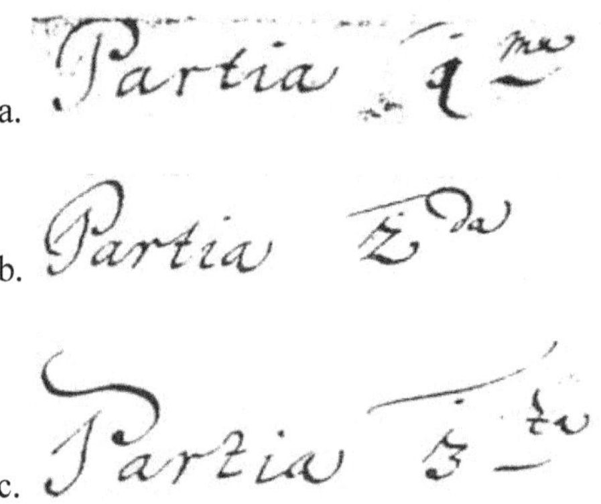

Neither the idea of progression through the partias nor even the covert signature is without parallel in the immediate context. We have already noted that the partias increase evenly from four to five and finally six movements, and a similar covert signature seems to appear in the title of the Menuet 1re of the E-major partia (Image 5.2).[20]

18. Wolfgang Ruf notes the care Bach invests in the physical score of the *Sei Solo*, calling it a "calligraphic masterpiece" ("Polyphonie in Bachs Sonaten für Violine solo," 221), and Tatlow observes that Bach's concern even with those elements of the score that cannot be heard in real time reflects the general concerns of a broader musical culture in which "the status of the written score, and the status of music as a written form, was higher than it is today" ("Bach's Parallel Proportions," 149). The subsequent erosion of the status and conception of the musical score is related to what Chafe describes as the nineteenth-century tendency to downplay (notated) appearance in favor of (abstract) "essence" as the locus of a musical work (Chafe, *Tonal Allegory*, 1). By contrast, he notes, the centrality in Bach's day of the interplay between these two dimensions at least partly accounts for the fundamentally allegorical conception of music held within Bach's culture (1–25).

19. Thoene makes this observation in *Bach: Sonata A-Moll*, 19.

20. On Bach's self-reference, see Tatlow, *Bach's Numbers*, 27–28, 61–72.

Image 5.2. Appearance of *J*, *S* in the *1* of "Menuet 1re," BWV 1006/4

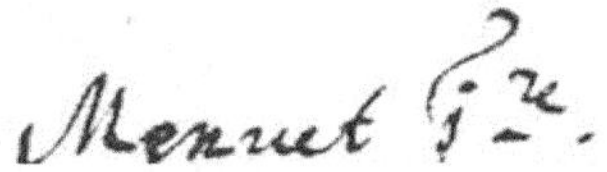

Note in Image 5.1a that Bach originally wrote the *1* of "Partia 1ma" similarly to the above but changed it, which is perhaps best explained by the hypothesis that he decided, while penning the manuscript, to represent a progressive clarification of the letters *J*, *S*, culminating in the third and final partia in E major.

Since the prospect of full knowledge in the age to come is likened in 1 Corinthians 10:12 to the degree to which one is known (which Luther translates *erkennet*, the same word rendered in English as "recognized"), could it be that by making himself recognized (*erkennet*) by his initials, Bach is expressing hope in the glories of the age to come, in which the present "shadows" come into focus in the true, heavenly realities?[21] In that case, the progressive development of the letter *P* throughout the partias would seem to correspond to the hope of growing in the transforming knowledge and grace of God here in this present life, not only the next.[22]

The B-minor Partia

In light of the strong possibility that the numbers 4, 5, and 6 in the latter two partias could have a dimension of symbolism, it is reasonable to consider whether the same might be true of the strongly emphasized number 2 in the B-minor partia.

As an initial but necessarily somewhat inconclusive observation, it is interesting to note that in Bach's vocal music, B minor is often associated with Christ's condescending to and identifying with sinful humanity in his incarnation,[23] perhaps in part because the two sharps (*Kreuze*) of the key signature can recall the dual nature of the incarnate Christ (*X*). For example, the only five movements of the Mass "in B minor" that are actually in B minor reflect this association. Most tellingly, of course, is the "Et incarnatus est," Bach's only setting of the portion of the Nicene Creed affirming that

21. Col 2:17; Heb 10:1. This is a prominent emphasis throughout the epistle to the Hebrews.

22. See Col 1:10; 2 Pet 3:18. Also Rom 12:2; Phil 3:12–14.

23. I am grateful to Karl Böhmer for drawing my attention to this association.

Christ "was made man." The "Benedictus qui venit in nomine Domini" sets the portion of Psalm 118 that the crowds shout at Jesus' triumphal entry into Jerusalem: "Blessed is he who comes in the name of the Lord!"[24] But Bach ironically sets the text to melancholy, sparsely scored music that anticipates Jesus' coming rejection and thereby doubly highlights the God-man duality, as the God-man Jesus, "who comes in the name of the Lord," is rejected by men. By welcoming the rejected King with a blessing, the participant in the Mass is acknowledging another duality fundamental to Lutheran thought, that of "God hidden in suffering" (*Deum abscondicum in passionibus*).[25] The remaining three B-minor movements of the Mass—the first "Kyrie," "Qui tollis," and "Qui sedes"—are supplications for mercy specifically addressed to Christ (as is, for example, the B-minor "Erbarme dich" from the St. Matthew Passion), the significance of which a devout Lutheran in Bach's context would without doubt strongly connect with the dual nature of Christ. According to Lutheran Christology, although the suffering of Christ means that God himself suffers, because Christ is God,[26] yet insofar as it concerns the two natures of Christ, it is in his human nature and not his divine nature that he suffers and dies[27]; and, significantly, it is therefore in his human nature that Christ is exalted to the right hand of God following the triumphant accomplishment of his work on the cross.[28] The significance, therefore, is that in crying out to the ascended Christ for mercy, the believer is calling out not to a disembodied spirit but to one who was and remains a man; who can sympathize with us by virtue of having shared in our brokenness to its bitter end, though without sin[29]; and who is therefore the mediator between God and man, able to intercede to God as God but yet for man as man.[30]

Outside of the Mass in B minor, two further examples that may briefly be noted are the hymn to "Immanuel" (meaning "God with us," a reference to Christ), BWV 123/1, and the aria "Es ist vollbracht" ("It is finished") from the St. John Passion, marveling at the accomplishment of the redeeming work for which Christ took on flesh, whose accomplishment utterly depends on Jesus' being God and man; as God, he absorbs the full wrath of

24. Matt 21:9; Mark 11:9; Luke 19:38; John 12:13.

25. *WA* 1:362.

26. See Althaus, *The Theology of Martin Luther*, 197–98.

27. Article VIII.10 of the "Solid . . . declaration of some articles of the Augsburg Confession" in *Concordia Triglotta*, 1019. *WA* 17 I:72.

28. Olearius, *Biblische Erklärung* 5:1453.

29. Heb 4:15.

30. 1 Tim 2:5–6.

God and saves to the uttermost,[31] and yet he does so as one of us and on our behalf. This is an emphasis that permeates Lutheran thought and teaching and is by no means confined either to academic Christology or to passion-specific contexts. Luther's popular Christmas hymn "Uns ist ein Kindlein heut geborn," for instance, explicitly identifies Jesus' being "true man and true God" as the reason that he is able to "help us out of all need" ("Ein wahrer Mensch und wahrer GOtt/ Daß er uns helf aus aller Noth").

Of course, it would be a fallacy to assume that any idea appearing to be associated with a particular key in the context of vocal music "should" apply to an instrumental work in the same key. However, if the evidence for thoroughgoing theological symbolism in the *Sei Solo* is credible, then the extensive repetition of the number 2 in the B-minor partia would most naturally seem to invite association with the dual nature of Christ and thus neatly coincide with this prominent association with B minor within Bach's vocal works.

There is a long-standing tradition in the visual arts called "the hand of God" in which Jesus is depicted with the thumb and first two fingers extended, representing the Trinity, and the third and fourth fingers curled together, representing the dual nature of Christ.[32] According to this tradition, then, Jesus' dual nature (as his belonging to the triune Godhead) is considered so important that it becomes an essential aspect of his depiction, superseding considerations of consistency with scene, theme, and so forth. Could the B-minor partia's emphasis on the number 2 be Bach's way of similarly referring to the dual nature of Christ, the second person of the Trinity, immediately following the possible representation of the nativity in the G-minor sonata? After all, as observed above, in Lutheran thought the dual nature is far from an auxiliary doctrine; rather, it lies at the heart of the nature of Christ and his role as savior of the world.

Accompanying the doctrine of the two natures of Christ is the idea not only of duality but of contrast. Many Biblical passages emphasize the contrast between God and man by presenting the two as a contrasting pair according to established literary technique. Among many examples, Numbers 23:19 reads:

> God is not a man, that He should lie,
> Nor a son of man, that he should repent.

Similarly, Isaiah 55:8–9 reads:

31. Heb 7:25. See my Chap. 3 n. 45.

32. *Nelson's Dictionary of Christianity*, s.v. "Hand of God."

For My thoughts are not your thoughts,
Nor are your ways My ways, declares the LORD.
For as the heavens are higher than the earth,
So are my ways higher than your ways
And My thoughts than your thoughts.

It is interesting, then, that the unusual titling of the movements in the B-minor partia suggests a similarly archetypal contrast. If the third movement's title "Sarabande" (rather than "Sarabanda") is indeed a mere typographical error, as is widely thought,[33] it would mean that the principal movements of the partia are given Italian titles while the variations that follow each movement are given the French title *Double* (bearing in mind that the Italian and French styles are the two principal and opposing styles of Europe in the decades leading up to Bach). The B-minor partia is the only work in the entire surviving Bach oeuvre in which an Italian-titled dance is paired with a French-titled *double*; and Bach does this with all four movements of the B-minor partia.

Although the mixing of French and Italian stylistic elements was common of German music in Bach's day,[34] the explicit and systematic juxtaposition of Italian-titled dances and French-titled *doubles* in the B-minor partia creates an uncommonly emphatic sense of duality. As such, it is yet another of the partia's many features that enunciate the number 2. I have suggested that the exceptional recurrence of the number 2 in the B-minor partia might best be explained as representing the dual nature of the incarnate Christ on the basis of its placement within the proposed Christological-allegorical schema of the *Sei Solo* coupled with the possible association of the key of B minor with Christ's incarnation. In that case, there is reason to consider whether the vivid if nominal juxtaposition of French and Italian elements might be employed, in the B-minor partia specifically, with this same significance in view, especially since this juxtaposition further parallels the idea of the hypostatic union of Christ's divine and human nature by representing not only duality but contrast.

Furthermore, if the title "Sarabande" is actually supposed to be "Sarabanda," it would mean that the contrasting elements of French and Italian are equally represented in the partia, at least linguistically, just as the historic Christian understanding of the incarnate Christ is that he is equally God and man. An Italian-titled Sarabanda would also mean that the Italian

33. See Ledbetter, *Unaccompanied Bach*, 115. Various typographical errors are to be found throughout the *Sei Solo*.

34. See, for instance, Zohn, *Music for a Mixed Taste*, 3–5.

and French titles run parallel to each other without mixture—the principal movements would exclusively have Italian titles, the variations exclusively French—exactly like what is said of Christ's dual nature in the Athanasian creed: "[He is] altogether one, not by the mixing of his natures, but as a unified person."[35] It is also interesting to note that in some places the harmony of the *doubles* does not match the harmony of the corresponding sections of the principal movements, though the correspondence of duration and the general harmonic concurrence remain unbroken (Ex. 5.2).

Ex. 5.2. Harmonic divergence between principal movements and their *doubles* in BWV 1002

35. "Unus omnino, non confusione substantiae, sed unitate personae." The intentionality of this significance must remain open to question, especially when considering how likely it is that Bach could write "Sarabande" rather than "Sarabanda" as a slip of the pen if the Italian title were part of an allegorical schema. It is not, of course, altogether inconceivable, and so I have put forward this theological parallel all the same, since it could still plausibly have been in Bach's mind.

In the same way, Christ's fleshly being differs in some respects from his divine nature without ever ultimately breaking concord with it. For instance, although God is self-sufficient,[36] as a man Jesus hungers and thirsts,[37]and although God is above temptation,[38] as a man Jesus is subject to temptation, though without sinning.[39]

There are two further contrasting pairs within the B-minor partia that evince correspondences with Lutheran (and historic Christian) theology. Whether these correspondences represent Bach's intentions or convenient coincidence, it is not possible to say; but the parallels are there, and I will explore them inasmuch as they could very plausibly represent Bach's designs. The first of these contrasting pairs with a possible theological parallel is the opposition of severe and tender gestures in the Allemanda. Ledbetter observes that the primary model of the Allemanda appears to be a particular vein of French allemande whose dotted rhythms should be played more gently than in various Italianate models with similarly notated textures.[40] But several features of the B-minor Allemanda are not typical of French models prior to 1720, notably the triplet figurations prominent throughout, as Ledbetter notes. Especially in the context of a German mixed-style work, this raises the question of the extent to which association with the French model is intended. If the Italian title "Allemanda" is not wholly irrelevant stylistically, it could in fact suggest that the dotted rhythms are to be played in the more Italian manner—that is, more sharply—so as to contrast with the slurred triplet rhythms that are in any case atypical of French allemandes. This would mean that the relationship between the B-minor Allemanda and the (later) Italianate aria "Komm, süßes Kreuz" from the St. Matthew Passion could indeed be deeper than the merely superficial one Ledbetter suggests.[41] In the obbligato viola da gamba part of "Komm, süßes Kreuz" ("Come, sweet cross"), a contrast between hard, often jagged dotted figures and smooth, slurred gestures allegorizes the paradoxical juxtaposition of "sweet" and "cross."

Could the Italianate title of the B-minor Allemanda indicate that Bach conceived it to exhibit a similar contrast of "hard" and "soft" gestures? If so, the ongoing alternation of these "hard" and "soft" musical gestures could be

36. Isa 43:10; John 5:26; Acts 17:25; Rom 11:36; 1 Cor 8:6; Col 1:17; Heb 2:10; Rev 1:8 and 22:13 (Isa 41:4). See my Chap. 6 n. 111.

37. See John 19:28.

38. Jas 1:13.

39. 2 Cor 5:21; Heb 4:15; 1 Pet 2:22.

40. Ledbetter, *Unaccompanied Bach*, 110–12.

41. Ibid., 111.

understood to continue the Christ-themed allegory by representing the idea that in the person and work of the dual-natured Christ, "hard" and "soft," judgment and mercy, are utterly intertwined. For Luther, it is impossible to separate the doctrine of the law and wrath for sin from proclamation of the mercies of Christ the redeemer, because Christ's purpose in coming to earth has been to fulfill the righteous requirements of the law in order to offer himself as a sinless sacrifice on the cross, vicariously bearing the wrath of God for the sin of humankind.[42] Accordingly, Lutheran theology has emphasized the dualities of law and gospel, justice and mercy, and so forth,[43] an understanding that permeates Bach's sacred works.[44] If the hard and soft musical gestures of the B-minor Allemanda could be understood to parallel the duality of law/judgment and gospel/mercy, it is interesting that the "soft" triplet gesture has the final word at the close of the Allemanda, just as the epistle of James remarks that "mercy triumphs over judgment."[45]

There is one final connection in the fourth movement of the partia that is rather oblique but not implausible. The title of the movement, Tempo di Borea, is unusual[46] and lends itself to a double entendre. *Borea* can mean either the dance borea (bourrée) or the north wind, named for the Greek god Boreas (referenced, for example, in Vivaldi's "Four Seasons"). And the word *tempo*, in addition to its musical usage, can also mean "weather." The title Tempo di Borea, then, can lend itself to being heard in terms of either dance or wind.[47] The connection with wind may not be entirely far-fetched. For instance, in *Der Streit zwischen Phoebus und Pan*, BWV 201, Bach uses bourrée-derived rhythms in the aria "Patron, das macht der Wind." [48] It is noteworthy that in this aria Bach is using bourrée elements to allegorize the idea of "mere" wind, entirely disconnected from Boreas or the North Wind. Indeed, within the context of the aria, "wind" is understood at two

42. See Chap. 3 n. 45; Chap. 6 n. 117.

43. In his funeral sermon for Luther, Bugenhagen identifies Luther's teaching on law and gospel as the key "by which the entire Scripture is opened and Christ is recognized, our righteousness and eternal life" ("durch welche die ganze Schrifft/ geöffnet wird/ und Christus erkand wird/ unser gerechtigkeit und ewiges leben"). Bugenhagen, *Eine Christliche Predigt*, 6, quoted in CB 6:1433.

44. See especially Chafe, *Analyzing Bach Cantatas*.

45. Jas 2:13.

46. Among the various bourrées composed by Bach, only in this movement does he use the Italian designation "Borea"; and within the *Sei Solo*, only in this movement does he preface the dance title with "Tempo di," typically used to distinguish a looser treatment of a dance from a stricter one.

47. In the following chapter I briefly elaborate on the use of word play by Bach and within his context.

48. See Little and Jenne, *Dance and the Music of J. S. Bach*, 216.

levels: literally, it is the breath with which Pan sings and plays his flute, and metaphorically, it is the vanity of Pan's claim to sing more beautifully than all others ("Pan singt vor allen andern schön").

If nothing else, the double entendre inherent within the title Tempo di Borea reinforces the emphasis on the number 2 that permeates the partia. But it is possible that this play between dance and wind may not be an end in itself. Whereas dance necessarily connotes the earthly and physical, wind is closely tied to the idea of spirit in biblical literature, because in both Hebrew and Greek a single word signifies "wind," "breath," and "spirit": *ruach* (רוח) in Hebrew, *pneuma* (πνεῦμα) in Greek. The association is not obscure, and indeed several biblical passages feature word plays on "wind" and "spirit" ("Wind" and "Geist" in Luther's translation) that make the connection both relevant and apparent to the student of theology (as we know Bach was), not merely the Greek scholar.[49] In Appendix B I present evidence that in his vocal music Bach sometimes uses wind instruments to represent spirit, especially the Spirit of God, and moreover that on at least three occasions he depicts the dual-natured Christ by means of shared material (whether by imitation or by doubling at the octave) between a wind instrument and violin or piccolo violin, the quintessential dancing-master's instrument. If this association is valid, it might suggest that the dual associations of wind and dance inherent in the double entendre of the title Tempo di Borea could possibly have been intended by Bach as an oblique allusion to the dual-natured Christ. If so—that is, if by 1720 Bach had considered the bourrée as a possible representation of *ruach/pneuma*—it may not be accidental that four years later the opening aria of Cantata 181, "Leichtgesinnte Flattergeister" ("light-minded frivolous spirits") should be cast to resemble a bourrée,[50] as it suggests not only the idea of spirit but also insubstantial vanity, for which wind was a long-standing metaphor (as, for instance, in BWV 201/3).[51]

49. See, for instance, John 3:5–8 and Heb 1:7, 14.

50. See Little and Jenne, *Dance and the Music of J. S. Bach*, 299.

51. The association is especially prominent throughout the book of Ecclesiastes.

6

A Hermeneutic Overview of the *Sei Solo*

To recapitulate what we have observed so far: musical elements of the D-minor Ciaccona and C-major Fuga, which are structurally related in various ways, respectively parallel the crucifixion and resurrection of Christ to a degree that seems less plausibly attributable to coincidence than to design. Considering the E-major partia and the A-minor Fuga in the context of the structure of the entire collection indicates the likelihood that the theological imagery extends beyond the D-minor partia and C-major sonata, possibly encompassing the entire collection. In this light, it is interesting that the final partia in E major appears to allegorize the end of the biblical Christ story with the coming of the kingdom of heaven, while the Siciliana of the first sonata in G minor could, in context, viably be associated with the nativity, so that the first and last works of the *Sei Solo* appear to represent the beginning and end of the Christ story respectively. Finally, we observed that symbolic associations with the numbers uniquely emphasized in the three partias correspond to theological themes that are appropriate to the respective positioning of each partia within the hypothesized allegorical narrative of the *Sei Solo*. In view of the fact that all six sonatas and partias now appear to have theological signifiers that sequentially parallel the Christ story, it seems reasonable to explore in more detail the hypothesis that the *Sei Solo* is conceived with a dimension of thoroughgoing theological allegory.

To this end, I will walk sequentially through the collection from the vantage point of this question: If, as I have proposed, evidence suggests that the Christ story could be the unspoken "text" of the *Sei Solo*, how might Bach be illustrating this text? This question highlights an important distinction between the kinds of evidences this study examines. The first type is evidence that can independently suggest the presence of an extramusical "text" by virtue of unique, strong correlations, often with the aid of established signifiers that are used in such a way as to suggest that their potential associations are warranted in the present case. I am treating the parallels with Christ's crucifixion and resurrection in the Ciaccona and C-major

Fuga preeminently as this type of evidence; that is, even in the absence of any other considerations or assumptions, the strength and uniqueness of these parallels would be sufficient, in my view, to establish the great likelihood that they represent Bach's intention. But there is a second important type of evidence that, incidentally, constitutes the majority of evidence in hermeneutic Bach studies, namely, evidence that can legitimately suggest a composer is representing a particular extramusical idea *only* if the pertinence of that musical idea has already been established. Vocal music is, of course, the perfect example. When a composer is setting a given text, certain musical features can appear clearly to be representing an idea in the text even though, if no text were given, there would be insufficient grounds for supposing that the same musical elements were intended to represent anything at all, much less the specific text or idea in question.

I have already presented evidence for the likelihood that the Christ story is intended as a "text" of the *Sei Solo*. In this chapter, then, I explore the extent to which this text might be illustrated musically. In doing so, I present a number of parallels between features of the *Sei Solo* and the Lutheran understanding of the Christ story that seem plausibly intentional to me, according to the five-point methodology spelled out at the end of Chapter 1, being cognizant of the inevitable possibility that some individual correlations may perhaps be no more than happy coincidence.

The Title of the Collection

The full designation Bach gives to his collection of unaccompanied violin works on the autograph title page is *Sei Solo a violino senza basso accompagnato*. It is often noted that Bach does not give the grammatically correct title *Sei Soli* but rather *Sei Solo*, which in fact properly translates not as "six solos" but "you are alone." Could this have been a simple error by a German writing an Italian title? Many of the headings Bach supplies in his manuscripts are in Italian, using words such as *violini* (violins), *voci* (voices), and so forth. He appears to have known that the plural of Italian nouns ending in –o and –e is formed by changing the suffix to –i. Ignorance of Italian does not seem to be a satisfying explanation for the curious title of the collection. Moreover, the words *Sei Solo* are separated from the remainder of the title by a greater space than one typically finds in Bach's title pages (Image 6.1).

Image 6.1. Title page of the *Sei Solo*

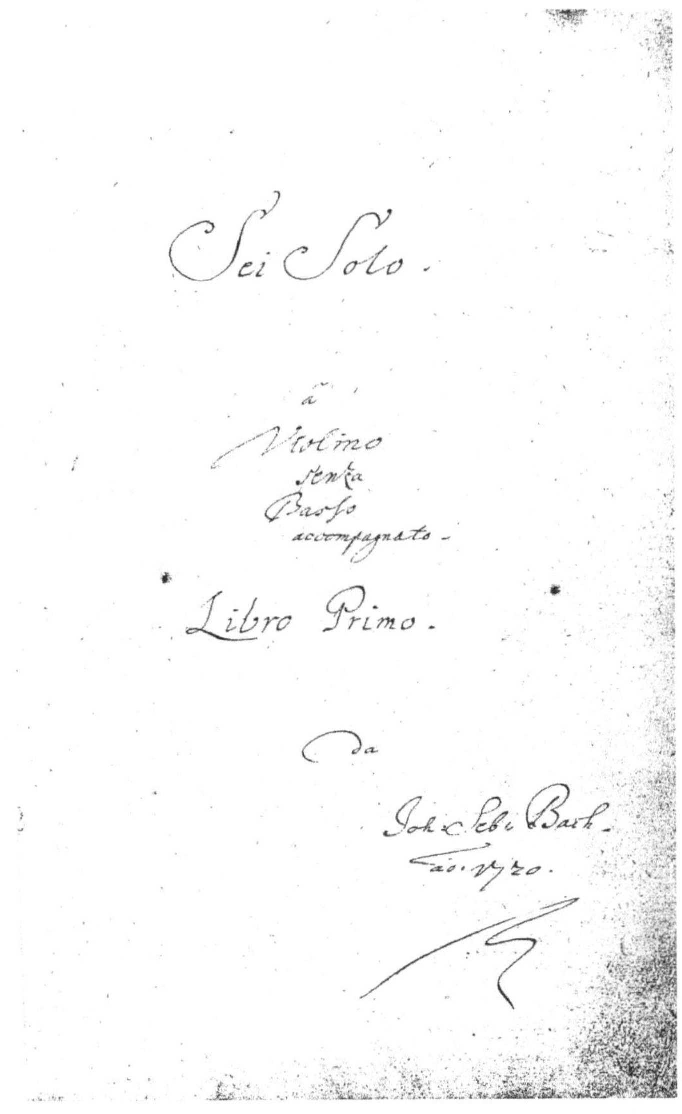
Sei Solo.
à
Violino
senza
Basso
accompagnato.
Libro Primo.
da
Joh. Seb. Bach.
ao. 1720.

In short, the phrase *Sei Solo* is made to stand alone. This not only draws attention to the phrase, with its curious grammar susceptible to the alternative reading "you are alone"; it could also be seen to allegorize this alternative reading and, to that extent, make it more viable. But to seriously consider that Bach might have intended a word play to indicate a cryptic second meaning requires, first, establishing a context against which such use of word play would be credible and, second, determining what the supposed cryptic meaning might reasonably refer to.

The use of word play in Bach's immediate setting and broader cultural context is so extensive that a separate study would be required to address it, but a few relevant examples may be noted. The Latin subheading Bach gives to his *Musical Offering* (BWV 1079) reads "Regis Iussu Cantio Et Reliqua Canonica Arte Resoluta" ("The theme given by the command of the king, and additions, resolved in the canonic style"). The title is an acrostic that creates the word *ricercar*, a fuguelike genre represented twice in the *Musical Offering*. More profoundly, however, the word comes from the Italian *ricercare*, meaning "to search out" (recalling the heading Bach gives to one of the canons of the *Musical Offering* with multiple solutions, "Quaerendo invenietis," "Seek and you will find.") There are, of course, many things to be sought out within the *Musical Offering*, including the realizations of its ten canons, the allegorical relationship between the musical devices of two of these canons to the Latin headings Bach gives to them,[1] and the theological meanings with which Bach appears to have imbued the collection (especially in light of its ten canons, resembling the ten "canons" or commandments of Biblical law).[2] But prior to all of this, there is a further complexity to be sought out within the "RICERCAR" acrostic itself, as the phrase "Canonica Arte" may have parallel meanings, alluding either to the parallel numerical structures of the collection as a whole (just as canon as a musical device is defined by melodic parallelism)[3] or to the "best possible way" in which the canons are constructed.[4]

Another particularly noteworthy example of Bach's word play is the F-major "Canon super Fa Mi," BWV 1078 (given the heading, "Fa Mi, et Mi Fa est tota Musica"). The canon appears to be dedicated to someone either called or represented by the name Faber,[5] as the name appears as an acrostic in the second line of a Latin verse accompanying the canon, while

1. To the canon by augmentation, Bach writes, "Notulis crescentibus crescat Fortuna Regis" ("As the notes increase, may the King's fortunes increase"); and to the canon that rises by a whole step with each repeat he writes, "Ascendenteque Modulatione ascendat Gloria Regis" ("As the modulation rises, so may the King's glory rise").

2. See Marissen, "The Theological Character of J. S. Bach's *Musical Offering*."

3. Tatlow, *Bach's Numbers*, 43; she presents these numerical parallels in 224–38.

4. Gardiner, *Bach: Music in the Castle of Heaven*, 227.

5. See Tatlow, *Bach and the Riddle of the Number Alphabet*, 126. Tatlow notes that, in addition to Benjamin Gottlieb Faber, several persons named "Schmidt" or "Schmid" have been proposed dedicatees of the canon, since "Schmid[t]" is the German translation of the Latin "Faber" (in English, "Smith"). Among the latter are Johann Michael Schmidt, Johann Christian Jakob Schmidt, and Balthasar Schmid.

the name "BACH" appears as an acrostic at the corresponding position in the second-to-last line:

Domin Possessor

[Honored possessor,]

Fidelis **A**mici **B**eatum **E**sse **R**ecordari

[that one is blessed to have a faithful friend]

tibi haud ignotum: itaque

[is not unknown to you: therefore]

Bonæ **A**rtis **C**ultorem **H**abeas

[accept a cultivator of the fine arts]

verum amIcum Tuum.

[as your true friend.]

Note that the name "FABER" appears at the point where the verse refers to the friend, while the name "BACH" appears in connection with the cultivator of the fine arts. The name "Faber" also appears encoded in the basso ostinato of the canon, which consists of the notes *f*, *a*', *b*♭' (*b* in German), *e*'—or, as Bach explicitly spells out, "F, A, B, E, Repetatur." Bach uses the properties of this name—specifically, that both A to "B" and E to F are a half-step apart and therefore represent the solmization syllables *mi* and *fa*—not only to give the canon a unifying conceptual theme but also to explicitly take sides in the contemporary debate about the continued relevance of hexachordal theory. In giving BWV 1078 the heading "Fa Mi, et Mi Fa est tota Musica," he is on the one hand describing the musical properties of the bass, the essential fundament of a musical texture, which in this case is made up entirely of two mutations of the syllables *mi*, *fa*; but at a deeper level he is recalling Johann Buttstett's defense of the hexachordal system in his treatise *Ut, Mi, Sol,/ Re, Fa, La,/ Tota Musica et Harmonia Aeterna* (1716). Bach's echoing this description of the hexachord as "tota Musica" (complete music) in 1749, the date of the "Faber" canon, must be heard as especially emphatic in light of Mattheson's taunt more than thirty years earlier that such theory represents not "tota Musica" but "todte Musica" (dead music).[6]

Two final examples are less intricate but more nearly resemble the manipulation of *sei soli* into *Sei Solo*. In a 1749 letter to Georg Friedrich Einike, Bach refers to the *Dreckohr* ("dirty ear") of the Rektor of Freiberg, Johann Gottlieb Biedermann, who wrote an essay (*Programma de Vita musica*)

6. See Chap. 4 n. 9.

demeaning musical education.[7] In the same year, Bach led a performance of the then-twenty-year-old cantata *Der Streit zwischen Phoebus und Pan*, which sets a libretto by Picander describing the proud and gifted but ultimately inferior Pan challenging Phoebus for musical mastery; and even though Pan is favored by Midas, Midas is rebuked by his fellow judges as having poor taste. Wolff sees "a scarcely hidden autobiographical undertone" in this performance on account of the fact that Johann Gottlob Harrer had recently auditioned to be Bach's successor at St. Thomas's in Leipzig.[8] This autobiographical element seems all the more likely in light of Bach's altering one of Picander's original lines for the 1749 performance in order to make reference to Orbilius, the notoriously violent teacher of Horace, whose name Bach subsequently jumbles in the last recitative from "Orbilius" to "Birolius," which Wolff notes comes remarkably close to a "dog-Latin" form of the name of Harrer's patron, Count Heinrich von Brühl.[9]

If this provides a sufficient linguistic foundation for the possibility that the title *Sei Solo* could likely be a word play, the next question is that of its plausible meaning or meanings. At the most immediate level, of course, it can refer to the violinist playing alone. But most word plays in Bach's context serve to imply a second, more covert meaning that is substantially different from the first and most obvious. Referring merely to the violinist playing alone would not suggest anything that was not already implied in the designation of the violin works as "solos," and therefore the paragrammatic manipulation of the title would seem rather pointless. Myles Jordan has suggested that it might refer to Bach's suddenly finding himself alone after the death of his first wife, Maria Barbara, in the same year as the *Sei Solo* were completed.[10] But this is proposed within the explicit context of the assumption that "sei solo" can be understood not only in the second person ("you are alone") but also the third ("he is alone"), which is not actually the case; "you are alone" is the only viable translation, and it would seem strange that Bach should be referring to himself in the second person, though it is not unthinkable in light of the fact that only the second-person construction resembles the phrase that translates as "six solos."

I suggest that the phrase *Sei Solo* might at least as plausibly have been intended as an invocation to the subject of the theological symbolism of the *Sei*

7. BD II, no. 592; NBR, no. 268.Wolff notes that the Saxon pronunciation "Rekdor" makes the pun with *Dreckohr* especially effective (*Bach: The Learned Musician*, 423). Bach insinuates that if the Rektor perceives any dirtiness in the learning and practice of music, the dirtiness is not in the music but in his ear.

8. Wolff, *Bach: The Learned Musician*, 445.

9. Ibid., 446.

10. Myles Jordan, "Realizations: A New Look at Old Music."

Solo, Jesus Christ, whose worthiness Bach would certainly have understood in terms of uniqueness or being "alone." Among the doxological literature in the Hebrew Scriptures, one of the primary devotional formulations is to extol the "alone-ness" or uniqueness of God,[11] bearing in mind that orthodox Christianity (including Lutheranism) holds this same God to be the Holy Trinity of whom Jesus is the second person. The New Testament continues in this strain, universally describing Jesus in terms consistent with "only" or "alone." Both the Gospel of John and the epistle of 1 John refer to Jesus as the "only begotten Son" of God,[12] and the New Testament contains several paeans in prose to the supremacy and uniqueness of Christ.[13] In his incarnation, Jesus becomes fundamentally alone in the sense of being rejected even by his own,[14] ultimately dying on a cross forsaken by man and God.[15] In doing so, however, he bears the guilt and curse of humanity's sin as the "one mediator . . . between God and men,"[16] becoming the one savior of humanity,[17] and is consequently given the "name that is above all names."[18]

Among the numerous liturgical and commentarial acknowledgments of the "alone-ness" or uniqueness of Christ, one that is particularly noteworthy comes from the Gloria, a prominent element of the Mass Ordinary that the Lutheran tradition preserved: "Quoniam tu solus Sanctus, tu solus Dominus, tu solus Altissimus, Jesu Christe" ("For you alone are holy, you alone are Lord, you alone are most high, Jesus Christ"). Also noteworthy are prominent Lutheran chorales that emphasize God or Christ as "alone" (*allein*): for instance, "Allein Gott in der Höh' sei Ehr'"[19] and "Allein zu dir, Herr Jesu Christ."[20] And of course there is the phrase whose initials Bach frequently pens at the bottom of his scores: "Soli Deo gloria" ("to God alone be glory").

11. See Deut 6:4; Ps 86:8 and 10, 113:5; Isa 37:16, 40:18 and 25, 43:10, 46:9; Jer 10:6; Neh 9:6; Zech 14:9.

12. See John 1:18, 3:16, 3:18; 1 John 4:9. The LB consistently translates this phrase as "eingeborenen [eingebornen/eingeborne] Sohn."

13. E.g., Col 1:15–23; Heb 1. See Matt 23:8–10; Rom 5:17; 1 Cor 8:6; Eph 4:5.

14. John 1:11. See Matt 13:57; Mark 6:4; Luke 4:24; John 7:5, 13:18, and 15:18.

15. See Mark 14:50, 15:34; John 3:14; 1 Cor 5:21; Gal 3:13.

16. 1 Tim 2:5.

17. Acts 4:12.

18. Phil 2:9.

19. "Allein Gott in der Höh' sei Ehr'/ und Dank für seine Gnade" ("Alone to God on high be glory and thanks for his mercy").

20. "Allein zu dir, Herr Jesu Christ,/ mein Hoffnung steht auf Erden" ("Alone on you, Lord Jesus Christ, my hope on earth depends").

In Appendix B I propose that the idea of "*X* alone"—encompassing both "Christ alone" and "the cross alone" (*CRUX sola*)—is prominently represented in the D-minor harpsichord concerto, BWV 1052. If that analysis is correct, BWV 1052—or, more precisely, its putative *Urform* dating from ca. 1714–1717[21]—would provide an important precedent against which to consider the possibility that the title of the *Sei Solo* may be a cryptic invocation to the Christ who is variously associated with the idea of being unique or alone.

In the end, the multiple possible meanings of "you are alone" probably need not be exclusive and need not even have been exclusive in the mind of Bach. It would, after all, be a fitting parallel to the multiple possible readings of the phrase *Sei Solo* if its more covert meaning, "you are alone," also had multiple significances. And although it would appear ironic that the title signifying oneness should have multiplicity of meanings, this too forms a ready parallel with Lutheran theology that might perhaps not have eluded Bach. We have observed three layers of applicable meanings of the phrase "you are alone": the aloneness of the violinist, the aloneness of Bach following the death of his wife, and the aloneness of Christ, whom I propose the collection of six solos allegorizes. This threefold meaning within the oneness-signifying title interestingly if accidentally recalls the triune nature of the (one) God to whom the invocation *sei solo* would be addressed.

Number and Genres

We have already noted that the *Sei Solo*'s containing six works would likely have been intended as a symbol of the completeness or perfection (*Vollkommenheit*) associated with the number 6.[22] But in light of the theological dimension of the *Sei Solo*, it may not be irrelevant that the perfection of the number 6 was associated with God himself as the source of perfection.[23] But even though the title of the collection refers to six works, the individual works are not numbered 1 through 6 but instead according to genre—*Sonata 1ma, Partia 1ma, Sonata 2da, Partia 2da, Sonata 3za, Partia 3za*—thereby emphasizing the constitution of the collection as three sonatas and three partias. This would likely evoke the common but in this case especially relevant association of the number 3 with the Trinity.[24]

21. See Appendix B n. 9.

22. See Chap. 4 n. 14.

23. See Tatlow, "Collections, Bars and Numbers," 54.

24. Prominent examples within Bach's tradition include Luther's describing the three hexachordal degrees *re, mi, fa* as a representation of the Trinity (*WA TR*, no. 815)

It is noteworthy that these two genres of sonata and partia carry distinct and contrasting associations. The three sonatas each contain four movements following the scheme slow—fugue—slow—fast, making them textbook examples of the sonata da chiesa or "church sonata." Thus their association with things "spiritual" becomes nearly unavoidable at some level, even if only nominally. Moreover, the fact that the partias differ markedly one from another in the number and type of their movements underscores, by contrast, the uniformity among the sonatas; Bach seems almost to be emphasizing that the works labeled "sonata" are to be understood distinctly as *da chiesa*. By contrast, the three partias are collections of dance movements and thus connote the physical and the worldly. While it would be erroneous to assume a hard and fast distinction between the musical styles deemed appropriate to each genre,[25] the conviction commonly expressed in the seventeenth century in words resembling those of Conrad Dieterich—that dance music in a church context can only "profane and desecrate the worship of God"[26]—carried over to some extent in the Germany of Bach's day in the form of the sentiment, expressed by Quantz, that "church music

---

and Joachim Burmeister's likening the Trinity to a triad in *Hypomnematum musicae poeticae* (see *Musical Poetics*, 212–13), an idea that would later be echoed by Werckmeister (*Musicae Mathematicae*, 147, in Appendix chap. 5). As early as the thirteenth century, Franco of Cologne speaks of the "perfection" of note values divisible by three, writing that "the ternary number is among numbers the most perfect, for it takes its name from the Holy Trinity, which is true and pure perfection" (". . . est enim ternarius numerus inter numeros perfectissimus pro eo quod a summa trinitate, quae vera est et pura perfectio, nomen sumpsit." Franconis, *Ars cantus mensurabilis*, chap. IV). The number 3 also had significances beyond the doctrine of the Trinity. It is, for instance, the number of days Christ spent in the tomb, corresponding to the amount of time Jonah spent in the belly of the fish (see Matt 12:40). In Pythagorean thought, with which Bach was certainly familiar, three, or the "triad," is considered the most noble digit by virtue of being the sum of all positive integers below it (see Dentler, *L'Arte della fuga di Johann Sebastian Bach: un'opera pitagorica e la sua realizzazione*).

25. For instance, Gregory Barnett has noted that dance *topoi* were used for "alleluia" settings in seventeenth-century Bolognese masses and motets and accordingly were also featured in the final movements of sonatas da chiesa, which were designed to be suitable for liturgical use. *Bolognese Instrumental Music*, esp. 231–42. I am grateful to Rebecca Cypess for bringing this to my attention.

26. ". . .den Gottesdienst profaniren und entheyligen." Dieterich, *Ulmische Orgel Predigt* (1624), 42. Bach seems clearly not to have held Dieterich's view, as much of Bach's own sacred music is driven by the rhythms of dance. But this only implies that he considered using originally secular-associated musical elements in a sacred context no more sacrilegious than appropriating melodies of secular songs to set sacred texts (*contrefactum*); it need not suggest the nonexistence in his mind of their associations with the secular. The following paragraph explores a possible Lutheran foundation for the intermingling of sacred and secular elements.

requires more majesty and seriousness than that for the theater, which permits greater freedom."[27]

It is not uncommon to find Baroque collections that incorporate genres with contrasting associations of sacred and secular, in keeping with the seventeenth- and eighteenth-century fondness for completeness and comprehensiveness. One particularly notable example before Bach is Corelli's Opus 5 violin sonatas, consisting of six sonatas da chiesa followed by six sonatas da camera that consist largely of dance movements. But even though equal inclusion of the contrasting genres of sonata da chiesa and partia would not be unusual, their thorough integration by systematic alternation is not only unusual,[28] it is also a fitting structural parallel to the theological content of the *Sei Solo*. After all, the Christ story, as understood by orthodox Christianity, is fundamentally marked by the infusing of the worldly with the sacred as God himself steps down into our fallen world, identifying with the poor, the outsiders, the broken, the unclean, and even the sinful[29] as part of God's redemptive plan "to reconcile all things to himself, . . . whether things on earth or in heaven"[30] with a commitment and intimacy that the New Testament repeatedly likens to marriage.[31] From this fundamental understanding of the implications of Christ's incarnation spring a number of Lutheran teachings that could similarly be expressed by the intermingling of symbols of the sacred and secular, perhaps most notably Luther's distinctive teaching on vocation whereby he argues that the calling of the monk is no holier than that of the farmer and, conversely, that the farmer's work is no less holy than

27. ". . . eine Kirchenmusik erfordert mehr Pracht und Ernsthaftigkeit, als eine theatralische, welche mehr Freyheit zuläßt." Quantz, *Versuch*, 245.

28. Sackmann, "Warum komponierte Bach BWV 1001–1006?" 1.

29. See Luke 6:20; Matt 2:23 in light of Isa 53:3–12; Matt 8:2–3 (Luke 5:12–13); 9:10 (Mark 2:15), 9:20–22 (Mark 5:25–34) in light of Lev 15:25; Luke 15:2. With Lev 12:8 in view, Luke 2:24 indicates that Jesus' family was poor, and the genealogy of Jesus that opens the Gospel of Matthew goes beyond conventions of genealogy to show that Jesus' lineage includes those not of the chosen people (Ruth, the Moabitess, v. 5) as well as infamous episodes of incest (Judah and Tamar, v. 3), prostitution (Tamar, v. 3, and Rahab, v. 5), and adultery/murder (David and "the wife of Uriah," v. 6; see 2 Sam 11). Luther not only acknowledges Christ's full identification with the lowly state of humanity but uses it toward one of his most striking emphases, that in Christ, God himself has suffered with humanity and, without ceasing to be the most high God, has become the lowest of the low through the humility and ultimately the humiliation of Jesus. For Luther, this is the key to salvation itself, because Christ's work on the cross—the zenith of his suffering and humiliation—can be nothing less than an act of God in order to bring salvation to the world. See Althaus, *The Theology of Martin Luther*, 197–98; Wood, *Captive to the Word*, 170.

30. Col 1:20.

31. 2 Cor 11:2; Eph 5:25–32; Rev 19:6–9. See Isa 54:5.

the monk's.[32] Indeed, it is this understanding that could best explain Bach's weaving theological symbolism into the *Sei Solo*, which clearly belong to the realm of secular music.

Instrumentation

Considering this Lutheran emphasis on the incarnation and its implications, it is interesting that the collection of *Sei Solo*, allegorizing the Christ story as I propose, should exhibit a relationship between notation and instrumentation that creates a perhaps uniquely apt image of the incarnation of Christ.

At some level, of course, every act of performance and composition can be likened to incarnation. In the theory of Bach's day, crafting an affecting piece of music on the requisite planned structural foundation[33] can be likened to motion from the realm of *ratio*, with its associations with the heavens and the divine order, into the realm of *sensus*, emotion, the human. Then the act of performance incarnates (in a more nearly literal sense) this abstract composition by giving it physical being in the form of sound waves.[34]

But the *Sei Solo* go considerably further. There is at once the incongruity between the scope of the grandest structures within *Sei Solo* and the single violin for which they are conceived. After all, Bach's sonatas and partias for solo violin contain some of his most majestic musical conceptions, especially the monumental Ciaccona and the C-major Fuga, while the instrument on which this vast structure and rich texture is to be realized—a solitary treble melody instrument—necessarily conveys a certain sense of finiteness and limitation, especially in Bach's age of continuo-driven harmony. Moreover, the *Sei Solo* contain a great deal of passagework that it is not possible to execute as notated on a violin, as in Example 6.1.

32. See Chap. 1 n. 20.

33. This applies equally to improvisation, in which the planning either occurs moments before the sounding of the notes or belongs to a collection of stock gestures, patterns, or structures that can be appropriated at will.

34. The physical phenomenon of sound waves moving through air was known from the time of Leonardo da Vinci and was the subject of further discoveries by Galileo, Mersenne, Boyle, and Newton in the seventeenth century. In fact, Bach's student Lorenz Mizler expressed skepticism at the popular idea (one might nearly say dogma) of heavenly music on grounds that "one must first substantiate that in eternal life there is air. One must have investigated the potency and properties of this same air." ("Man muß zuvor darthun, daß im ewigen Leben eine Lufft ist. Man muß die Kräfften und Eigenschafften selbiger Lufft untersuchet haben.") Mizler, *Neu eröffnete musikalische Bibliothek*, vol. 1, 30.

Ex. 6.1. Quadruple stopping in BWV 1005/2

At other times, Bach writes a single line of music that is fully idiomatic for the violin and can be played straightforwardly on it but that at the same time contains an embedded polyphonic texture that the written notes can only imply, as in Example 6.2.

Ex. 6.2. Implied polyphony in BWV 1001/4, with realization below

In both cases, the violin seems as though it is called on to "incarnate" something too big for it to contain, as with the premise of God taking on a human frame.

But here the connection with theology becomes both subtler and more striking. The irony of Bach's "impossible" violin writing is that, when played on a violin, it *is* fully and sufficiently realized. Indeed, it is one of the marvels of the *Sei Solo* that its implied polyphony sometimes *cannot* be realized beyond what is given for one violin without having to change the melodic or harmonic profile of the music.

One example is measure 198 of the Fuga from the A-minor sonata (BWV 1003), show in Example 6.3.

Ex. 6.3. "Illicit" $^6_4$ chord in BWV 1003/2

Bach apparently intends the common bass gesture $\hat{8}$, $\hat{6}$, $\hat{3}$ but yet wants what modern theory, following Rameau, would call a G-minor chord (ii in F major) on the second beat. But this requires that the second beat contain an "illicit" $^6_4$ chord. Although this unconventional voicing has apparently left many musicians perplexed through the years,[35] the effect is nonetheless agreeable when played as part of a polyphonic texture on a single violin. However, if this passage were given a different scoring—almost any other scoring—the "illicit" $^6_4$ chord would sound much more vividly like a $^6_4$ chord as such and would likely be troubling to the listener. In other words, even though the texture may seem to ask for instrumental forces greater than a single string instrument, nevertheless one cannot score it for anything other than this "limited" string instrument while preserving the integrity of the passage. This bears a strong conceptual resemblance to how Luther conceived the mystery of Christ's incarnation: that although God is so vast that the heavens cannot contain him,[36] yet one cannot look anywhere but at the human frame of Christ to see God truly,[37] because it is in the incarnate Christ that the invisible God is made visible.[38]

Thus far, we have noted that various general components of the *Sei Solo*, considered individually, either markedly resemble or else have established associations with theological ideas Lutheranism embraced. But it is worth considering that the most prominent associations or implications of the number content, structure, and instrumentation of the *Sei Solo* converge

35. The manuscript copy by E. L. Gottschalk (*D-B Mus. ms. Bach P 968*), copied from Bach's 1720 autograph shortly after its completion, already changes the lowest from *d'* to *e'*. Many nineteenth- and twentieth-century editions changed the middle note from *g'* to *f'*, creating a first-inversion B♭-major chord. Joseph Silverstein plays (and advocates playing) the chord as *g*, *f'*, *b*♭' on account of the ascending line it creates in the bass, resembling what is found in the D-minor keyboard transcription, BWV 964.

36. 1 Kgs 8:27; Jer 23:34; Isa 66:1; Eph 1:23. A similar idea is expressed, for instance, in BWV 91 and BWV 121/3.

37. For a summary of Luther's treatment of this idea, see "The New Element in Luther's Christology," in Althaus, *The Theology of Martin Luther*, 181–93.

38. See Col 1:15; John 1:1, 16, 18.

to collectively suggest a possible association with the incarnation of Christ. The numbers 6 and 3 have traditional associations that refer to God—6 by virtue of perfection, and 3 by way of the Trinity. And as noted in Chapter 4, the key structure of the collection is chiastic (thus possibly signifying Christ) and also represents fullness or totality by virtue of being bounded by extremes on multiple levels. By accident or design, the concurrence of these potential significances bears striking resemblance to the succinct description of the incarnation of Christ in Colossians 2:9: "in Him [that is, *Christ*] all the *fullness* of *Deity* dwells in bodily form" (emphases mine). It is interesting, then, that the collection of *Sei Solo*, with its intimations of *X*, fullness, and deity, should be realized on an instrument that I will propose in Appendix B has distinct associations with the human in Bach's vocal works and that in any case had its origins in the most bodily of genres, dance music.[39]

One final aesthetic consequence of the relationship between music and instrumentation in the *Sei Solo* is that it creates a sense of inversion, as a treble melody instrument is responsible for realizing the fullness of an essentially bass-driven polyphonic texture. In the aria "Wie jammern mich doch die verkehrten Herzen" from Cantata 170, Bach depicts the inverse relationship between the world, with its "backward hearts" (*verkehrten Herzen*), and the kingdom of God by creating a musical texture that is the inversion of well-ordered propriety; the solo alto voice is accompanied by organ obbligato playing two upper obbligato lines while the bass line is supplied by violins and violas. In other words, the instrument typically associated with the bass group and responsible for filling in harmony is instead given a melodic role—two, in fact, so that the left hand is prevented from doubling the bass line!—while the bass line is denied its typical chord-playing contingent and is given solely to those instruments that usually play the upper melodic voices. Naturally, this is not to suggest that the intimation of role reversal inherent in polyphonic solo violin music indicates that all such music is meant to represent the idea of inversion. But what it does indicate is that expressing inversion through reversing instrumental roles is not an alien idea to Bach, and therefore polyphonic writing for a solo violin would a suitable medium for a work or collection that deals with the Christ story, since the idea of inversion is absolutely central to it.

39. In 1556, Philibert Jambe de Fer rather derogatorily writes that "there are few persons who use [the violin] save those who make a living from it through their labour"—that is, accompanying dances. This is in contrast to the viola da gamba, the instrument of choice by which "gentlemen, merchants, and other virtuous persons pass their time." Jambe de Fer, *L'Epitome musical*, quoted in Boyden, *The History of Violin Playing from its Origins to 1761*, 32.

Key Structure of the Collection

The principle of inversion is also evident in the key structure of the *Sei Solo*: g—b—a—d—C—E. We have already observed that the succession of the tonic pitches of this sequence is chiastic. But it is not the simplest way of forming chiastic symmetry, which would be to reverse the order of tonic pitches, as in the key structure of the cello suites (Fig. 6.2). Bach's choosing to incorporate a less simple chiasm in the *Sei Solo* is likely owing to the other attributes he wished the collection to have: that the respective tonic pitches of the violin solos should create a shuffled hexachord and that the outermost works of the collection represent extremity, neither of which would be possible within a simple chiastic structure (such as g—b—a—A—B—G). But even if only as a consequence of needing a more complex chiastic structure to realize the foregoing structural features, the second half of the key sequence is not merely the retrograde of the first (which is how simple symmetry is created) but a transposition of the retrograde inversion, shown in Example 6.4.

Ex. 6.4. Tonic pitches of successive works of the *Sei Solo*

In short, whatever its immediate impetus, the key structure of the *Sei Solo* features inversion; and as such, it forms a parallel with the inversion-connoting relationship between notation and instrumentation discussed above.

The reason this is particularly interesting in the context of a collection of works allegorizing the Christ story is that the idea of inversion or turning upside-down could be described as the essential shape of the Christ story: the high King becomes a low servant in order to raise the lowly up to glory[40]; the beloved Son becomes an outcast in order to turn outcasts and enemies into beloved sons[41]; the Judge becomes the judged and the carpenter becomes nailed to a piece of wood to die in the stead of those who have crucified him[42]; the God whose purity is reflected in the strict regulations of

40. Exaltation of the lowly through the humiliation of Christ is explicit and implicit throughout the New Testament, but it is a particular emphasis in the Gospel of Luke. See Kimbell, *The Atonement in Lukan Theology*, 9.

41. See John 17:1, 24. Also Matt 27:46; Rom 5:10, 8:15; Gal 4:4–7; Heb 13:12.

42. In his commentary on Galatians, Luther emphasizes that those who have sought

the Mosaic Law becomes accursed under the law in order to purify defiled sinners[43]; the one in whom is life[44] becomes obedient to death[45] in order to give eternal life to those to whom death is due[46]; the invisible God whom none may see and live[47] becomes visible in Christ,[48] yet it is he, not his beholders, who dies; Jesus conquers precisely through what appears to be his defeat, disarming the spiritual powers of evil through his bodily death on the cross[49] and putting death to death through death,[50] so that the death of the righteous one may give life to the sinful many.[51] So the principle of inversion seen in many of Jesus' teachings (for instance, that the least shall be great and the last shall be first)[52] goes beyond mere moralizing; it represents the very shape of the world the gospel depicts.

There is one other aspect of the key structure of the *Sei Solo* that is particularly noteworthy. Eric Chafe observes that "the two modulatory directions—the sharp or dominant and the flat or subdominant—were to a very considerable degree perceived as opposite in their affective characters, the former direction widely associated with the idea of ascent and the latter with descent."[53] He notes that the descent-ascent pattern has numerous theological, liturgical, and devotional applications and accordingly was used extensively to theological ends in Bach's sacred vocal works.

---

to justify themselves by works—and for Luther, this means everyone—are responsible for crucifying Christ (*WA* 40 I:324). He repeatedly emphasizes the believer's own culpability in the death of Christ, for instance, in the 1519 "Meditation on Christ's Passion" ("Ein Sermon von der Betrachtung des heiligen Leidens Christi," *WA* 2:136–142). The familiar Lutheran chorale "Herzliebster Jesu" by Johann Heermann expresses the idea thus: "Ach! meine sünden haben dich geschlagen! Ich, ach Herr Jesu! habe dies verschuldet, was du erduldet" ("Ah! my sins have smitten you! I, ah, Lord Jesus, am guilty for what you endured.") Bach was very familiar with this chorale, having written a setting for organ (BWV 1093) ca. 1703, while still a teenager, later incorporating the chorale into the St. John and St. Matthew Passions.

43. Deut 21:23; Heb 9:14; 1 John 1:7; Rev 7:14.

44. John 1:4.

45. Phil 2:8.

46. Rom 6:23.

47. Exod 33:20.

48. Col 1:15.

49. Col 2:15.

50. See Appendix B n. 72.

51. See Rom 5:6–19. For Rambach's similar observations of ironic inversions, albeit specific to the cross, see my Chap. 4 n. 40.

52. See Chap. 4 nn. 33 and 34; also Matt 20:27–28 (Mark 10:43–45; Luke 22:26–27) and 23:11–12; Luke 1:52–53 and 14:8–11.

53. Chafe, *Analyzing Bach Cantatas*, xi–xii.

What is interesting is that the D-minor partia—which I suggest represents the passion of Christ, the nadir of his humiliation and suffering—is the midpoint (that is, the low point) of a symmetrical scheme of tonal descent and ascent, shown in Figure 6.1. Of the five works making up this schema, the D-minor partia, the innermost, is the only one to have a "flat" key signature. Framing the D-minor partia are two sonatas with neutral key signatures: A minor and C major. The outermost works in this schema, both partias, have "sharp" key signatures. That the outermost, middle, and innermost terms are distinguished by sharp, neutral, and flat key signatures respectively is sufficient to create a sense of tonal symmetry, even though the precise key signatures of the outer terms do not correspond. But their difference may itself be significant.

If the low point of this descent-ascent pattern is the partia corresponding to Christ's ultimate debasement, then it would be reasonable for the first piece in the schema (the B-minor partia) to represent the height from which he descended and the last piece (the E-major partia) to represent the height to which he subsequently ascended. The validity of this interpretation is reinforced by the independent evidence considered in Chapter 4 supporting the idea of the E-major partia as a representation of heaven, which is where the New Testament repeatedly describes Jesus as seated at the right hand of the Father following his resurrection and ascension. In this case, it is potentially significant that the last work in this schema has two sharps more than the first, because Lutheran theology has understood the New Testament to teach that, whereas Christ has always been the most high God, there are two senses in which he becomes glorified still more on account of his redeeming work as a man. First, he is glorified in and for what he accomplished on the cross,[54] by virtue of which Luther understands Christ to reign as "Lord over all angels and creatures [as well as] death, the devil, and hell."[55] Secondly, with his ascension to the right hand of the Father, Jesus is proclaimed to be Lord no longer only as God but also as man[56]; the human nature that Jesus assumed with his incarnation has become eternally joined to his divine nature in hypostatic union, and therefore the glorification of Christ following

54. See, e.g., Acts 5:31; Phil 2:6–11; Heb 1:3–4; Rev 5:9.

55. ". . . daß er über alle Engel und Creatur/ Tod/ Teuffel/ Höll/ Herr sey." CB 6:714.

56. Olearius, *Biblische Erklärung* 5:1453.

the accomplishment of his redeeming work is glorification of his human nature,[57] by which, being God, he was able to redeem humanity as a man.[58]

Since this descent-ascent pattern we have observed bears all the hallmarks of intentionality, several further points may be drawn from it. First, according to this schema, the D-minor partia, the work representing Christ's crucifixion, is the crux of a five-part tonal chiasm. And of course within this partia, the movement in which the crucifixion imagery comes into sharpest focus is the Ciaccona, which itself is structured as a five-part chiasm. This creates a fractal-like parallelism that is interesting in light of the extent to which the Ciaccona in particular features the Golden Section, a ratio that preeminently creates fractal-like parallelism and in fact does so within the Ciaccona with the proportions 12:19:31.[59]

Second, this tonal descent-ascent schema helps to clarify the role of the B-minor partia within the *Sei Solo*. It is initially puzzling that the B-minor partia should seem to suggest the incarnation of Christ when the Siciliana of the previous sonata in G minor has already most naturally lent itself to representing the nativity. On further reflection, there is a difference of function; the G-minor Siciliana recalls the event of Christ's birth, whereas the B-minor partia seems more of a theological reflection on the incarnation. Nonetheless, the conceptual overlap is perhaps not what one would expect. The descent-ascent pattern we have just observed, however, appears to confirm the association of the B-minor partia with the incarnation; if the nadir of the tonal descent occurs with the partia that independently recalls the passion of Christ, the darkest moment of the Christ story, and if the "exalted" culmination of the tonal ascent corresponds to the partia that independently appears to represent his heavenly destination, then it is only natural that the B-minor partia that begins the descent-ascent schema should represent the beginning of Christ's descent, namely, the incarnation. The somewhat curious overlap

57. Article VIII.12 of the "Solid . . . declaration of some articles of the Augsburg Confession" from the definitive Lutheran *Book of Concord* reads, "We also believe, teach, and confess that the assumed human nature of Christ not only has and retains its natural and essential properties but moreover also—by the personal union in which it is most marvelously coupled with divinity, and afterward by glorification—is exalted to the right hand of majesty, power and authority above all that is named, not only in this but also in the age to come." ("Credimus quoque, docemus ac confitemur, assumptam humanam naturam in Christo non tantum essentiales et naturales suas proprietates habere et retinere, sed praeterem etiam per unionem personalem, qua cum divinitate mirando modo copulata est, et postea per glorificationem exaltatam esse ad dexteram maiestatis, virtutis, et potentiae super omne, quod nominatur, non tantum in hoc, sed etiam in future saeculo, Eph. 1.21"). *Concordia Triglotta*, 1019.

58. 1 Tim 2:5–6. On the centrality of the dual nature of Christ to Luther's understanding of his redeeming work, see Wood, *Captive to the Word*, 170.

59. See "The Problem of Structure in the Ciaccona" in Chap. 2.

of subject matter with the G-minor sonata could be explained in any number of ways, perhaps most convincingly as a quirk of Bach's endeavoring to combine multiple structural schemas with various significances. But it would seem that here, as ever, Bach is mindful of redemptive possibilities; if any idea should appear to be a doubling of another, how appropriate that it should pertain to a concept touching on the idea of duality (that is, the dual nature Christ assumes in his incarnation).

Third, this tonal descent-ascent pattern could offer two potential explanations—one theological and one structural—for Bach's notating the G-minor sonata with only one flat instead of the customary two, especially when various source evidence suggests that at least the first two movements might originally have been notated with two flats.[60] Since the correspondence between the tonal and theological properties of the D-minor partia depend on its being the tonal low point of the descent-ascent schema—that is, the furthest toward the enharmonic or "flat" end of the tonal spectrum—it is possible, though of course entirely speculative, that Bach might have felt the impact of this tonal descent would be diminished if the one work of the *Sei Solo* outside this schema were in a key that had still more flats. Of course, various other patterns and significances that we have already observed within the key structure of the *Sei Solo* depend on the collection's beginning with G minor; Bach could not change that without ruining these other designs, and therefore it would not be possible to find a perfect solution to the problem of a work more enharmonic than the D-minor partia. But at least there could be the compromise of using a key signature of a single flat for G minor, reflecting the older practice by which minor was associated with the Dorian mode.[61] This has the added effect, whether intended by Bach or not, of causing the key signature of the passion-associated D-minor partia to "identify" with the G-minor sonata, which not only is alienated from the descent-ascent structure in which the remaining five solos participate but also, as I will explore shortly, may contain connotations of fallenness and wrath for sin. This would seem to invite a parallel with Christ who, preeminently in his passion, associates with us in our fallen, alienated, and wrath-destined state, bearing the curse of our sin and nailing it to the cross[62] in order to reconcile us to God.[63]

60. See Chap. 5 n. 1.

61. See Chap. 5 n. 2.

62. John 3:14–17; 1 Cor 5:21; Gal 3:13; Col 2:14. On Christ's coming to us in our broken and fallen state, see this chap. n. 29.

63. Eph 2:12–13, 16.

At the same time, there could also be a structural impetus for the key signature of the first sonata. We have already noted in Chapter 5 that its single flat creates a 1:2 relationship with the number of *Vorzeichen* of the B-minor, a small auxiliary to the 1:2 proportions evident at various levels between this first and second work of the *Sei Solo*.[64] But the tonal descent-ascent schema may illuminate another possible structural incentive for Bach's decision.

The structural parallels this schema creates are shown in Figure 6.1, yielding a form remarkably similar to that of the six cello suites, BWV 1007–12, given in Figure 6.2.

Fig. 6.1. Key structure of the *Sei Solo*

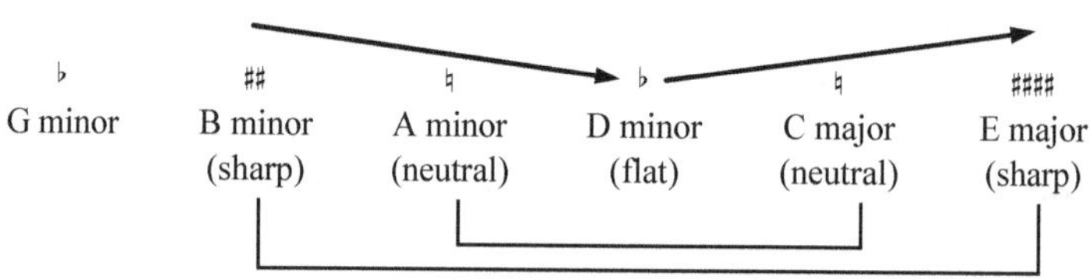

Fig. 6.2. Key structure of Bach's six cello suites

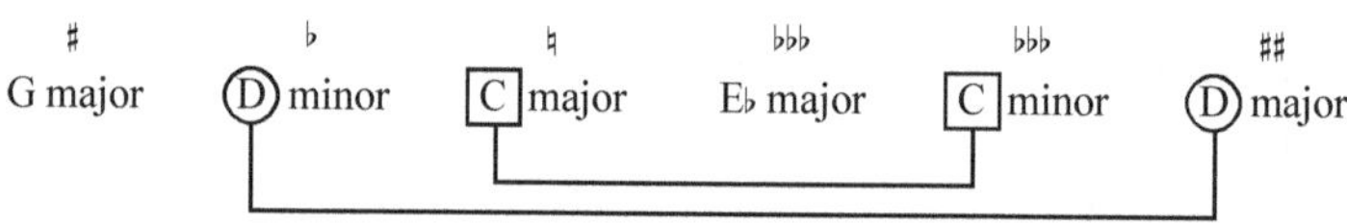

The properties of both schemas can be seen to suggest tonal unity in ways that are similar in concept, albeit slightly different in mechanism. In the cello suites, a consideration of the total sharp-flat content of each set of paired works yields one sharp for the outer pair (d/D, consisting of one flat and two sharps) and three flats for the inner (C/c, the three flats of C minor being unmodified by the neutral key signature of C major). The two resulting "sums," one sharp and three flats, correspond to the key signatures of the two works that remain unpaired in this schema, the first suite in G major and the fourth in E♭ major.

Approaching the pairings in the violin works from the perspective not of totality but of balance, there is a difference of two sharps between the key signatures of the outermost pair (B minor and E major), while the inner

64. See "The Number 2 in the B-minor Partia, BWV 1004" in Chap. 5.

pair are perfectly balanced both in relation to each other and in relation to the entire tonal spectrum, since neither has sharps or flats. Between the two pairs collectively, then, is a difference of two sharps, which is balanced by the fact that the two unpaired works collectively contain two flats, one apiece, which of course is a product of the notation of the G-minor sonata with only a single flat. In isolation, either of these schemas might conceivably be the product of coincidence. It is, after all, usually possible to detect relationships within a random series of six digits, if not always to this degree. But the fact that the schemas of both collections exhibit such a similar structure and concept of tonal balance suggests that Bach likely intended the parallel, which would further strengthen the longstanding assumption that the cello suites were intended as a complementary volume to the violin solos, which are labeled *Libro Primo* (Book 1) in the autograph, with no *Libro Secondo* specified.[65]

Interestingly, in the key structures of both collections, the means by which tonal balance is achieved can be seen only by reference to the pairings by which the chiastic structure of each is formed. Could this refer to Luther's understanding that it is only through the cross that one sees truly?[66]

Although both of the schemas observed above in connection with the *Sei Solo* appear individually compelling to me, their simultaneity is reason for pause. It is not uncommon in Bach to find such simultaneous schemas or processes that could each conceivably account for a particular compositional or structural feature, but there remains the difficulty of ascertaining which of these schemas or processes has been the primary impetus in forming the broader musical fabric and which arose merely secondarily. It must be noted, though, that it is not always necessary to assume one schema must represent the composer's primary intention to the exclusion of others. Admittedly, the presence especially of simultaneous structural schemas that appear likely to be intentional—as in the tonal plan of the *Sei Solo* with its multiple embedded patterns (seen in Ex. 6.4 and Fig. 6.1), each having

65. Tatlow has compellingly argued, on the basis of proportional parallelism, that the sonatas for violin and obbligato harpsichord might well be the intended *Libro Secondo* and the cello suites a *Libro Terzo* that was never revised and perfected to the level of his finished collections (*Bach's Numbers*, 146–58).

66. For instance, Theses 20 and 21 of the Heidelberg Disputation state: "[He deserves to be called a theologian] who understands the visible and manifest things of God seen through suffering and the cross. [21] A theologian of glory calls evil good and good evil; a theologian of the cross calls the thing what it actually is" ("[Ille digne Theologus dicitur], qui visibilia et posteriora Dei per passiones et crucem conspecta intelligit. [21] Theologus gloriae dicit malum bonum et bonum malum, Theologus crucis dicit id quod res est"). *WA* 1:354. On Luther's contrast of the theology of the cross (*theologia crucis*) with the theology of glory (*theologia gloriae*), see Chap. 2 n. 11.

its own compelling and apropos theological applications—can at first seem superhuman and thus raises the question of how reliable the assessment of the apparent intentionality of each schema is. But this in turn raises the question of how essential the manifestation of a particular idea is to the idea itself. Specifically, it is not necessary to assume that Bach's schemes are organic, unique, and perfect outgrowths of the ideas and shapes they seek to represent. If they were, the appearance of simultaneous schemas such as these and the ones I observe in Appendix B in connection with the D-minor harpsichord/(violin) concerto, BWV 1052, would seem nearly miraculous indeed. Rather, the creation of such simultaneous schemas is conceivable (though of course still most impressive) if constructed from the ground up, starting with the most basic shapes and concepts each schema could be hoped to exhibit and working from there toward greater specificity.[67] The results of such processes are not always "perfect"; but the wonder of Bach is his ability to find seemingly the greatest possible complexity, significance, and perfection within systems that are necessarily finite—and, in the process, to identify and reinforce other concurring elements that have sprung up by coincidence but that parallel or complement his essential intentions and that, with some strategic cultivation (through development, parallelism, and so forth), can be made to seem not much less essential to the total concept of the work than the designs he originally conceived.

The Music of the Six Solos

Having considered the general features of the *Sei Solo*, I will now walk sequentially through the sonatas and partias themselves, considering various plausibly symbolic or allegorical devices whose mention has not seemed warranted thus far. In the course of this sequential discussion, for purposes of clarity and coherence, I briefly recapitulate material discussed in previous chapters so that it can be more easily situated within the flow of the *Sei Solo*; but I keep such recapitulation as brief as possible, focusing instead on points not yet addressed.

Sonata in G Minor, BWV 1001

If the Siciliana of the G-minor sonata can most naturally be seen as representing the birth of Christ, it is notable that the two movements that precede

67. For a detailed analytical discussion of Bach's compositional process from a "mechanist" perspective, see Dreyfus, *Bach and the Patterns of Invention*.

it—that is, the first two movements of the *Sei Solo*—contain musical features that correspond to what Lutheran theology would understand to be important contextual elements of the Christ story. It is interesting that among the twenty-seven movements of the *Sei Solo*, only two contain a standard opening formula that prolongs the tonic by two intermediate chords, which in both instances within the *Sei Solo* takes the form i/I—vii(6)—V—i/I. The first of these movements is the G-minor Adagio that opens the collection, and the second is the E-major Gigue that concludes it (Ex. 6.25).[68] The fact that it is the first and last movements alone that contain this prolongation of the tonic harmony[69] by means of three distinct chords could recall the Christian conception of the one triune God as the Alpha and Omega, the first and last, the beginning and the end.[70] The association may perhaps not be as fanciful as it could initially appear; a similar device within the D-minor partia is discussed below.

We have already observed multiple ways in which the G-minor sonata and E-major partia represent extremity. Thus, to the extent that the E-major partia represents the culmination of history and the end of the biblical story, beginning the G-minor sonata with a chord progression that recalls the attributes of God corresponds neatly to the very beginning of the biblical story: "In the beginning, God . . ."[71]—or, as presented in John 1:1, "In the beginning was the Word, and the Word was with God, and the Word was God."

The association is not arbitrary, especially in the context of Lutheran theology, since Luther emphasizes that the fact of creation—that is, "the beginning"—inevitably points toward not only the person but the nature of God. Althaus writes, "For Luther, being God and creating are identical. God is God because he and only he creates."[72] Of course, whether the opening of the G-minor sonata is intended to have any association with the triune God must remain a matter of speculation; but it is at least interesting that the G-minor Adagio conforms most nearly of all the movements of the *Sei Solo* to the preluding formula that Emanuel Bach describes in his *Versuch über*

68. The Giga of the D-minor partia opens similarly, but its harmony, by the half-measure, is i—V—V—i.

69. C. P. E. Bach advocates beginning the (improvised) prelude by firmly establishing the tonic (he mentions the use of a pedal point as being convenient, but many of Sebastian Bach's preludes begin with a simple closed chord progression) before proceeding with stepwise motion in the bass accompanied by various harmonic figurations. C. P. E. Bach, *Versuch* 2, 328 (chap. 41, §7).

70. See Isa 44:6, 48:12; Rev 1:8, 21:6, 22:13.

71. Gen 1:1.

72. Althaus, *The Theology of Martin Luther*, 105.

die wahre Art das Clavier zu Spielen and that he almost certainly inherited from his father.[73]

The G-minor Adagio therefore most distinctly represents the idea of "beginning," which is musically fitting for its position at the very beginning of the *Sei Solo*; and to the extent that Bach intends a thoroughgoing theological allegory within the *Sei Solo*, the G-minor Adagio could also most naturally represent the beginning of the biblical story or indeed of history itself.[74] More concretely, the G-minor Adagio is arguably the most concentratedly dissonant movement of the *Sei Solo*, aptly paralleling the fallen and sorrowing state of humanity and of the world into which Christ descends.

Perhaps the most noteworthy compositional feature of the following Fuga is its chiastic exposition with successive voice entries on *d*'', *g*', *g*'', and *d*''.[75] The subject elaborated in this chiastic exposition also contains embellished *X* shapes, as noted in Chapter 3; and even though purely musical logic could conceivably account for such gestures, their presence in the two other fugues of the *Sei Solo* may be more than coincidence (Ex. 3.10). Since these *X* shapes intensify in the subject of the C-major fugue, whose inversion likely represents the resurrection of Christ, the subject in prime form can be all the more readily associated with the cross, which could suggest its melodic cross-shapes may have been intended as such by Bach. If the *X* shapes of the G-minor Fuga are similarly viable as such, it would mean that the content of the subject as well as the form of the exposition that introduces it are calculated to exhibit the same shape.

This is especially interesting because the idea of something appearing at multiple levels of structure also surfaces in the motivic content of the fugue subject as it is paralleled in the tonal design of the entire fugue. The very first pitches of the fugue subject (and therefore of the fugue itself) are *d*'', *c*'', *b*♭'. Throughout the course of the fugue, this portion of the subject is primarily decorative; it is, in other words, typically not essential to the basic contrapuntal and harmonic profile of any given texture in which it appears. By contrast, the structural pillars of the subject—in terms of both melodic

73. C. P. E. Bach, *Versuch* 2, 327–30 (chap. 41, §7). See Lester, *Bach's Works for Solo Violin*, 27; and Lester, "Bach Teaches Us How to Compose."

74. As noted in Chap. 4, the death of Christ is the focal point of history in Lutheran thought, and the representation of this event some two-thirds of the way through the *Sei Solo* corresponds to the chronological situating of the death of Christ within the course of history as Bach would have understood it (see Chap. 4 nn. 25–27). This could indicate that at some level the span of the *Sei Solo* can be associated with the span of the history of the world.

75. See the discussion of the exposition of the G-minor Fuga under "Sonata in A Minor, BWV 1003" in Chap. 4.

contour and contrapuntal function—are the notes that fall on the quarter-note beats. These, too, are *d*'', *c*'', *b*♭' (Ex. 6.5).

Ex. 6.5. *d*'', *c*'', *b*♭' at two levels of structure in the subject of the G-minor Fuga, BWV 1001/2

Because of the presence of the subject throughout, the melodic content of the Fuga is dominated by this three-note motif not only on the surface but also in its essential structure. Finally, at the deepest levels of the Fuga's form, the three cadences preceding its final close on G minor fall on D minor, C minor, and B♭ major (mm. 24, 55, and 64 respectively). When the ninety-four-measure movement is divided into twelve equal parts, the D-minor cadence falls at the end of three parts (at the middle of m. 24, or after twenty-three-and-a-half measures), the C-minor cadence after four more (after fifty-four measures), and the B♭-major cadence after one more (after sixty-three measures), with the remainder of the movement being in G minor. This is interesting because, according to the contrapuntal treatment of the subject that defines the exposition and predominates throughout the fugue, the final *d*'' is treated like a suspension. This means that, from a harmonic perspective, *d*'' as an essential tone remains in force for three eighth notes, while the essential note of the next four eighth notes is *c*'', with a single eighth-note *b*♭' concluding the subject, corresponding exactly to the proportions describing the general harmonic disposition of the entire fugue (Ex. 6.6).

Ex. 6.6. Parallelism between the subject and structure of BWV 1001/2

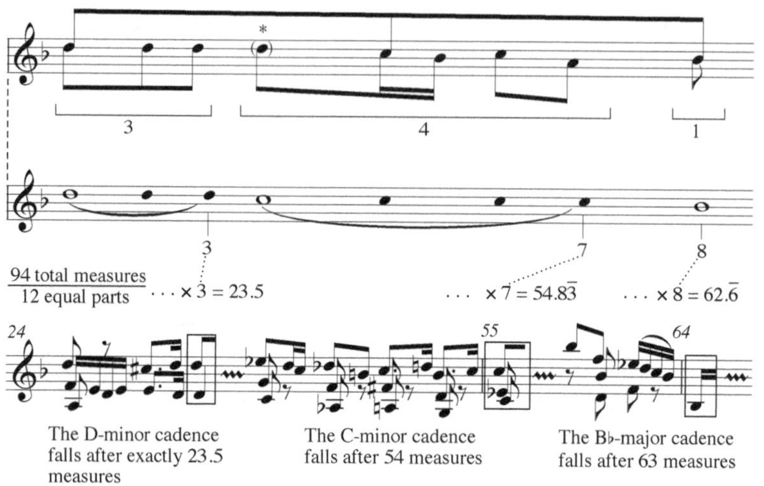

* Frequent suspension

These prominent instances of applicability at multiple structural levels are fascinating, especially in connection with *X* imagery, because they correspond to the historic Christian understanding of Christ's representation in biblical literature prior to his birth, namely, that prophesies and other writings of the Hebrew Scriptures not only have immediate fulfillment in the events the writer describes but also point forward ultimately to Christ and his redemptive work.

If the following Siciliana represents the nativity of Christ, its atypical tonal structure might be a product of tonal allegory of the type Eric Chafe has documented extensively in Bach's vocal works. The Siciliana consists of three parallel sections delineated by three cadences: the first is on B♭ major (m. 4, beat 3), the second is on G minor (m. 9), and the third is the final cadence on B♭ major.[76] Two features of this cadence structure are somewhat atypical for Bach. First, the opening section concludes with a tonic cadence. More typical in Bach's practice is that the first principal cadence falls in a contrasting key area, especially when there are so few structurally important cadences in the movement. Second, equally atypical for a through-composed movement is that there is no cadence falling outside the domain of B♭ major and its relative minor. Instead, there are three cadences

76. For a more detailed discussion of the form of the Siciliana, see Lester, *Bach's Works for Solo Violin*, 87–107.

in one essential tonal region, the second of which has descended below the other two.[77] This scheme, unusual as it is, recalls the Christian doctrine of the incarnation: of the three persons of the one unified God, the second of these persons (Christ, who is God the Son)[78] has descended—that is, to human form.[79]

If the tonal structure of the Siciliana is understood thus, it is perhaps noteworthy that the interval of descent is a minor third (*kleine Terz* or "small third"), which, as I observe in Appendix B, appears with unusual prominence in both BWV 1052/2 and 1046/2 within the context of apparent representations of Christ's debasement. Could this perhaps suggest that Bach sometimes uses the interval of a minor third to represent the member of the Trinity who has made himself small by assuming human form and submitting himself to death for our redemption?

The idea of descent is reinforced throughout the Siciliana by the ubiquity of the four-note descending figure introduced on the second beat of measure 1, whose importance is underscored by its threefold repetition in increasing augmentation within the opening phrase (Ex. 6.7).

Ex. 6.7. Progressive augmentation of the major-mode tetrachord in BWV 1001/3

This double augmentation of the descending motif could arguably recall Paul's teaching that Christ is magnified precisely because of his willing descent to incarnation and death on a cross.[80]

77. The second cadence can legitimately be described as "lower" than the others for two reasons: first, when the roots of the chords on which the cadence falls are written in closest proximity, the G is a minor third below B♭ rather than a major sixth above; second, the actual pitches of treble and bass alike are noticeably lower in the second cadence than in any other.

78. Christ is traditionally referred to as the "second person" of the Trinity, and thus is he listed in the three chief creeds embraced by Lutheranism and included in the definitive *Book of Concord* (i.e., the Apostles' Creed, the Nicene Creed, and the Athanasian Creed).

79. See John 3:13 and 6:38; Eph 4:9; Phil 2:7–8.

80. See Phil 2:6–11. The idea that Bach might use augmentation for such representative ends is not far-fetched. In the *Musical Offering*, for instance, he connects a canon by augmentation with a wish for the augmentation of the king's fortunes, writing "Notulis crescentibus crescat Fortuna Regis" ("As the notes increase, may the King's

The Presto that concludes the G-minor sonata is the most furious movement of the *Sei Solo*. This may initially seem curious, coming on the heels of the serene nativity imagery of the Siciliana, but it does indeed parallel the fact that the gospels of Matthew and Luke preface the ministry of Jesus with an announcement by John the Baptist that connects the coming of the Christ with fiery judgment,[81] whose broader significance for the Christ story has been explored above in connection with the B-minor partia.[82] Since fire is an image of destruction repeatedly associated with divine judgment throughout the Bible, it may not be accidental that the G-minor Presto features several prominent images of destruction. One of these is corrosion of the metric order. For example, the movement is in $\frac{3}{8}$ time but frequently features sequenced groupings of three or even four sixteenths (Ex. 6.8).

Ex. 6.8. Metric crosscurrents in BWV 1001/4

Full barlines are found only after even-numbered measures, with partial barlines closing the odd-numbered measures, thus creating pairs of two measures; yet musical material often falls into odd-numbered groups of three or five measures (Ex. 6.9), and changes of harmony falling on hypermetrically weak downbeats but extending more than a full measure create a sense of metric displacement (Ex. 6.10).

fortunes increase").

81. Matt 3:10–12; Luke 3:9, 17.

82. See "Possible Implications of Prominent Numbers: The B-minor Partia" in Chap. 5.

Ex. 6.9. Hypermetric crosscurrents in BWV 1001/4

Ex. 6.10. Metric displacement in BWV 1001/4

Metric instability is created elsewhere throughout the movement by various means. At measures 117–21, for example, slurs beginning on weak beats and ending on strong beats undermine the metric pulse that coincides with harmonic rhythm (Ex. 6.11).

Ex. 6.11. Slurring contrary to harmonic rhythm in BWV 1001/4

A more localized image of destruction could arguably be heard in the downward arpeggiations, at three levels of structure, that begin the movement (Ex. 6.12).

Ex. 6.12. Three levels of downward arpeggiation at the beginning of BWV 1001/4

Lester has observed that taking the first sixteenth note of each beat for the first four bars yields a downward arpeggiation of exactly the same chord, voicing and all, as the one that begins the first movement of the sonata.[83] Though this chord that begins the sonata is notated as four simultaneous notes, nonetheless in performance it would have been expected to be arpeggiated from the bottom up. Thus the downward arpeggiations that begin the final Presto could be heard as an undoing of the chord with which the sonata began.

In the discussion of the G-minor Adagio above, I speculated that the prolongation of the initial tonic harmony by means of two intervening chords (thus creating a three-chord prolongation of a single tonic harmony) could perhaps be understood as a symbol of the triune God whose being begins the biblical narrative, especially since this formula recurs in the final movement of the *Sei Solo* (and only there), just as historic Christianity has understood God to be "the Alpha and the Omega, the first and the last, the beginning and the end."[84] To the extent that this association is valid, it is possible to read the metaphorical destruction or melting[85] of this opening G-minor chord at the beginning of the Presto as an image of God submitting

83. Lester, *Bach's Works for Solo Violin*, 111.

84. Rev 22:13.

85. Melting is another image frequently associated with the burning wrath of God (see, for instance, Ps 97:5; Mic 1:4; Nah 1:5; 2 Pet 3:12).

himself to the consuming fire of his own wrath[86] as Christ, the lamb of God, hung on the cross.[87]

Partia in B Minor, BWV 1002

Following the G-minor sonata, the B-minor partia, I have suggested, might represent a second introduction of the Christ figure with a theological rather than narrative orientation, constituting a meditation of sorts on the dual nature of the incarnate Christ. To the extent that the partia could be heard as a second introduction to the dual-natured Christ, it could be understood as a kind of conceptual *double* to the G-minor sonata, which is interesting, because the B-minor partia alone in the surviving canon of Bach features a *double* after every one of its movements. That is to say, the internal mirroring in the B-minor partia could be seen to mirror the partia's conceptual mirroring of the G-minor sonata. The various 2:1 structural relationships between the B-minor partia and the G-minor sonata—including their relative positions within the *Sei Solo*, their respective bar sums with repeats, and the number of *Vorzeichen* (sharps or flats) in the key signature of each—could likewise be seen as mirroring one another, as could the various parallels between the pairs of movements discussed in Chapter 5. These multiple mirroring effects are certainly unusual, far exceeding the typical manifestations of symmetry and parallelism whose value was so deeply ingrained in the Baroque aesthetic. And although a comparison with the Versailles-type "halls of mirrors" found in palaces throughout Germany (including Cöthen) in Bach's day may be fanciful, it might not be wholly inappropriate. What can at least be said is that, in the elegant complexities of the B-minor partia, Bach has created a structure fit for a king.

Sonata in A Minor, BWV 1003

With the A-minor sonata, the theological connections come increasingly into focus. We have already noted that the descending tetrachord that permeates the sonata will be brought into ultimate focus in the Ciaccona of the D-minor partia, where I propose it contributes to a representation of the passion of Christ (as it does in the C-major Fuga, inasmuch as the inversion

86. On the Lutheran understanding of the atonement, see my Chap. 3 n. 56.

87. Under the Mosaic law, a lamb without blemish is offered as a propitiation for sin and is destroyed by fire (Lev 4:32–35). Jesus' title "the lamb of God," used heavily within the Lutheran tradition of Bach's day, necessarily recalls this image of fiery destruction.

of its tetrachord-infused subject likely corresponds to the resurrection). The musical connection forged by the prominence of the descending tetrachord in all three of these works invites the passion associations attending the tetrachord in the D-minor partia and the C-major sonata (specifically, the Fuga) to be heard in the A-minor sonata as well, especially as these works are grouped together both by *ambitus* and by the fact that their outstanding movements—the A-minor Fuga, the D-minor Ciaccona, and the C-major Fuga—add up to a round 900 measures.[88] In view of these possible passion overtones in connection with the tetrachord in the A-minor sonata, it appears all the more significant that in the opening Grave of the A-minor sonata Bach uses the descending tetrachord to what could be described as redemptive ends, as I will explain.

By way of context, the A-minor sonata bears several marked similarities to the G-minor sonata,[89] particularly in the first two movements, that effectively group the G-minor and A-minor sonatas together in contrast with C-major (see Ex. 6.16). Among the features that create a sense of connection between the first two sonatas are similarity of the texture and structure of their opening movements, a curious correspondence between the subjects of their fugues (to which I will return shortly), and the most atypical chiastic structure of voice entries in the exposition of each fugue (which has already been discussed).[90] It is precisely because of these similarities that any difference in the presentation of these elements in the A-minor sonata immediately creates a sense of reference to and contrast with the corresponding parts of the G-minor sonata.

The first movement of the G-minor sonata has a chiastic structure, albeit one whose constitution is far too commonplace to consider it an intentional (or at least uniquely intentional) *X* image. Measures 1–9 correspond to measures 14–22, each passage modulating down a fourth; measures 1–8 move from G minor to D minor (v, one step from G minor toward the chromatic or "sharp" side of the spectrum), and measures 14–22 move from C minor (iv, one step from G minor in the enharmonic or "flat" direction) back to G minor, concluding with the same chord with which the movement began—a compositional feature that, incidentally, is unique among the *Sei Solo*.[91] The material in between these two sections, in measures 9–13, is

88. Tatlow, *Bach's Numbers*, 141–42. See my Chap. 3 n. 50.

89. Schröder refers to these sonatas as "the Castor and Pollux of the six solos" for this reason. *Bach's Solo Violin Works*, 53.

90. See "Sonata in A Minor, BWV 1003" in Chap. 4.

91. The E-major Preludio concludes with a single note, not a chord; but it, too, ends with the same note with which it began, although Ruth Tatlow suggests this might not originally have been the case ("Bach's Parallel Proportions," 141–42). See my discussion

primarily transitional, though it is perhaps noteworthy that the transition from D minor to C minor is decisively completed in measure 11, half of the total twenty-two-measure structure and itself the midpoint between the end of the opening material (downbeat of m. 9) and its reprise (downbeat of m. 14). The resulting structure can be diagrammed as shown in Figure 6.3.

Fig. 6.3. Structure of the G-minor Adagio, BWV 1001/1

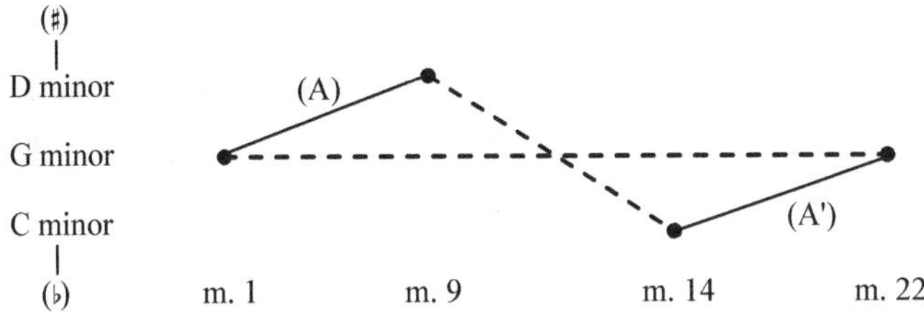

The Grave that begins the A-minor sonata lacks the "triune" prolongation formula that opens the G-minor sonata, instead directly introducing the lamenting tetrachord in the bass (see Ex. 4.5a). Like the Adagio of the G-minor sonata, the first major cadence of the A-minor Grave is on v (m. 12) before a variation of the opening material is introduced on iv a few bars later (m. 14), creating a chiastic structure similar to that of the G-minor Adagio.

But there are important differences. Whereas in the G-minor Adagio the entire opening section (mm. 1–9a) is reiterated in full (albeit transposed and embellished) in measures 14–22, in the A-minor Grave the reprise on iv beginning in measure 14 ends prematurely in measure 16, and the correspondence with the opening material (mm. 1–12a) does not resume until the cadential approach in measure 18b, which corresponds to measure 9. But the imperfect reprise has caused the second "half" of the movement to fall short. Even with a measure-and-a-half between the conclusion of the first section at measure 12a and the beginning of the reprise at measure 14, the material following the end of the first section has not yet equaled the latter's length as of the cadence at measure 21a, which corresponds to the cadence at measure 12 and therefore, especially by comparison with the Adagio of the G-minor sonata, "should" be the final cadence of the movement. The shortness of the second section is unusual for such structures; far more typical is that the second section is longer than the first. And if the structural deficiency were not clear enough, the material of the renewed reprise is now displaced by half a measure, meaning that what should be the

of the E-major partia below and Ex. 6.27.

ultimate A-minor cadence (m. 21a) is due to fall weakly on the half-measure rather than the downbeat. Its weakness is accentuated by the fact that the cadence consists of a single bass note that leaves the melodic voice essentially unresolved at the point of cadence. But rather than actually concluding the movement, this weak cadence begins the final tetrachordal descent in the bass, which adds two-and-a-half measures to the end of the movement, not only realigning the emphasis from the weak third beat to the downbeat but also creating a twenty-three-measure structure whose exact midpoint is the end of the cadential E-minor chord that concludes the first section after eleven-and-a-half measures.

Many slow movements of the high and late Baroque conclude with a codetta built over a simple Phrygian descent, like that which concludes the A-minor Grave. Such "Phrygian codettas," as they might be called, are typically little more than appendages on the end of the movement with little relation to what precedes them; they are more or less peripheral to its essential musical content. In the A-minor Grave, however, this seemingly peripheral figure brings a kind of redemption to the entire structure, rectifying the metric displacement of what would otherwise be the final cadence, completing the durational shortcoming of the second half of the movement, bringing numerical perfection to the entire structure so that it consists of two times eleven-and-a-half measures, and doing so in a way that brings melodic unity to the whole, since the Phrygian tetrachord that concludes the movement is also the motif with which it began (both times in the bass). The parallels with the New Testament understanding of the marginalized Christ[92] atoning for the sins of the world in such a way as to bring the types and prophesies of the Old Testament to perfect fulfillment[93] are at least inviting.

We have already substantially considered the implications of the A-minor Fuga as it appears to point forward to Christ's impending crucifixion while plausibly representing (or at least paralleling) the motto *Christus Coronabit Crucigeros*. Two points remain to be mentioned. First, as noted briefly above, there is a striking correspondence between the subjects of the A-minor and G-minor fugues, shown in Example 6.13.

92. All four biblical gospels repeatedly describe Jesus' rejection by various communities with which he comes into contact. The broader image of Jesus as a Messiah rejected by man is conveyed, for instance, in Matt 21:42; Mark 12:10; Luke 20:17; John 1:11; Acts 4:11; Heb 13:12; 1 Pet 2:7; see Isa 53:3 (on the reading of Isa 53 as a reference to Christ, see Appendix B n. 25).

93. See Chap. 2 nn. 24–29.

Ex. 6.13. Similarities between the subjects of the fugues in G minor (BWV 1001/2) and A minor (BWV 1003/2)

Both subjects are five beats long. The first two beats of each subject consist of an eighth rest and three eighth-note repetitions of scale degree $\hat{5}$ (slightly embellished in the A-minor fugue). The remainder of both subjects consists of two cross-shapes formed by identical interval structures with inverse contours, both moving essentially in steady eighth notes. In light of the striking similarity between these two subjects, the inverse motion of the A-minor subject to that of the G-minor not only suggests the principle of reversal that is central to the idea of *Christus Coronabit Crucigeros* but can also imply a further, abstract dimension of chiasm, since reversal is the operation by which chiastic structure is generated. Second, considering the cross imagery that pervades the A-minor fugue, it is interesting that this movement contains the most plausible chorale allusion anywhere in the *Sei Solo* outside the subject of the C-major fugue, namely, the passion chorale "O Haupt voll Blut und Wunden," popularly approximated in English as "O sacred head now wounded" (Ex. 6.14), somewhat recalling the treatment of the same chorale in the opening chorus of the 1723 cantata "Es ist nichts gesundes an meinem Leibe," BWV 25.

Ex. 6.14

a. Opening of "O Haupt voll Blut und Wunden," melody alone

O Haupt voll Blut und Wun - den,

b. Allusion to "O Haupt voll Blut und Wunden" in BWV 1003/2?

273

277

I have proposed in Chapter 4 that the general tonal pull of the A-minor sonata toward E, as well as the unique incomplete cross of the exposition of the Fuga, suggest the idea of "going"—specifically, Jesus' going toward the cross and ultimately toward his Father. If this is valid, it might not be coincidence that Bach crafted the third movement of the A-minor sonata to be an andante, meaning, literally, "going"—the only such movement within the *Sei Solo*. Though necessarily speculative, the correlation is not tenuous; the three synoptic gospels emphasize the resolution with which Jesus goes toward Jerusalem, knowing that he will be killed,[94] and the Gospel of John adds the further dimension of depicting Jesus' progression toward the cross as going to the Father, as if the crucifixion, resurrection, and ascension were part of a single upward sweep.[95] From a literary perspective, the central motion of all four gospels is toward the cross, the empty tomb, and the ascension. Moreover, as noted in connection with the C-major Fuga, Luke 9:31 fascinatingly refers to Jesus' atoning work on the cross itself as a "departure" or literally "exodus"—a description that necessarily has overtones of "going."

All of this fits neatly within the association of andante with the path from birth to death that Gerhart Darmstadt documents in connection with the Baroque era.[96] In light of this frequent (though by no means necessarily universal) association, it is interesting to note that of Bach's relatively few andantes one is from the *Actus Tragicus* of 1707–1708, setting the words "Es ist der alte Bund: Mensch, du musst sterben" ("It is the ancient covenant: man, you must die"); another is the opening chorus of "Ich hatte viel Bekümmernis" ("I had much grief"), BWV 21, whose text and its setting recall Roger North's association of the andante with "a walking about full of concerne."[97]

At the same time, the Andante of the A-minor solo violin sonata is exceptional in several ways. First, unlike most of Bach's andantes, whether vocal or instrumental, it is in a major key.[98] Second, although its bass line consists of the standard steady eighth notes, these do not form the typical walking figure but remain stationary on a single note for up to a measure at a time. On the whole it conveys much more of the "hope" (*Hoffnung*) that Mattheson attributes to the andante than is typical of those of Bach.[99] Concretely, for instance, the essential bass motion that begins the solo violin Andante is a major-mode statement of the descending tetrachord that permeates the rest of the sonata (see Ex. 4.4).

But to the extent the implications of andante are meant to contribute to a tapestry of theological allegory, this major-mode statement of the tetrachord could illustrate an important hermeneutic point: the association with hope need not exclude connotations of death and mortality (to whatever extent each may be present), nor vice versa. Theologically, the combination

94. Matt 16:21, 20:17–19; Mark 8:31, 10:32–33; Luke 9:51.

95. John 13:1, 13:36–14, 16:10 and 28.

96. Darmstadt, "Andante und Mystik," 43–104.

97. North, "Of Composition in Generall," 123.

98. A similar exception in this regard is the third movement of BWV 1014.

99. Mattheson, *Der vollkommene Capellmeister*, 208 (part II, chap. 12, §34).

is in fact perfectly apt in connection with Christ's approach to the cross,[100] just as the major-mode statement of the descending tetrachord could suggest the specter of suffering transformed by the hope of glory. Expressed according to Lutheran theological emphases, it could be seen to represent a hope that does not evade the cross but comes precisely from it.

In order to express this tension in performance, it is probably advisable that the repeated bass notes be played very evenly and distinctly (as indeed a number of sources from the period prescribe for andantes),[101] so that it recalls less the gentle consolation of "Vergnügte Ruh, beliebte Seelenlust" (BWV 170/1), for instance, than it does the steady ticking of a clock numbering the hours to Golgotha, much as Bach represents the eerily steady trembling of bells in "Der Glocken bebendes Getön" from the *Trauer Ode*, BWV 198.

The final Allegro of the A-minor sonata begins with a series of brilliant gestures consisting of arpeggiated and scalar figures over static harmony that are each repeated in *piano* in what David Ledbetter calls a "*trompe l'oreille*," suggesting antiphony from a distant gallery (shown in Ex. 6.22a).[102] These combined elements—the flamboyant gestural cells containing majestic arpeggiations (recalling the accustomed figuration of natural brass), the static harmonies, the implied antiphony—could all suggest a fanfare. But it is certainly an ironic fanfare, set as it is in the minor mode (an impossibility for natural trumpets, the proper kingly instrument) and followed immediately in measure 7 by the lamenting tetrachord that recurs throughout the movement. I suggest the possibility of hearing it as an ironic fanfare for a rejected, suffering king.[103] This ironic fanfare ends not with pomp and brilliance but with repeatedly elided cadences that leave the dominant, E, feeling substantially unresolved as the music recedes into *piano* and ultimately disappears into the depths with only the most minimally implied resolution to the last dominant chord.

100. Heb 12:2 states that Jesus endured the cross "for the joy set before him."

101. For instance, Bach's cousin Johann Gottfried Walther states that the andante should "promenade with equal steps" ("mit gleichen Schritten wandeln"). *ML*, s.v. "Andante" (p. 35). For a convenient collection of primary source excerpts on the subject, see Dornenburg, "Andante: What's the Rush?" 56, 54.

102. Ledbetter, *Unaccompanied Bach*, 128.

103. Jesus' kingship in the context of the crucifixion is an important theme of all four biblical gospels as well as of Lutheran theology and commentary. Rambach, for instance, calls the cross "the throne of grace" (*Gnaden-Thron*), evoking the recurring idea in historic Christian theology of Jesus the sovereign king figuratively reigning from the cross. *BLC*, 963.

Partia in D Minor, BWV 1004

The sense of "going" in the A-minor sonata is answered in the following partia, in the historically solemn key of D minor,[104] by means of structural devices that suggest a coming into focus. Specifically, the descending tetrachord that represents the tonal trajectory of the A-minor sonata returns in the D-minor partia in the form of a lamenting bass-motif that opens all five movements, coming into focus as the initial manifestation of an essentially tetrachordal *basso ostinato* in the final movement of the partia, the enormous Ciaccona having a five-part chiastic form.

I proposed in Chapter 2 that the coming into focus of an adumbrated (or "foretold") lament motif within the context of a structural chiasm, a shape traditionally associated with Christ and the cross, warrants the hypothesis that Bach conceived the D-minor partia in general and the Ciaccona in particular as a symbol of the long-foretold passion of Christ, which according to Lutheran theology is the coming-into-focus of all preceding biblical history. In Chapter 5 we observed the prominence of the numbers 4 and 5, noting their respective associations with the world and the five wounds of Christ and considering the possibility that they could represent Christ who dies for the redemption of the world as its representative head, the second Adam. We also observed that the proportions of all five movements of the partia are based on the numbers 4 and 5, and that these proportions within individual movements relate to those of other movements in two distinct ways: one unites movements 1 with 5 and 2 with 4, and the second unites movements 1 with 4 and 2 with 3, so that both schemes create chiasms, the first spanning the whole partia and the second spanning its

104. Although Bach usually notates minor-mode works with a key signature corresponding to the Aeolian mode (as in modern practice), the earlier association of the minor scale with the Dorian mode remained in force into Bach's lifetime (see Lester, *Between Modes and Keys*, 12, 90, 100); and since the untransposed Dorian scale begins on D, the key of D minor was associated all the more with the Dorian mode. Accordingly, German theorists of the generations leading up to Bach generally describe the affective properties of D minor in terms recalling Zarlino's view that "by its nature [the Dorian mode] is rather sad . . . optimally accommodat[ing] those words that are full of gravity and that deal with things high and meaningful" ("per sua natura è alquanto mesto. Però potremo ad esso accommodare ottimamente quelle parole, le quali saranno piene di gravità, & che trattaranno di cose alte & sententiose." Zarlino, *Le Istitutioni Harmoniche*, 322 [part 4, chap. 18]). French writers tend to give more uniform descriptions of the Dorian mode and the key of D minor in terms of seriousness and gravity; certain German writers attribute to it what seems like a conflicting quality, a certain cheerfulness—but these writers almost invariably understand this cheerfulness to be solemn or religious in character, coexisting with what is often called a "wondrous gravity" (borrowing again from Zarlino). See Steblin, *A History of Key Characteristics*, 23–25, 27; Bartel, *Musica Poetica*, 40–46.

first four movements (which is roughly the first half of the partia in terms of duration). The fact that the Ciaccona (the second half of the partia) is also chiastic means that the D-minor partia consists of three crosses, two that span each half of the partia and one that spans the whole, possibly corresponding to the three crosses of Golgotha, one of them bringing redemption to the entire world.

It may also be conceivable that Bach's curious penmanship in the title "Ciaccona" (Image 6.2) could represent the acronym "CCC," standing for *Christus Coronabit Crucigeros* ("Christ crowns those who carry the cross").[105]

Image 6.2. Curious penmanship of the title *Ciaccona* in the autograph of BWV 1004/5

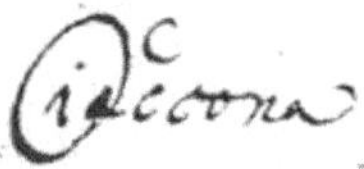

Rutger van Randwijck goes so far as to suggest that what appears to be an oddly closed initial "C" is not intended to be a "C" at all but rather a circle around the "i," and that the additional "c" written above the other two in the middle of the word replaces the missing initial one. He believes Bach is making the motto even more explicit by implying "*Iesus* Christus Coronabit Crucigeros."[106] Ledbetter likewise sees a circle in place of a standard letter *C*, basing his observation on analysis of Bach's handwriting.[107] He proposes various possible interpretations of this circle ranging from an image of totality[108] to a symbol of perfection (by reference to the antique signature for perfect time)[109] to the letter Omega, such that the first and last movements of the partia are represented by the letters Alpha (Allemanda) and Omega.

The latter might perhaps not be as fanciful as Ledbetter suggests.[110] The Allemanda that begins the D-minor partia is the only movement of

105. On the importance of notation and concerns of the written score, see Chap. 5 n. 18.

106. Randwijck, "Music in Context," 51.

107. This analysis is found in Lindley and Ortgies, "Bach-style Keyboard Tuning," 614–15.

108. ". . . as if this piece is a microcosm that can include a whole world of styles and emotions." Ledbetter, *Unaccompanied Bach*, 143.

109. Ibid., 311 n. 100.

110. Ibid. What appears more likely fanciful is the second part of his observation: that between Alpha and Omega are fourteen letters of the Latin alphabet, fourteen

the *Sei Solo* to begin with a unison, and the Ciaccona that concludes the partia is the only movement of the *Sei Solo* to end with a unison. Among Werckmeister's various allegorical interpretations of harmonic numbers and intervals, he consistently associates the unison, embodying the number 1 (*die Unität*), with God: "For the *Unität* exists in and of itself and has its beginning in no [other] number but is itself the beginning of all numbers, and has no end. Likewise, God is the one ultimate being from all eternity, the beginning without beginning and agent behind all things, whose being and power encompasses all eternity and has no end."[111] That is to say, had Bach indeed intended his strange penmanship to connect Alpha with the beginning of the partia and Omega with its end, it would correspond neatly to the fact that the partia begins and ends with an interval associated with God himself, the Alpha and Omega, in the allegorical thinking of Bach's day.

It is also interesting that all of the possible interpretations of Bach's penmanship Ledbetter cites have to do with representations of perfection or totality, just as the music of the Ciaccona itself would seem to exhibit the fondness of its composer for comprehensiveness (not to mention perfection). If the passion of Christ were indeed in view in the Ciaccona, such imagery of perfection and totality would be an appropriate complement to the representation of the finished work of Christ on the cross,[112] which represents "the whole counsel of God for our salvation."[113]

Little remains to be said about the D-minor partia that is relevant to the present argument. I will simply make three small observations about the Ciaccona. As noted in Chapter 2, the first time the ostinato takes the form of a diatonic descending tetrachord is at measure 49 (that is, 7 x 7), and it recurs seven times consecutively, remaining in force longer than any other single bass motif anywhere in the movement. If the prominence of the diatonic descending tetrachord in the A-minor sonata is indeed intended to adumbrate the D-minor partia, then in light of the biblical associations of the number 7 with fulfillment or completion, the marked connection of the diatonic descending tetrachord with the number 7 in the Ciaccona could

being the alphanumeric sum of the name "Bach" (that is, B + A + C + H as 2 + 1 + 3 + 8).

111. "Denn wie die Unität vor sich selber ist/und von keiner Zahl den Anfang hat/ sondern der Anfang aller *Numerorum* selber ist/ und kein Ende hat. Also ist Gott ein einziges Wesen von Ewigkeit/ der Anfang ohne Anfang/ und Fortgang aller Dinge/ deßen Wesen und Kraft sich in Ewigkeit erstrecket/ und kein Ende hat." Werckmeister, *Paradoxal-Discourse*, 92 (chap. 19); see *Musicae Mathematicae*, 142 (Appendix, chap. 2) and 146 (Appendix, chap. 5).

112. "opus Christi pro nobis impletum." *WA* 39 II:188. See John 19:30 and Luther's commentary at my Chap. 3 n. 56.

113. "der ganze Rath GOttes von unsrer Seligkeit." *BLC*, 1037.

emphasize that the work toward which Jesus appears to be going in the A-minor sonata is brought to completion in the passion.[114]

Similarly, the fact that the Ciaccona, which I am proposing represents the most seemingly catastrophic event in Scripture, is given such a clear and elegant mathematical design according to *Sectio Divina* (the "Divine Section" or Golden Section) could reinforce the idea that, despite all initial appearances, the cross is the perfect design of God for the salvation of the world, a revelation of the wisdom of God, even though it seems like foolishness according to human wisdom.[115]

Finally, perhaps more than any other movement of the *Sei Solo*, the Ciaccona represents the intersection of contrasting elements: the dynamic versus the static (in the form of rich variations over a repeating ostinato), D minor versus D major, French versus Italianate stylistic tendencies, and so forth. Ledbetter calls the Ciaccona "perhaps the ultimate Baroque oxymoron, exploiting the tension of opposites inherent in the solitary violin recreating not only social court dance [one of the primary associations of the chaconne] but the final, or close to final, number of a Lully opera, involving orchestra, chorus, soloists, corps de ballet, in a form that is not conventionally limited but (in theory at any rate) indefinitely extensible."[116] There is no way to know whether the following idea was on Bach's mind, of course, but it is interesting that in two-dimensional space perhaps the most perfect representation of this paradoxical union of contrasting elements is the intersection of two perpendicular lines, that is, a cross—just as the cross of Christ unites the contrasting axes of justice-mercy and heaven-earth,[117] because the judgment for man's sins that falls upon the sinless God-man, Christ, enables mercy to be extended to sinful man without travesty of justice.

Sonata in C Major, BWV 1005

After the awesome majesty of the D-minor Ciaccona, the beginning of the C-major sonata has the feeling of something entirely new. Tonally, it represents a turning point in the *Sei Solo* from the former dominance of the minor mode to a new "reign" of major, with not a single remaining movement

114. John 19:30.

115. See 1 Cor 1:18–30.

116. Ledbetter, *Unaccompanied Bach*, 137.

117. Although the confluence of the contrasting strains of justice and mercy in the cross is a readily evident emphasis in Lutheran theology, the meeting of heaven and earth in the cross may also have played a role in Bach's thinking. Rambach, for instance, writes that in the cross "peace is established between heaven and earth" ("an diesem Creuz ist der Friede zwischen Himmel und Erde gestiftet"). *BLC*, 963.

being in minor. Texturally, in contrast to the nearly incomparable variety in the Ciaccona, the C-major Adagio opens with a single, slowly pulsating note that unfurls a spacious structure of similarly slow-moving pulsating harmonies that extends almost to the very end of the movement (Ex. 6.15).

Ex. 6.15. Opening of BWV 1005/1

This texture is unlike anything else to be found in the *Sei Solo*, and its sense of uniqueness is further heightened by the corresponding movements of the first two sonatas being texturally very similar to one another, jointly contrasting with the C-major Adagio (Ex. 6.16).

Ex. 6.16

a. BWV 1001/1

Adagio

b. BWV 1003/1

Grave

The sense of newness following the representation of the passion of Christ seems especially appropriate considering that historic Christian theology has understood the crucified Jesus' proclamation "It is finished" to refer not merely to atonement for sin but to inauguration of a new creation cleansed from sin (apropos to the "pure" key of C major).[118] Just as the first creation, culminating in the creation of man, is completed at the end of the sixth day of the week,[119] so too the new creation, culminating in the new

118. 2 Cor 5:17; Gal 6:15; Col 3:10. See John 1:13, 3:3–14; Rom 6:4; Jas 1:18; 1 Pet 1:3–4, 24.

119. Gen 1:24—2:1.

man,[120] is declared from the cross by Jesus the Creator[121] at the waning of the sixth day.[122]

Despite the spacious, almost timeless feeling of the C-major Adagio—and despite the associations of purity with the key of C major—there is nonetheless an unsettled quality to the movement. Ledbetter notes that the rising sixteenth note at the end of every beat throughout most of the movement recalls the French *accent*, which Montéclair (1736) describes as a "sob" (*sanglot*) to be used in "plaintive airs" (*airs plaintifs*).[123] The Adagio is also quite harmonically unstable, as consideration of the first fifteen measures (Ex. 6.17) will illustrate.

Ex. 6.17. The harmonically unstable beginning of BWV 1005/1

The movement begins with what initially sounds like a standard tonic prolongation akin to what opens the G-minor sonata (or, still more nearly in terms of voice leading and key, the first prelude of *The Well-Tempered Clavier*, whose earliest surviving form is in the *Clavier-Büchlein vor Wilhelm*

120. Eph 2:15, 4:24; Col 3:10.

121. John 1:3, 10; Heb 1:2.

122. That is, according to the chronology historically accepted by the church, including Lutheranism, according to which Jesus is crucified on Friday and raised on Sunday. Though that chronology has recently been questioned by some in favor of a Wednesday crucifixion, the traditional Friday-Sunday timing remains favored by most biblical scholars.

123. Montéclair, *Principes de musique*, 80, cited in Ledbetter, *Unaccompanied Bach*, 146.

Friedemann Bach, which Bach began compiling in January 1720, the year of completion of the *Sei Solo*). But this gesture, which we expect to prolong and establish the tonic, comes unhinged in measure 4 and instead pulls the tonality away from C major toward D minor. This in turn yields to a D-dominant-7 chord with a very dissonant minor ninth in measure 7, pulling the tonality further afield in the enharmonic or "flats" direction toward the distant key of G minor. However, this chord is alarmingly followed in measure 8 by a $^{6}_{3}$ chord built on *d#*'—what today we would call a first-inversion B-major chord—that respells the E♭ of the previous measure and abruptly pulls the tonality toward the chromatic or "sharps" end of the spectrum. The tonality shifts suddenly and rather dramatically from the realm of G minor to the distant realm of E minor, making it the most radical, tonality-threatening harmonic motion to be found in the *Sei Solo.*[124]

But in the end, an E-minor chord is never even heard, and what follows is instead a chain of diminished chords: after the *d#*' diminished-7 chord that increases the pull toward E minor, the next sonority is a $^{6\#}_{3}$, chord built on *e*', which then sinks to a $^{6}_{4}$ chord on *e*♭' (thus returning the E♭ that had become D# to its original spelling). This pulls the tonality back to G minor, where it rests most atypically (for a movement in C major!) until the cadence at measure 15—although even this is ambiguous, as no third is heard until the very last sixteenth note of the measure. The resulting bass-harmonic motion has a sense of directionless wandering or even futility. After drifting away toward *d*' during the opening bars, where we expect to find it anchored around *c*', it then ceases to make any meaningful motion that will not be canceled shortly. When *d*' yields to *d#*', it seems that a definite motion toward *e*' (and E minor) has been undertaken; but even though the bass does eventually ascend to the note *e*', its harmonic goal of E minor is never reached, and the bass sinks again through *e*♭' into the *d*' that it left four bars earlier. After a nearly three-measure effort, it has succeeded in moving only the space of a whole step. This sense of futility contrasts with the far more pronounced sense of direction with which all the previous sonatas and partias in the collection have begun.

The root of the word *bass* and its equivalents in German (*Baß*), Italian (*basso*), and French (*basse*) is the Greek word *básis* (βάσις), which has two distinct albeit related classes of meaning. One of these is the what we most naturally associate with the word *bass* today, a foundation, or in music, the lowest voice of a musical structure. But a second sense of the word comes from its derivation from the verb *bainó* (βαίνω), "to go" or "to walk," according to which *básis* can mean "step," "rhythm," and "foot," connoting motion and direction. In the Baroque era, this second sense of *básis* appears to have

124. In Appendix A, I note the association of enharmonic respelling with emotional extremes, especially of sorrow.

remained in the general musical consciousness not only through the many learned writers on music who spoke Greek but also by virtue of its forming the root of two very important musical-rhetorical terms: *anabasis* (*ana* [upward] + *basis* [going]) and *catabasis* (*cata* [downward] + *basis*), which appear in numerous German writings from the period.[125] To whatever extent this second meaning of *básis* can be associated with eighteenth-century attitudes toward the essential nature of bass-driven harmony, the sense of aimlessness and even futility that characterizes the bass-harmonic motion in the opening of the Adagio of the C-major sonata can be interpreted not merely as stagnation but as a kind of teleological frustration of the bass.

Placed within the Christ story, this sense of teleological frustration coupled with the threat of dissolution of tonal coherence suggests something akin to the typical ending point of a Lutheran passion, exemplified, for instance, in Bach's St. Matthew Passion: redemption has been won and sin atoned for, but the one who is Meaning himself, the one who holds the world together, lies dead in the tomb.[126] Similarly contributing to this general impression is the chain of sustained, chromatic, dissonant chords (again what we would call diminished chords in various inversions) in measures 40–42, which draw special attention to themselves by prominently interrupting the established pattern of pulsations at the quarter-note. These pull the tonality toward C minor for the two measures preceding the final tonic cadence at measure 45. But at this point there is a special connection with the corresponding point in the A-minor sonata. The A-minor Grave concludes with a descending Phrygian tetrachord, a gesture that is common enough but in this case appears specially to lend itself to representation of the suffering of Christ. Now, at the close of the first movement of the C-major sonata, the same gesture comes back but in the major mode, hinting (as it could be heard) at the glorification of the suffering Christ through the resurrection that, I propose, is represented in the following Fuga.

In Chapter 3 I put forward the idea, which I only summarize here, that just as Christ is raised two days following his crucifixion—that is, on the third day—so the C-major Fuga, which comes two movements after the passion-associated Ciaccona, creates a striking image of the resurrection of Christ after exactly two hundred measures by the decisive inversion[127] of its chorale-derived subject ("An Wasserflüssen Babylon"), which, together

125. See Bartel, *Musica Poetica*, 179–80, 214–15. My thanks to Panagiotis Linakis for drawing my attention to this.

126. In John 1:1, the title applied to Jesus and typically translated as *Word* in English (*Wort* by Luther) is a much weightier and more specific philosophical term, *Logos* (λόγος), essentially designating the governing principle of existence—what in today's language might be expressed as "the meaning of life." See Heb 1:3.

127. On the contrast with the intermingling of prime and inverted statements in the A-minor Fuga, see "Sonata in A Minor, BWV 1003" in Chap. 4.

with its lamenting countersubject, can be associated with the plight from which Christ redeems us. Therefore the return of the prime forms of this subject and countersubject to conclude the fugue in a slightly varied reprise of the exposition with which it began corresponds most naturally to the historic Christian understanding of the time since the resurrection of Christ: the fallenness of this world remains in effect, but something has changed; Christ's redemptive work has been completed and his victory decisively won, the effects of which will be fully realized with his return in glory at the end of the age.

Also in Chapter 3, we observed that the seven-part structure of the C-major Fuga could suggest assurance of the completion of Christ's redemptive work in the face of the paradoxical persistence of the fallenness of the world for a time. But a somewhat subtler application is invited by the subsequent observation in Chapter 5 that the prominence of the number 5 in the D-minor partia might signify the suffering of Christ by reference to the traditional five wounds. If, therefore, the five-part chiasm of the Ciaccona could imply the suffering of Christ on the cross, could the seven-part chiasm of the Fuga in the "pure" key of C major represent the vindication of Christ at his resurrection bringing his work on the cross to perfection?[128] If so, the chiastic structure of the C-major fugue, might reasonably be construed as a symbol not only for Christ (Χριστός) but also for the cross, a notable and theologically rich gesture that would not be without a notable precedent, albeit one Bach appears not to have known.

In Biber's collection of "Mystery" Sonatas, the only one calling for strings to be crossed is, curiously, the sonata representing the resurrection. Although it could be argued that the visual image of the two middle strings crossed recalls only the letter *X* and thus could represent either Christ or cross, the verbal association with what is required—that the strings be "crossed" (*gekreuzt*)—necessarily recalls the cross (*Kreuz*). It is conceivable that Biber—and perhaps Bach, if he intended the same association—meant to emphasize that the significance of the cross is not negated by the resurrection but retains a central role in the life of the believer.[129] Such an idea would have been consciously recognized at least as much by the Lutheran

128. See 1 Cor 15:14–22.

129. See Chap. 2 n. 11; Chap. 3 nn. 66 and 67; Matt 10:38 and 16:24 (Mark 8:34, Luke 9:23); 1 Cor 1:22–24 and 2:2; Gal 2:20, 5:24, and 6:14. In the Lutheran tradition of Bach's day, the cross is associated with the trials and tribulations the believer faces. For instance, chap. 2 of book 5, part 1 of Arndt's *Wahren Christenthum* (which Bach owned) is entitled "Vom Creuz und Verfolgung des heiligen christlichen Lebens" ("Of cross and persecution in the holy Christian life"). "Von Creuz/ Verfolgung und Anfechtung" ("Of cross, persecution, and the assault of temptation") was a common heading under which hymns were organized in the Lutheran songbooks of Bach's day, among which was the 1713 Weimar hymnal Bach would have known, *Schuldiges Lob Gottes.*

Bach as by the Catholic Biber, since Luther's *theologia crucis* explicitly emphasizes the centrality of the cross to faith and theology.

Whether such an idea is in view in the gentle cross shapes and melodic symmetries that open the following Largo (Ex. 6.18) must remain a matter of speculation.

Ex. 6.18. Melodic crosses in BWV 1005/3

If they were, their presence in the context of the serene and pastoral-like F-major texture[130] might suggest the idea that it is precisely in the

130. F-major is frequently used to convey mellow tranquility perhaps not least because of its association with the pastoral; for instance, the one work Bach explicitly labels "Pastorale," BWV 590, is in F major. A particularly famous example contemporary to Bach is Handel's aria "He shall feed his flock" from *Messiah*, whose mellow grandeur recalls that of the earlier "Ombra mai fu" (also in F major) from *Serse*. Mattheson is of the opinion that F major "is capable of expressing the most beautiful sentiments in the

cross that the believer finds the peace that Jesus promises to leave with his followers.[131]

In any case, as noted in Chapter 3, the setting of this third movement in F major makes it the only movement of the *Sei Solo* whose key signature differs from the general tonic of the piece as a whole. It is interesting that this gives the entire sonata a pattern of tonal descent and ascent, that is, descending from the neutral key signature of C major into the single flat of F major and ascending back to C, a microcosm of the descent-ascent patterns Chafe notes are so commonly used to theological ends in Bach's vocal music.[132] This is by no means to suggest that every instrumental piece by Bach in which a movement is set in the subdominant should be seen as having theological significance. But it is at least interesting that the one work of the *Sei Solo* using such a schema should be the sonata appearing to represent the resurrection of Christ, the ultimate descent-ascent narrative that is the very reason the same shape is applicable to so many aspects of Christian theology and faith.

The Allegro aßai that concludes the C-major sonata has a sense of triumphant celebration that comes in part from its evocation of the texture of a full Baroque orchestra complete with trumpets and timpani. The stark alternations between I and V beginning the movement recall textures that prominently feature the timpani, such as the chorus "Jauchzet, frohlocket" that opens the Christmas Oratorio. At the same time, leaping out from the busy sixteenth-note surface of the Allegro aßai, as if in relief, are melodic gestures moving at a slightly slower pace, whose distinctive rhythmic properties and relationship to the quicker musical foreground are characteristic of Bach's orchestral trumpet writing. I give a few illustrations in Examples 6.19 and 6.20.

world, be it magnanimity, steadfastness, love, or whatever else stands high in the list of virtues, without any constraint necessary to do so" ("F. dur . . . ist capable die schönsten Sentiments von der Welt zu exprimiren, es sey nun Großmuth, Standthafftigkeit, Liebe, oder was sonst in dem Tugend-Register oben an stehet, und solches alles mit einer der massen natürlichen Art und unvergleichlichen Facilité, daß gar kein Zwang dabey vonnöthen ist"). Mattheson, *Das Neu-Eröffnete Orchestre*, 241 (part 3, chap. 2, §13).

131. John 14:27; Col 1:20; Eph 2:16.

132. See this chap. n. 53.

Ex. 6.19

a. BWV 1005/4 with rhythmic profile emphasized

b. Sinfonia to "Wir danken dir, Gott," BWV 29/1

* For ease of reading, I have notated trumpets and timpani in concert pitch, though Bach always notates them in C.

c. "Cum sancto Spiritu" from the Mass in B Minor, BWV 232

Ex. 6.20

a. BWV 1005/4 with implied voicing realized

b. BWV 29/1. Similar figuration occurs in mm. 51–52, 55–56, 67–69, and 121–24.

Ex. 6.20 (cont.)

c. "Et resurrexit," from the Mass in B Minor, BWV 232

The unusually high violin writing toward the end of the movement, in measures 89–92, can be heard as the culmination of progressively intensifying exultation. As was briefly mentioned in connection with the C-major Fuga, the highest note found in the *Sei Solo* is *g*''', which occurs rarely throughout the collection and indeed fairly rarely in all of Bach's surviving violin writing. Its first occurrence in the *Sei Solo* is in the Ciaccona, where it appears once, in measure 87. Two movements later, in the C-major Fuga, it is heard twice in succession in measure 263. Two movements after that, in the Allegro aßai, we find it three times in succession, in measures 89–92.

But this intensifying exultation nonetheless remains earthbound by virtue of the parallel minor that asserts itself at the end of each half of the movement, as it has asserted itself toward the end of each previous movement, until finally in measure 101 the accelerated resolution to C major, in contrast with measure 41, could be heard as a victory over the parallel minor mode, a victory that remains in force through the end of the *Sei Solo* (see Ex. 3.15d).

Partia in E Major, BWV 1006

The symbolic banishment of the minor mode in the E-major partia, coupled with the partia's representing the culmination of an ascending *X*-shaped structure spanning the entirety of the *Sei Solo*, provides a concrete foundation for viably associating the E-major partia with the kingdom of heaven, as discussed above. In addition, the partia is full of musical imagery that can be heard, subjectively, as illustrations of biblical descriptors of the kingdom of heaven and the return of Christ at the end of the age.

Following the C-major sonata, the E-major partia feels like a transfiguration. The Allegro aßai of the C-major sonata already seemed like the height of exuberance and triumph; but with the E-major Preludio, a similarly rapid and virtuosic texture reappears shifted upward two steps from the pure C major to the highly chromatic E major, which, especially coupled with the brightness of the violin's (extensively used) open *e*''-string, transcends what had seemed to be the zenith of exuberance and suggests an other-worldly brilliance that is nearly disorienting in its intensity, especially the fantastically ambiguous bariolage figuration in measures 17–28 and 67–78 (Ex. 6.21).

Ex. 6.21. Metrically disorienting bariolage in BWV 1006/1

It is easy to associate this with what Paul writes in 1 Corinthians 15:51–52: "Behold, I tell you a mystery; we will not all sleep, but we will all be changed, in a moment, in the twinkling of an eye, at the last trumpet; for the trumpet will sound, and the dead will be raised imperishable, and we will be changed." If the trumpet can be heard in the fanfarelike figure that opens the Preludio before its *moto perpetuo* begins, then the steady stream of sixteenth notes—much like what Bach uses to depict the four rivers in "Schleicht, spielende Wellen" (BWV 206)—might well recall the River of Life,[133] especially considering the harmonic richness springing from this musical "stream."

Perhaps even the key of E-major itself can recall the resurrection of the dead by virtue of its associations with resurrection and salvation in Bach's vocal works.[134] Although Chafe observes that Bach's apparent associations with E major differ sharply from those famously articulated by Mattheson, the two actually share some interesting common ground. Whereas for Bach E major is a key of joy and exuberance, Mattheson describes it as "incomparably expressing a desperate or downright deathly sadness . . . and . . . in some cases so piercing, severing, suffering, and penetrating that it can only be compared to a fatal separation of body and soul."[135] What the two views share is an association of E major with something beyond (or something

133. Rev 22:1–2; see Ezek 47:1–12.

134. Chafe, *Tonal Allegory*, 152 n. 1.

135. "E. dur . . . drucket eine Verzweiflungsvolle oder ganz tödliche Traurigkeit unvergleichlich wol aus . . . und hat bey gewissen Umständen so was schneidendes, scheidendes, leidendes und durchdringendes, daß es mit nichts als einer fatalen Trennung Leibes und der Seelen verglichen werden mag." Mattheson, *Das Neu-Eröffnete Orchestre*, 250 (part 3, chap. 2, §21).

pointing beyond) this mortal life. Of course, we can only speculate as to whether Mattheson's view or something similar to it was known to Bach, but if so it might add an interesting dimension to our reading of Bach's use of E major.

A further point of interest is the handful of correlations that exist between the E-major partia and other works of the *Sei Solo*. We have already observed that the A-minor sonata exhibits a strong tonal pull toward E, as if toward the E-major partia; the plausibility of this association is reinforced by several features of the E-major partia appearing to refer back to the A-minor sonata. If the beginning of the last movement of the A-minor sonata (Allegro) can seem to resemble a fanfare on account of its harmonic stasis, gestural brilliance, and arpeggiation (recalling figuration typical of natural brass), then surely the beginning of the E-major Preludio can equally be heard as such (Ex. 6.22).

The inverse relationship between the ironic minor-mode fanfare of the A-minor Allegro and the "proper" fanfare of the E-major Preludio is paralleled by their opposite positions within their respective works (the last movement as opposed to the first movement) as well as by the inverse motion of their initial arpeggiated gestures. A second possible connection with the A-minor sonata is the identical returning-note figure following an eighth rest that begins both the E-major Preludio and the subject of the A-minor Fuga (Ex. 6.23).

Ex. 6.23

A third similarity between the two works is the presence throughout the E-major partia of a transformation of the lamenting tetrachord that permeates the A-minor sonata. This transformation can be considered from two perspectives. With regard to mode, the transformation is from the Phrygian mode (or, functionally, minor) to major. From a motivic perspective, it is a retrograde inversion. Both carry similar significances in the context of the patterns of meaning we have already observed in the *Sei Solo*. A particularly vivid example of this transformed tetrachord is found at the beginning of the Bourée, where it begins not on its tonic pitch but on *a*"—in short, where the tetrachord most typically begins in the A-minor sonata (Ex. 6.24).

Ex. 6.24. BWV 1006/5

Just as the A-minor sonata could be seen to look heavenward (that is, toward E) in the face of the specter of the cross, so amid the triumphant glories of heaven the E-major partia continues to bear the marks of the A-minor sonata, albeit transformed, just as the glorified Christ continues to bear the scars of his crucifixion in his risen, glorified body.[136] This touches on a heady concept in Christian theology: redemption entails the sufferings of this present age being not merely erased or negated but rather transformed into glories that would not exist had the suffering not been.[137]

136. Luke 24:40; John 20:20, 27; see Rev 5:6.

137. See Rom 11:32; Gal 3:22. Luther is reported to have said, "If God were asked at the last judgment, 'Why did you permit Adam to fall?' and he responded, 'So that my goodness to the human race would be understood when I gave my Son for the salvation of humanity!' we would say, 'Let all mankind fall once again, that your glory

It was noted earlier in this chapter that the E-major Gigue shares its opening chord progression, in its most essential form, with the Adagio of the G-minor sonata (Ex. 6.25).

Ex. 6.25. Harmonic similarity between the beginnings of the first and last movements of the *Sei Solo*

In both cases, the harmonic rhythm moves consistently in two-beat intervals with melodic filigree connecting these harmonic pillars. But if this connection is intentional, it would seem as though Bach establishes it in order to represent an inverse relationship between the two movements. Whereas the G-minor Adagio began with an (implied) upward arpeggiation of its initial chord,[138] the E-major Gigue begins by arpeggiating its tonic downward. After the initial arpeggiation, the melodic voice of the G-minor Adagio flows downward by step from scale degree $\hat{1}$ to scale degree $\hat{7}$; by contrast, following the initial arpeggiation in the E-major Gigue the melody runs upward by step from $\hat{1}$ to $\hat{7}$. In the G-minor Adagio, the melodic filigree then circles upward to the seventh degree of the dominant chord, but the E-major Gigue proceeds downward by leap to its root. And finally, the G-minor Adagio concludes the progression by resolving the melody downward to scale degree $\hat{3}$, while the E-major Gigue moves upward, also resolving on $\hat{3}$.

be known! For you have brought about so much through Adam's fall that we do not understand your ways.'" ("Si Deus interrogaretur in iudicio extremo: Quare permisisti cadare Adamum? et ille repondebit: Ut bonitas mea erga genus humanum possit intelligi, cum Filium meum do pro salute humana! diceremus nos: Laß noch ein mall fallen alles geschlecht, ut tua gloria innotescat! Weil du so vill ausgericht hast casu Adami, so verstehen wir deine wege nicht.") *WA TR*, no. 5071. Luther does not embrace the idea of *felix culpa* ("the fortunate fall"), still less the idea that God engineered the fall. Rather, Luther understands God's sovereignty to encompass Adam's fall with eternal redemptive intentions, even while not being the agent of Adam's sin.

138. Because the violin is unable to play four notes simultaneously, the performer must arpeggiate upward, beginning with the bass.

Indeed, these two movements exemplify the idea of inversion or contrast in many respects. One is the solemn opening movement of a sonata da chiesa, the other the exultant concluding movement of a dance suite; one begins the collection of *Sei Solo*, the other concludes it; one is in a slow common time, the other in a rapid $\frac{3}{8}$; one is in minor, the other in major; one is perhaps the most dissonant movement of the *Sei Solo*, the other perhaps the most consonant; one is through-composed, the other in repeating binary form; one is given an Italian title, the other French; one is primarily chordal, the other entirely monophonic (at least on the surface); and one represents the lower extremity of the gamut as well as of the strings of a violin, while the other represents the upper extremity of both.

The connection of these disparate movements, especially as they represent the outer extremes of the collection, brings a sense of narrative unity to the whole. From another perspective, the inverse relationship between these two connected movements suggests that the latter aligns itself with the former but inverts its content. In view of the association of the G-minor sonata with Christ's descent into our fallen world, the E-major Gigue can be seen as representing the undoing of the brokenness of the world into which Christ enters[139] as well as symbolizing that Christ's humiliation in his incarnation is precisely what has become his glory.[140]

To conclude, I find it noteworthy that the piece I suggest represents the kingdom of heaven should be not a church sonata but a dance suite bursting with *joie de vivre*. It is, for one thing, a particularly life-affirming gesture. Many of the texts Bach sets in his cantatas present what seems like a rather dismal view of life, with statements like these:

Mir ekelt mehr zu leben,	It disgusts me to live any more,
Drum nimm mich, Jesu, hin![142]	So take me away, Jesus!

or

Ich freue mich auf meinen Tod,	I am looking forward to my death,
Ach, hätt' er sich schon eingefunden	Oh, that it were already here!
Da entkomm ich aller Not,	Then I will escape all the hardship
Die mich noch auf der Welt gebunden.[143]	That still binds me to the world.

139. See Rev 21:4.

140. Phil 2:6–11.

141. From the final aria of "Vergnügte Ruh," BWV 170. Text by Georg Christian Lehms.

142. From the final aria of "Ich habe genug," BWV 82. The author of the text is unknown.

The perspective represented at the end of the *Sei Solo* provides what I suspect many will find to be a welcome qualifier for these strong statements by anchoring the longing for release from suffering within the context of the hope of an indestructible and sorrowless life. In other words, it suggests that the cantata texts in question may best be heard as a longing to be rid not of life but rather of the death that is with us even in the midst of this mortal life.[143]

The emphasis on the departure of the soul at death evident in the texts cited above, among countless others from within and outside Bach's immediate context, can foster (and often has fostered) a Platonized view of the afterlife within the Christian tradition, in which ultimate hope is placed in escaping this material world and being taken away to a bodiless spiritual existence. But the idea that the eternal heavenly existence is disembodied and removed from the world contrasts sharply with the eschatological assumptions that the New Testament writers held in common, which included the coming of the kingdom of heaven to earth[144] with the bodily return of Jesus,[145] the resurrection of the dead (with what Paul calls a "spirit-driven body" but a body nonetheless),[146] the passing away of the present material order,[147] and the creation of the glorified new heavens and new earth[148] that are nonetheless continuous with the present creation.[149] For Paul, this eschatology is the basis for an affirmation of the importance both of the body[150] and of the activities of this present life; he concludes his lengthy discourse on bodily resurrection in 1 Corinthians 15 with the assurance that "your toil is not in vain in the Lord."[151]

It is thus all the more interesting that the piece signifying the heavenly kingdom should be a dance suite, with its inescapable associations with the

143. This idea is expressed in the antiphon *Media vita in morte sumus* ("In the midst of life we are in death"), translated by Luther as "Mytten wir ym leben synd mit dem todt umbfangen" and set by Bach in BWV 383. Leaver makes a similar observation in *J. S. Bach and Scripture*, 139.

144. Rev 21:2–3.

145. Acts 1:11. See Matt 24:30 et al.; Matt 26:64 et al.; 1 Thess 4:16; Rev 22:20 etc.

146. 1 Cor 15:44. See John 5:28–29 and 11:24–5; Rom 8:23; 1 Cor 15:12–58; Rev 20:5–6 and 12–13; Dan 12:2; etc.

147. 2 Pet 3:7, 10; Rev 6:14; see Isa 51:6.

148. Rev 21:1, 5; see Isa 65:17.

149. See Rom 8:21. The CB commentary emphasizes the continuity of the present world, which will be destroyed by fire, with the new heavens and new earth that will be formed out of its ashes by drawing a comparison with the departure of the immortal soul from the body at death, later to be reunited with the resurrected body (6:95).

150. See Rom 8:23; Eph 5:28–29.

151. 1 Cor 15:58.

body. The relationship between the Preludio that opens the E-major partia and the C-major Allegro aßai that preceded it is one of change and transformation but also of continuity, particularly in their common texture of rapid sixteenth notes. (This is, incidentally, the only point within the *Sei Solo* where juxtaposed movements exhibit such textural relationship.) Another small point that may not be wholly insignificant is that this "heaven partia" begins not with an ascent, as if flying up into the clouds, but rather a two-octave descent from above, as if heaven were coming down to earth (Ex. 6.26a). The final Gigue also begins and ends with descending figures that span an octave and a fifth (Ex. 6.26b).

Indeed, if Tatlow is correct, Bach may initially have intended the final arpeggiation of the Preludio to return from its high *e'''* back down to the *e'* two octaves lower (resembling what is found in BWV 1006a for lute) but later eliminated the last measure as part of the process of manipulating measure counts in the interest of creating proportional relationships within and among works of the *Sei Solo* (see Ex. 6.27).[152]

152. Tatlow, "Bach's Parallel Proportions," 141–42.

Ex. 6.27

a. Conclusion of BWV 1006/1 for violin

b. Conclusion of BWV 1006a/1, probably for lute

c. Speculative original conclusion of the E-major Preludio, BWV 1006/1

If this is accurate, it would mean that both the opening Preludio and the final Gigue could originally have been conceived to end as they began—the former with a descent of two octaves, the latter with a descent of an octave and a fifth—creating a sense of the general descending of a structure bursting with gestures in a seemingly infinite variety of directions, like the new Jerusalem descending from heaven as described in Revelation 21.

It seems evident from even the scant surviving biographical information that Bach enjoyed the good things in life, which he would have identified as blessings from the Lord, whether it be family (he was the father of no fewer than twenty children), a well-working musical instrument, or even a good wine. Could the E-major partia suggest that Bach's appreciation of God's gifts in the present was grounded in his eschatology, rooted in the hope of redemption not *from* but *of* God's creation? John Eliot Gardiner observes a particular connection between the legacy of religious dancing and Bach's Christmas music, that is, celebrating the first coming of Christ.[153] Could the E-major partia represent dancing at the second coming of Christ, this time not as a weak and vulnerable baby but as the King of Glory who comes to make all things new?

153. Gardiner, *Bach: Music in the Castle of Heaven*, 474.

Appendix A

An Examination of Helga Thoene's Premise of Symbolism in the Sei Solo

Johann Sebastian Bach: Ciaccona—Tanz oder Tombeau? Eine analytische Studie. Oschersleben: Ziethen, 2001.

Johann Sebastian Bach: Sonata A-Moll, BWV 1003—Eine wortlose Passion. Analytische Studie. Oschersleben: Ziethen, 2005.

Johann Sebastian Bach: Sonata C-Dur, BWV 1005—Lob sey Gott dem Heiligen Geist. Analytische Studie. Oschersleben: Ziethen, 2008.

~ ~ ~

In October 2013 an article titled "The New Mythologies: Deep Bach, Saint Mahler, and the Death Chaconne" appeared in the *Los Angeles Review of Books.* In it Michael Markham reflects on the process by which compositions become "mythologized" as well as the role of such mythologizing in their continuing appeal. His principal example of how a work can be endearingly and enduringly mythologized, even when that mythology has minimal basis in discernible fact, is Helga Thoene's theory of hidden chorales and gematria in Bach's Ciaccona. But because systematic review of Thoene's theory is not his intention—and because, as he observes, Thoene's general premise has permeated the collective musical (and to some degree popular) consciousness, even among those who have never read her volumes, which are published exclusively in German—it seems appropriate to investigate her premises with somewhat more specificity than has yet been done in print. This is not undertaken to discredit Thoene. Markham is quite right to observe that, irrespective of the historicity of her claims, she has "done us all, and the Chaconne, a great service" in providing a contemporary interpretation that artists and listeners today can identify with. Rather, I mean simply to clarify the extent to which the various devices she describes might be better attributed to her own remarkable creativity than to Bach's design, since considerable confusion appears to linger on that front. Nor is it necessarily my intent to remove what Markham calls "the historical rumor needed to sanction [the next generation's] emotional listening," though I respectfully question whether a historical rumor is indeed needed for a meaningful listening experience or the forging of a stirring interpretation; after all, if Markham is correct that the justification of a particular hearing of (in this case) the Ciaccona "will have little to do with Bach [but] will come from our own tendency to turn art into autobiography," then insofar as we truly believe that, we will altogether obviate the need to look to history, illusory or otherwise, to justify our interpretive impressions. But to the extent that these interpretive impressions might be stimulated or honed by an accurate awareness of historical fact (to the best that it can be discerned), discussions like the following might hopefully not be altogether fruitless.

The idea that the *Sei Solo* contain religious significances is not new but has long been the object of speculation, although Thoene has produced the most extensive study of the subject to date. Following a methodology of Friedrich Smend that has been called into significant question by Ruth Tatlow,[1] Thoene proposes that Bach uses a number alphabet (A = 1, B = 2, etc.) to create equivalences of alphanumerical sums between fragments of music and excerpts from liturgical texts as well as names. She also proposes that Bach has woven hidden chorale melodies into at least four of the solo violin works: the three sonatas and the Ciaccona (she does not analyze the partias in B minor and E major or the first four movements of the D-minor). Using evidence produced by these methods, she argues that the Ciaccona from the D-minor partia (BWV 1004) is a *tombeau* for Bach's first wife, Maria Barbara,[2] and that the three sonatas (BWV 1001, 1003, 1005) are intended to represent the three foremost holidays in Lutheran observance: Christmas, Easter, and Pentecost.[3]

The often abstruse nature of the relationships Thoene detects has led many to question whether they are "really there." In one sense, of course, they are certainly there. But the deeper question is whether they are *uniquely* there, such that similar methods would uncover these significances and not others. I will briefly consider this question with regard first to gematria and then to hidden chorales.

1. See my Chap. 1 n. 6.
2. Thoene, *Bach: Ciaccona.*
3. Thoene, *Bach: Sonata A-Moll*, 42; *Bach: Sonata C-Dur*, 12.

First, regarding gematria: the more direct the numerological correlation, the stronger the argument that the correlation is uniquely present and not merely a more or less arbitrary interpolation. Equating sums of collections of alphanumeric note values with sums of phrases from among myriad ecclesial documents is quite a weak correlation. And even if one genuinely admires the virtuosity, so to speak, with which Thoene observes these correlations, one also wonders whether correlations with other subjects could be found in equal number if a similarly observant analyst were so inclined. If so, then the credibility of her analyses would require substantive prior evidence for the likelihood—not merely the possibility—that Bach did indeed encode theological equivalencies into the *Sei Solo*. Lacking this, her analyses demonstrate at best that it is possible to find correlations Bach could speculatively have intended. Even this, however, is called into question by two considerations. One is the substantial research conducted by Tatlow on Bach's fabled use of numbers, which seriously challenges some of Smend's theories of alphanumeric encryption in Bach that Thoene adopts as a foundation for her study.[4]

A second consideration to bear in mind regarding gematria is that if its presence is detected extensively at the surface level of the music, and if such is thought to be the intent of the composer, then it is most likely (especially given the natural finiteness of the musical language) that the gematria was the driving force in constructing the passage in question. If, however, there are other, more immediate compositional features and operations that can explain the form of the passage, it necessarily raises the question of whether perhaps the number correlation might be coincidence and therefore an interpolation, especially if the correlation is weak in the manner discussed above.

One example that could suggest the potential of searches for number symbolism to go rather startlingly astray is Thoene's derivation of several significances from what I propose is an incorrect reading of the Ciaccona's opening bass line. The Ciaccona opens as shown in Example A.1a. From this, Thoene extracts the bass line shown in Example A.1b. However, this seems to me to be incorrect; the *c#'* at the end of measure 4 appears to belong not to the bass but to an inner voice, resolving an implied *d'* suspended from the first beat of the measure into the second, as shown in Example A.1c.[5]

4. Tatlow, *Bach and the Riddle of the Number Alphabet* (see esp. her summary on pp. 126–29).

5. Bach's notating m. 4 as he has, as opposed to writing the second bass note (*a*) as a half note, is readily explainable in that throughout the *Sei Solo* Bach's notation balances the practical with the theoretical or ideal, often leaning toward the side of practicality (this is probably least so in the C-major Fuga). Understanding the *c#'* in the fourth measure as belonging to a middle voice rather than the bass necessarily has important implications for performance, since one would then not want the *c#'* to receive the same

Ex. A.1

a. Opening of the Ciaccona, BWV 1004/5

b. Thoene's representation of the Ciaccona's opening bass line

c. Realization of the implied voicing of mm. 4–5

Indeed, to the extent that a standard $^6_4$ chord is implied on the second beat of measure 4, the implied *d'* in the tenor must resolve to *c#'*; and if *c#'*, the leading tone, is present in the tenor, it is contrapuntally inconceivable that it would be doubled by the bass. Beyond considerations of counterpoint, we have already observed in Chapter 2 that the bassline appears crafted to reflect that of older and more rapid ciacconas (see Ex. 2.4), a parallel that would exclude the *c#'* both rhythmically and melodically. Together with the fact that the *c#'* is absent from the bass register in measure 8 when the bass line repeats (Ex. A.2), these considerations indicate beyond reasonable doubt that the *c#'* must belong to the tenor voice and not the bass.

Ex. A.2. Ciaccona, BWV 1004/5, second iteration of the ostinato

kind of weight as would be given to the true bass notes *g* and *a* on the first two beats.

I emphasize this so heavily because even from this apparently inaccurate reading of the bassline Thoene materializes a number of supposed significances. According to her realization of the bass, she concludes that it consists of 17 notes rather than 16 (or merely 8), which she numbers progressively from 1 to 17 and adds up to 153, the *numerus electorum*, signifying chosenness and blessedness.[6] She then similarly assigns numbers to what she considers each half of the ostinato (1, 2, 3 . . . 9; 1, 2, 3 . . . 8) and, adding them, arrives at 81, which is the sum of the letters of Maria Barbara, the name of Bach's deceased wife.[7] Next, she groups by measure the digits she has assigned to the supposed first half of the bass line: 1 (the first measure contains a single note) + 23 (the second measure contains notes 2 and 3) + 45 (the third measure contains notes 4 and 5) + 678 (the fourth measure, Thoene supposes, contains notes 6, 7, and 8) + 9 (the statement ends in the next measure with the supposed ninth note), totaling 756, which is the alphanumerical sum of "Ex Deo nascimur, In Christo morimur, Per Spiritum Sanctum Reviviscimus" ("Of God we are born, in Christ we die, by the Holy Spirit we are revived")[8]—a formulation that, I note parenthetically, is probably Rosicrucian in origin and thus would likely have been viewed with no little suspicion by an orthodox Lutheran like Bach. Finally, she assigns numbers to the pitches themselves according to the gematria she uses elsewhere (A = 1, B = 2, etc.), yielding the sequence 4, 4, 30, 4, 2, 7, 1, 30, 4. By grouping the notes in the second and fourth measures together (4 and 30 in the second measure, forming 430; and in the fourth measure 7, 1, and 30, forming 7130) to total 7560 (which is ten times the number that her previous operation had associated with the Trinity) and by adding the remaining numbers—symmetrically arranged as they are, with two in the middle and one each on the outer ends—she obtains 14, the sum of B-A-C-H.[9] All of this is derived from what I am proposing is a faulty reading of the bass line, which raises the question of whether the ability to detect relevant numerological equivalencies necessarily suggests that those equivalencies reflect Bach's intentions.

Regarding the premise of embedded chorales, several observations suggest that chorale melodies may fairly easily be read into music where no such association is intended. First, it is important to note that chorales are generally stepwise, as is much of the essential voice leading of the music of Bach's time (including the works in which Thoene alleges the presence of hidden chorales). Second, the musical language of Bach and his German contemporaries was certainly shaped to a considerable extent by these

6. This significance comes from the miraculous catch of 153 fish in John 21.

7. Thoene, *Bach: Ciaccona*, 91.

8. Ibid., 100.

9. Ibid., 101.

chorales and the musical possibilities they elicited in the countless chorale settings of various types since Luther's day. Third, it is reasonable that there should be substantial parallels between the expressive contours of chorale melodies and expressive gestures in other works within a musical tradition to which these chorales profoundly relate. From this perspective, the ability of a chorale fragment to coincide with a musical texture of Bach is not especially remarkable. However, if in the process of detecting chorales their rhythm can be distorted and their metrical and textual weights displaced (Ex. A.3), and if they may create poor counterpoint with the musical texture in which they are supposedly embedded (Ex. A.4), and if they may alter the necessarily implied harmony of the passage in question (Ex. A.5), then to that degree it becomes more and more possible to "find" melodies that may not be uniquely present in any given musical texture.[10]

Ex. A.3

a. First melodic phrase of "Jesu, meine Freude" (Crüger), transposed to G minor

b. Thoene: "Jesu, meine Freude" purportedly embedded in BWV 1005/3 (*Bach: Sonata C-Dur*, 162)*

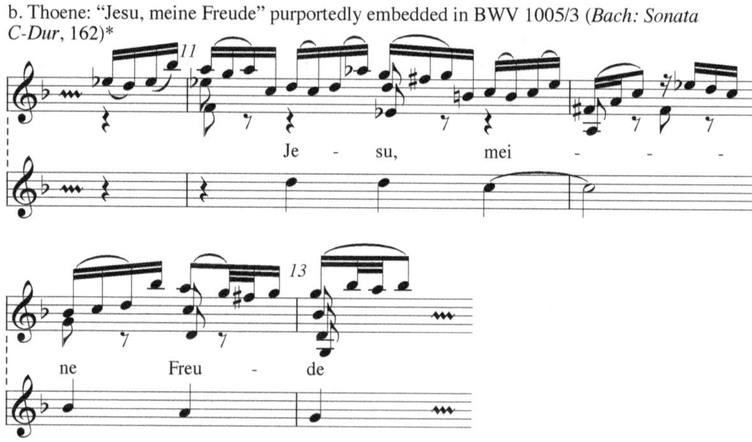

* In m. 11, note that the metrical strength of beat 1 over beat 2 and beat 3 over beat 4 is heightened by suspensions on beats 1 and 3 resolving on beats 2 and 4. The placement of the text is therefore directly at odds with not only the metrical but also the contrapuntal properties of the music.

10. Since Thoene likens the solo violin works to chorale arrangements, it should be noted that in none of Bach's elaborated chorale settings, whether choral or for organ, are comparable distortions to be found.

Ex. A.4

a. Thoene: "Herr Jesu Christ, du höchstes Gut" purportedly embedded in BWV 1001/2 (*Bach: Ciaccona*, 59)

b. Contrapuntal infelicities of Thoene's proposed chorale melody against the bass line of the violin's texture

* The dissonant 7th, *g*', wants to resolve down by step to *f*♯'.
** The chorale creates a direct fifth with the bass.
*** The chorale phrase ends on an unresolved fourth above the implied bass *d*'.

Ex. A.5

a. Thoene: "Herr Jesu Christ, du höchstes Gut" purportedly embedded in BWV 1001/1 (*Bach: Ciaccona*, 57)

b. Harmonic reduction of BWV 1001/1 against Thoene's chorale backdrop, revealing a clash on beat 2 of m. 3

* The implied bass *f* ' precludes a *b*♭' from being heard above it, as it would constitute an improperly treated fourth.

c. Rhythmic alteration of Thoene's chorale citation to fit the implied harmony of BWV 1001/1. The result, while harmonically acceptable, is undesirable rhythmically.

It is true that, particularly in the D-minor Ciaccona, the "hidden" chorales Thoene cites have considerable commonality of subject matter, and this may indeed be owing to more than mere coincidence. Modes (and later keys) were widely held to have diverse affective properties; and although individual writers within Bach's broader tradition may differ on the specific affective properties of each mode or key, there is nonetheless considerable agreement among them—largely, perhaps, because many simply accept associations put forward by previous influential theorists.[11] For that reason, chorales whose texts deal with similar ideas are likely also to share modal properties. From this it follows that among chorales that can be interpolated within a piece of music in any given key, one is likely to be able to find considerable commonality of subject matter. In other words, it is not surprising that, among chorales lending themselves to being heard within the fabric of the D-minor Ciaccona, one could find a number of them sharing themes of suffering and death, as prevalent as these subjects are in the chorale literature.

Thoene's suggestion that "the three sonatas can be seen as representations of the three high feasts of the church year: G-minor—Christmas . . . A-minor—Easter . . . C-major—Pentecost"[12] follows rather loosely from the evidence she presents. Her strongest piece of evidence is that the subject of the Fuga from the C-major sonata is, as she claims, a quotation from the beginning of the Pentecost hymn "Komm, heiliger Geist" ("Come, Holy Spirit"). But especially in view of the at-least-equally strong resemblance of the subject to "An Wasserflüssen Babylon," any supposed association with "Komm, heiliger Geist" must be rigorously established, especially if it is to play a critical role in a hermeneutic approach to the *Sei Solo*. But no such critical comparison of the two chorale possibilities appears; and indeed, as I have already discussed, I believe "An Wasserflüssen Babylon" to be by far the more likely association. If this is correct, it alone would place Thoene's premise in need of fundamental revision.

Thoene posits that fragments of "Komm, heiliger Geist," especially the opening phrase and the closing "Alleluia," are to be found throughout the sonata. Aside from the slipperiness of her method of chorale detection, it is curious that none of the other chorales she cites within the C-major sonata—including "Wachet auf," "Es ist das Heil uns kommen her," and "Jesu, meine Freude"—are associated with Pentecost. Indeed, "Vom Himmel hoch" is a Christmas hymn; and thus, according to Thoene's proposed scheme, one would sooner expect to find it in the G-minor sonata. And the line "Ich will dich preisen ewiglich," which she repeatedly cites, comes from the final stanza of "Herzlich lieb hab' ich dich, O Herr," which pertains to the hope of eternal life after death and thus would seem most fitting for

11. For a more detailed treatment of this subject, see Steblin, *A History of Key Characteristics in the Eighteenth and Early Nineteenth Centuries.*

12. ". . . die drei Sonaten [dürften] als Repräsentation der drei Hochfeste des Kirchenjahres anzusehen sein: G-Moll—Weihnachten . . . A-Moll—Ostern . . . C-Dur—Pfingsten." Thoene, *Bach: Sonata A-Moll*, 42.

the A-minor sonata, which Thoene connects with the phrase "In Christo morimur" ("in Christ we die"), as I explain below.[13]

Equally curious is that none of the excerpts from liturgical texts that Thoene connects with fragments of the C-major sonata through gematria have any direct connection with Pentecost; three are broad references to the Trinity, one is the Nicene Creed's confession of baptism (to which Peter enjoins the crowd in his Pentecost sermon),[14] one is a general statement of praise to God from the Gloria, and only one pertains uniquely to the Holy Spirit, namely, the portion of the Nicene Creed confessing the Spirit. This latter association is derived by adding the alphanumerical values of all the letters in the portion of the Nicene Creed dealing with the Holy Spirit,[15] equaling 1,652, and finding this to be the sum of the number of notes in the first and last fugal passages combined with the first and last episodic sections (that is, the first, second, penultimate, and last sections of the C-major Fuga's well-defined seven-part form). Notably, the number associated with the text represents not the number of letters but their collective alphanumeric value (A = 1, B = 2, etc.), whereas Thoene locates this number in the score of the C-major sonata using not alphanumeric valuation but a simple tallying of notes. All of the texts she cites are from either the Latin Mass Ordinary or the Latin Magnificat, neither one particularly associated with Pentecost.

As ambivalent as the connection of the C-major sonata to Pentecost therefore appears, it would seem that the connection of the other two sonatas to Christmas and Easter respectively is still more difficult to substantiate by her methods. If the third sonata corresponds (as Thoene supposes) to the third Person of the Trinity (the Holy Spirit), which in turn corresponds to the third principal feast of the church year, it would be convenient if the same associations applied to the first two sonatas. Although the second feast of the church year, Easter, does focus on the second Person of the Trinity (namely, Christ and his resurrection), the actual connection Thoene cites between the content of the A-minor sonata and Easter or the resurrection is tenuous. Perhaps her most direct connection is in measures 236–56 of the A-minor Fuga, where she considers a chromatic passage frequently passing through *c*, *b*' (that is, *h*' in German), *b*♭', and *a*' to contain a series of permutations of B-A-C-H. She observes that the notes between the respective ends of the second-to-last and last of these permutations, in addition to the notes

13. Ibid., 39.

14. Acts 2:38.

15. Et in Spiritum Sanctum, Dominum et vivificantem: Qui ex Patre Filioque procedit. Qui cum Patre et Filio simul adoratur et conglorificatur: Qui locutus est per prophetas.

sounding simultaneously on the downbeat of the following measure, have a collective alphanumerical value of 261, which is the alphanumerical sum of the phrase "Et resurrexit tertia die" ("and was resurrected on the third day"). Most of her analysis, however, focuses on passion associations in general. And though it is true that the passion of Christ is associated with the feast of Easter, it is curious that any proposed reference to Easter as such would have only scant associations with the second and equally important event commemorated by the feast, Christ's resurrection.

But whereas the connection between the three Persons of the Trinity and three church feasts applies to some degree to the second and third feasts (Pentecost and Easter), even this breaks down when considering the first feast (Christmas) because in no meaningful way can Christmas be associated with God the Father over and above the Son (whose incarnation Christmas celebrates) or, for that matter, the Holy Spirit. So Thoene widens the pool of associations. She notes that the number of measures contained in each fugue subject added to the total number of measures in all three fugues adds up to 756, which is the alphanumerical value of the previously cited Rosicrucian formulation "Ex Deo nascimur, In Christo morimur, Per Spiritum Sanctum revivimus."[16] (This is why Thoene connects the A-minor sonata to the phrase "In Christo morimur," as mentioned above). In the context of Thoene's main argument, the connection of the three fugues with this (theologically dubious) Rosicrucian formulation provides an association whose first of three terms describes birth and can therefore be likened to Christmas, which celebrates Christ's birth. The association is indeed quite loose, which is why it is especially curious that Thoene cites no connection between the actual content of the G-minor sonata and the celebration of Christmas (or even the idea of birth); the one supposed hidden chorale that she cites, "Herr Jesu Christ, du höchstes Gut," does not pertain to Christmas, nor do the various gematria whose presence she alleges.

I cannot, of course, escape the irony that the point at which I must question Thoene's methodology most is precisely where her conclusions most closely correspond to the schema I have suggested in the present study. My reason for engaging in this discussion, therefore, is not to gratuitously challenge the methods leading to a conclusion that, insofar as it concerns

16. In support of using number symbolism in connection with the latter quotation is her observation that numerology appears inherent in the text itself: because "Ex Deo" and "In Christo" have the same alphanumeric sum as "reviviscimus" it follows that the sum of the dative phrases ("Ex Deo," "In Christo," "Per Spiritum Sanctum") must equal the sum of the third clause ("Per Spiritum Sanctum reviviscimus"), while the verbs ("nascimur," "morimur," "reviviscimus") are equal to the first two clauses ("Ex Deo nascimur, In Christo morimur"). See Thoene, *Bach: Sonata A-Moll*, 40; *Bach: Sonata C-Dur*, 47.

the association of the G-minor sonata with the coming of Christ, I would generally agree with; on the contrary, the methods by which she arrives at this particular conclusion also lead her to other conclusions that are at odds with those to which the present study has led me, and therefore I could not responsibly put forward the propositions that I have without engaging Thoene's in the process.

In sum, although admittedly being skeptical that the connections Thoene cites represent Bach's design, I reemphasize that I do not mean to diminish either the astonishing operations Thoene performs with numbers or the artistic merit, in their own right, of the scores she has produced that superimpose chorale fragments on the solo violin works. Irrespective of whether these reflect any intention of the composer's, they are certainly beautiful and fascinating creations that give us yet another lens—and a particularly interesting one—through which to approach the music of Bach.

Appendix B

Further Applications: Two Case Studies

Concerto in D Minor, BWV 1052

Bach's D-minor harpsichord concerto, BWV 1052, has long been the center of considerable debate. Even the question of the original solo instrument is contested. Preceding the 1738 autograph composing score of BWV 1052[1] is an earlier version of the same essential musical material in the hand of Carl Philipp Emanuel Bach, also in the form of a harpsichord concerto, dating from 1732–1734 and labeled BWV 1052a.[2] But preceding both of these are movements distributed among Cantatas 146 ("Wir müssen durch viel Trübsal in das Reich Gottes eingehen") and 188 ("Ich habe meine Zuversicht") in which the solo voice is played by obbligato organ. All three of these incarnations appear to have been created independently of one another.[3]

Notwithstanding that all surviving versions of the concerto's musical material give the solo voice to a keyboard instrument, many scholars point to the concerto's highly violinistic figurations (including extensive use of the actual open strings of the violin in bariolagelike passages), as well as the fact that the earliest two keyboard versions lacked an independent left-hand part, as evidence that the work originated as a now-lost violin concerto.[4] Christoph Wolff, however, has pointed out that this lack of an independent left-hand part is common among early keyboard concertos and that the violinistic figuration could be no more than *imitatio violistica*, a technique

1. *D-B Mus. ms. Bach P234.*

2. *D-B Mus. ms. Bach St350.*

3. See NBA KB VII/7:42; Dreyfus, *Bach and the Patterns of Invention*, 197.

4. See, for instance, Fischer, "Konzert für Violine d-moll," NBA KB VII/7:39; Breig, "Bachs Violinkonzert d-Moll," 32.

frequently found in German keyboard music of the seventeenth and early eighteenth centuries.[5]

But in fact the strongest evidence for the original solo instrument comes from consideration of the original range of the solo voice. The concerto in Emanuel Bach's hand appears to be an often-clumsy attempt to make a solo voice that exceeded the upper range of the harpsichord playable on that instrument. One example among many is shown in Example B.1.

Ex. B.1. C. P. E. Bach: BWV 1052a/1 (1732–34), mm. 139–44 and 152–57, harpsichord part

5. Wolff, "Sicilianos and Organ Recitals," 110.

BWV 1052 avoids such clumsiness by moving entire sections an octave lower. In the case of the material in Example B.1, for instance, he moves the entire passage beginning at measure 136 down an octave, thus avoiding the awkward leaps found in BWV 1052a (Ex. B.2), though it is telling that the autograph manuscript of BWV 1052 reveals that the passage in question was originally begun in the upper octave and only after three full measures did Bach scratch it out and write it in the lower octave (Image B.1).

Ex. B.2. J. S. Bach: BWV 1052/1 (1738), mm. 139–44, 152–57 (corresponding to Ex. B.1), harpsichord part

Image B.1.

a. Autograph ms. of BWV 1052/1, mm. 133b–38, showing evidence of octave transposition from m. 136

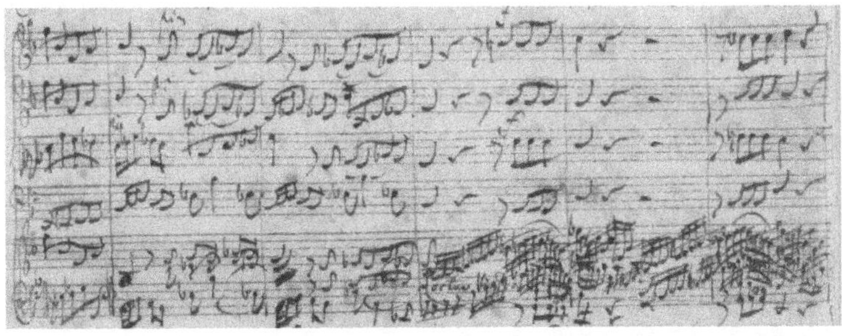

b. Ms. harpsichord part of BWV 1052a, mm. 132–136a, showing the apparently original register at m. 136

In Cantata 146, the organ presents the solo voice *in toto* an octave lower than the register in which it appears in the harpsichord concertos, thus enabling preservation of what appears to be the original contour without internal changes of register. But neither can this organ version plausibly be original, as the lower octave creates a number of contrapuntal infelicities, including an egregious string of parallel fifths in measures 142–45 of the sinfonia, which would have been fourths (that is, part of a chain of $^{6}_{3}$ chords rather than $^{5}_{3}$) had the solo voice been an octave higher (Ex. B.3).

Ex. B.3

a. BWV 146/1, mm. 142–45

b. BWV 146/1, m. 142: voicing condensed to show the striking series of parallel fifths

c. Placing the solo voice above the ripieno yields the $^{6}_{3}$ sonorities shown below

Also noteworthy is that, in this register, the solo voice doubles violin 1 at the unison rather than the octave when the two come together (Ex. B.4); and in the second movement, there are two points at which the solo voice crosses below all notated bass lines, which is most atypical of Bach's instrumental writing (Ex. B.5).

Ex. B.4. The organ doubles the uppermost ripieno voice an octave below in BWV 146/1

Ex. B.5. The solo organ part crosses below all notated bass lines in BWV 146/2

d.

Therefore it seems overwhelmingly likely from the sources that the original solo voice sat in the general register in which it appears in the harpsichord concertos but followed the contour given to the organ in BWV 146. This yields a range extending from *g*, the lowest open string of the violin, upward to *a*''', the highest note in Bach's surviving violin writing.[6] No other eighteenth-century instrument possesses this range, suggesting that the original solo instrument must indeed have been the violin.

An issue that comes closer to the heart of the work is its potentially disconcerting anomalies of style: its sheer size and gravity of tone, the withering intensity of its sometimes almost obsessive figurations, the jagged monophony that begins and ends the first two movements, and the *two* substantial capriccios (sometimes called cadenzas) found in each of the outer movements, which, as a pair, are without parallel in Bach's oeuvre.[7] Against those who have argued that such anomalies call Bach's authorship into ques-

6. This *a*''' is found in the "Laudamus Te" from the Mass in B Minor; the D-major sinfonia, BWV 1045; the opening chorus of "Erfreut euch, ihr Herzen," BWV 66 (played by ripieno violin 1 and 2 in unison, no less!); and the disputed A-major sonata, BWV Anh 153.

7. Mm. 153–71 in the first movement and m. 250 through the final ritornello in the third. The identity of these capriccios as such is especially evident in BWV 1052a, where they appear wholly unaccompanied, presumably reflecting the putative original (see this appendix n. 12).

tion, Laurence Dreyfus has contended that the concerto exhibits elements of structural design, particularly in the treatment of the ritornello, that to our knowledge are unique to Bach.[8]

Nonetheless, even at a structural level, anomalies remain. In particular, the tonal schemas of all three movements are uncommonly discursive, doubling back on themselves in ways not typical of the mature Bach. It is tempting to attribute this supposed lack of formal sophistication to the comparatively early genesis of the D-minor concerto. After all, the view endorsed by Wilfried Fischer, Werner Breig, and Christoph Wolff and generally accepted by Bach scholars is that Bach must have composed the putative *Urform* of the D-minor concerto between 1714 and 1717, after encountering Vivaldi's Opus 3 but before he left Weimar—in short, when Bach was no older than his early thirties, having only recently had his formative first encounter with Vivaldi's revolutionary ritornello treatment.[9] Even so, I maintain it would be mistaken to attribute to the D-minor concerto a youthful incoherence of form; although it *is* indeed a relatively early concerto, its form is not, on further analysis, incoherent after all.

The sequence of keys traversed in the first movement initially appears circuitous: D minor, A minor, F major, A minor, E minor, C major, G minor, D minor, B♭ major, D minor. But this appearance of circuitousness is only superficial. As shown in Figure B.1, the sequence comprises three groups of three, each of which consists of i, v, and III relative to the first key of each group. The latter are D minor (i), A minor (v), G minor (iv), and D minor (i).

8. Dreyfus, *Bach and the Patterns of Invention*, 202–8. Ralph Leavis has similarly argued that, despite the concerto's anomalies, Bach is the only conceivable composer ("Zur Frage der Authentizität von Bachs Violinkonzert d-Moll").

9. NBA VII/7:39; Breig, "Bachs Violinkonzert d-Moll," 32; Wolff, "Sicilianos and Organ Recitals," 109.

Fig. B.1. The tonal design of BWV 1052/1

Measure	Key	Deeper tonal relationships	
1	D minor	i	in D minor (i)
22	A minor	v	
40	F major	III	
56	A minor	i	in A minor (v)
70	E minor	v	
91	C major	III	
95	G minor	i	in G minor (iv)
116	D minor	v	
134	B♭ major	III	
146	D minor	i	in D minor (i)

The more fundamental shape that emerges from this apparently roundabout tonal scheme, therefore, is i—v—iv—i, the symmetrical pattern that is most typical of Bach's essential tonal trajectories.[10] The midpoint of this structure is articulated by rapid modulation between the most tonally disparate of any juxtaposed keys found in the movement, shifting the tonality from the chromatic/"sharp" side of D minor toward the enharmonic/"flat" side. This strongly articulated midpoint of the tonal structure is also the numerical midpoint of the whole movement: measure 95 of a total of 190.

The following Adagio consists of six repetitions of a jagged ostinato that, excluding its last note, is twelve measures long, the same number of measures as the ritornello of the third movement and twice the length of the six-measure ritornello of the first movement. Even though the tonal scheme of the Adagio is characteristically less intricate than that of an Allegro-type movement, it too is somewhat less economical than is typical of Bach. The beginning and ending of each statement of the ostinato articulates an important local tonality within the course of the movement. These are shown in Figure B.2.

10. This schema is symmetrical because v is one step to the chromatic or "sharp" side of the tonic, whereas iv is one step to the enharmonic or "flat" side within a fifths-based system as represented in Heinichen's *musicalischer Circul.* See my Chap. 4, Image 4.1 and n. 19.

Fig. B.2. Keys defining the beginning and end of the six ostinato statements in BWV 1052/2

Ostinato statement	Measures	Beginning and ending keys
1.	1–13	G minor—G minor
2.	14–26	G minor—C minor
	[27–29: three-measure modulation]	
3.	30–42	D minor—B♭ major
	[43–44: two-measure modulation]	
4.	45–57	C minor—C minor
	[58–60: two-measure modulation]	
5.	61–74 (elongated)	G minor—G minor
6.	75–87	G minor—G minor

If not for the strongly articulated motion to C minor at the end of the second ostinato statement, the tonal structure would be very typical, exhibiting a trajectory similar to that of the first movement, namely, tonic, motion toward the chromatic ("sharps") end of the spectrum, motion toward the enharmonic ("flats") end of the spectrum, and finally return to the tonic. But the motion to C minor at the end of the second ostinato statement (m. 26) seems decidedly premature, creating a kink in the otherwise seamless and systematic tonal scheme, especially given the stark modulation to D minor that follows. However, this tonal disjunction is accompanied by extreme melodic disjunction in all voices going into measure 28, which raises the question of whether the disjunction may actually be intentional. The melodic disjunction is as follows: the solo voice leaps an octave and a seventh to a strikingly dissonant minor ninth over the bass, the first and second ripieno violins both leap up a startling augmented octave, the viola leaps up a sixth (the only consonant interval in the ensemble, though still a notable space), and the bass leaps down a seventh (see Ex. B.6).

Ex. B.6. BWV 1052/2, 1052a/2, 146/2: melodic disjunction into m. 28

* Grace notes appear in BWV 1052 only

If the coinciding of the tonal and melodic disjunction is not accidental, it would suggest that the tonal design may be attributable to something other than a youthful lack of systematic thinking, even if Bach's specific intentions remain mysterious.

As in the first movement, the tonal scheme of the third movement seems quite discursive. It is common for Bach to recycle a single cadential formula throughout a ritornello movement, using it to articulate the main pillars of the tonal structure. This cadential formula is typically not heard twice in the same key, except in cases when the first and last statements both fall on the tonic. In the third movement of BWV 1052, however, the cadential formula appears in the succession of keys shown in Figure B.3.

Fig. B.3. Sequence of keys outlined by statements of the principal cadential formula in BWV 1052/3

Occurrence of the cadential formula	Measures	Key
1.	12–13	D minor
2.	40–41	A minor
3.	54–55	F major
4.	72–73	D minor
5.	83–84	D minor
6.	113–14	F major
7.	129–30	G minor
8.	158–59	B♭ major
9.	176–77	G minor
10.	186–87	G minor
11.	212–13	B♭ major
12.	292–93	D minor

Especially considering the sequence of musical ideas in the movement, to which I return shortly, it seems best to understand this tonal structure as consisting of two halves. The first half begins with a D minor cadence, and the following local tonics articulated by the cadential formula (a—F—d—d—F) outline a D-minor triad. The second half begins with the cadence on G minor, and the subsequent tonics (B♭—g—g—B♭—d) outline a G-minor triad. In terms of this function, the D-minor cadence at measures 12–13 and the G-minor cadence at measures 129–30 correspond. The remaining cadences, however, exhibit a retrograde pattern: a—F—d—d—F retrograded and transposed yields B♭—g—g—B♭—d. As if to emphasize this retrograde, the last cadence of the first group (F major, mm. 118–19) and the first cadence of the second group (B♭ major, mm. 158–59) are the only two cadences in the movement in which the cadential pattern is heard between solo and continuo alone, both times being present in the continuo while the solo voice has running sixteenth notes overtop. This yields the generally palindromic relationship shown in Figure B.4.

Fig. B.4. Symmetry in the key sequence outlined by the twelve statements of the cadential formula in BWV 1052/3

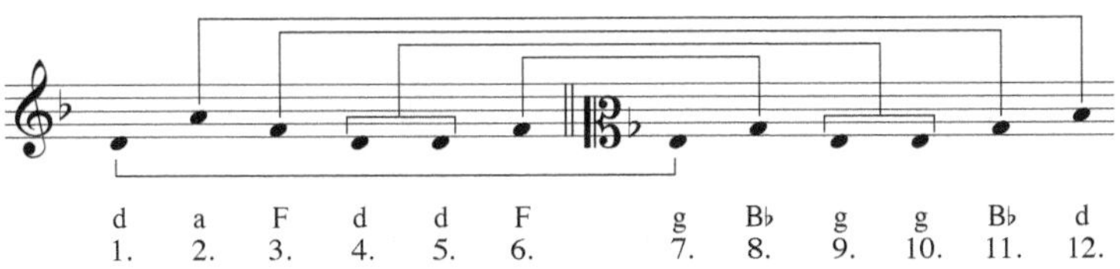

The concern for symmetry and balance evident in the tonal schemes of all three movements, despite their anomalies, is reflected also in the treatment of musical events at various levels of the structure of the concerto, perhaps most noticeably at the level of the concerto as a whole. There is of course a certain degree of symmetry inherent within the fast-slow-fast Vivaldian concerto model, and BWV 1052 appears to intentionally emphasize this symmetry in several ways. Foremost among these is the presence of a sizeable capriccio in both of the outer movements, which creates a strong sense of correspondence between them.

In fact, source material suggests that in the presumably original violin concerto the two capriccios bore greater similarity to each other than they ultimately would with the creation of BWV 1052 some twenty years later. All sources agree that the first capriccio ends with sustained arpeggiations driving into the following ritornello. However, none of the three surviving transcriptions of the third movement (BWV 188, 1052a, and 1052) agrees with another as to how the second capriccio is to end. BWV 1052 reintroduces the ripieno at measure 264, leading into a series of rapid written-out arpeggiations before a dramatic unaccompanied Adagio that ushers in the final ritornello (Ex. B.7a). The sinfonia of Cantata 188, of which the capriccio is the only portion that survives, introduces the continuo at measure 265 to reinforce a series of arpeggiations in the obbligato organ with a quarter note on the downbeat of every bar until the reintroduction of the ripieno at the final ritornello (Ex. B.7b). BWV 1052a leaves the ripieno fully silent until the reprise of the ritornello and simply gives the harpsichord a measurelong $^{\#4}_{2}$ chord over *g* (or third-inversion A-major dominant-7) at measure 265 with the instruction "ad libitum" (Ex. B.7c).

Ex. B.7. Three endings to the capriccio in the third movement of the D-minor concerto

a. BWV 1052/3

Ex. B.7 (cont.)

Ex. B.7 (cont.)

b. BWV 1052a/3 (C. P. E. Bach)

* The continuo rests for the duration of this excerpt

c. BWV 188/1

Ex. B.7 (cont.)

* The organ part is originally notated in C minor to accomodate the higher *Chorton* tuning of the organ.
** The manuscript continues to spell out the arpeggiation in sixteenth notes.
*** The manuscript indicates *Da capo* for the ensemble but spells out the organ part alone through m. 282. On these grounds, and on the assumption that the ripieno should double the organ at the unison, the NBA assumes that the uppermost voice of the ripieno would have sounded in the organ's lower octave at m. 282 and thus also in the opening ritornello, for which no notation survives (NBA I/25:270). But this is likely mistaken. The best explanation is that Bach continues writing the organ part into the second measure of the *DC* (unlike BWV 1052 and 1052/a) because there it diverges from the ripieno, returning to doubling the upper voice an octave lower, as in BWV 146/1.

It is attractive to consider that BWV 1052a likely represents the original form of the passage and that Bach wrote out two possible realizations of the *ad libitum* when creating BWV 188 and 1052, as necessitated by his adding some or all of the ripieno. And this may be so, but there are two counterconsiderations. First, leaving the low *g* of measure 265 unresolved at the entry of the ritornello, as in BWV 1052a, is not typical of Sebastian Bach and raises the question of whether the *ad libitum* of BWV 1052a might reflect not the source from which it was copied but Emanuel Bach's wish to improvise his own, perhaps more modern, cadenza.[11] Second, if Bach had conceived measure 265 as an *ad libitum* in the violin concerto, it is strange that when adapting it for organ as BWV 188 his written-out realiza-

11. It is worth noting that Emanuel Bach does appear to make several alterations to the concerto in various places, judging by concurrences among other surviving versions, and some of these appear to be in the interest of modernization. One example is his eliminating the lowered second scale degrees with their intimations of the Phrygian mode in mm. 62–63 and mm. 70–71 of the first movement.

tion should be both so regular (simply a series of arpeggios) and so much less idiomatic for the organ than for the violin. This seems to suggest that the original concerto might likely have contained a set of arpeggiations of which those in BWV 188 are an approximation (Ex. B.8).

Ex. B.8. Arpeggiations resembling what might have concluded the third-movement capriccio in the lost D-minor violin concerto, derived from BWV 188/1

If this were so, it would mean that both capriccios would originally have concluded with a brilliant series of arpeggiated chords.

Moreover, it appears most likely from the sources that both capriccios were originally unaccompanied from their beginning through their concluding arpeggiation—that is, until the start of the next ritornello. The ripieno is treated thus in BWV 1052a, and although the cantata sources as well as BWV 1052 variously accompany the latter portion of each capriccio, discrepancies between these accompaniments suggest that none had any precedent in the source from which the transcriptions were made.[12] This means that the capriccios would originally have been starker and still more imposing than they would become in BWV 1052—and if starker, then more anomalous; and if jointly more anomalous, then all the more strongly corresponding to one another in the listener's mind, heightening the sense of correspondence between the outer movements.

But this, of course, begs the question of why Bach would subsequently diminish the starkness of the capriccios in the cantatas and, later, in BWV

12. See NBA KB VII/7:48, 57. Tellingly, in the composing score of BWV 1052, the monophonic ritornello at m. 172 in the first movement originally began with *d'* or *d* in all voices, but in order to accommodate voice-leading considerations raised by the apparently newly composed accompaniment of the previous measures, the first note of the viola is changed to *f*.

1052 by adding ripieno accompaniment prior to the ritornello. It is impossible to give a definitive answer, but there are various plausible reasons, including the practical and the mundane. Perhaps he initially wanted to avoid too extensive a capriccio within the genre of the church cantata. Perhaps, given the static volume of the organ, he wanted to reinforce the approach to the ritornello with an increase of intensity (which seems to be a likely impetus in adding continuo at m. 265 in the sinfonia of Cantata 188).

In any case, what is especially interesting is that the alterations made to the two capriccios in BWV 1052 are done in such a way that they correspond to each other, preserving or perhaps even heightening the connection between them. Whether by accident or by design, the first capriccio is structured according to the Golden Section,[13] which is articulated by changes of texture in the solo voice. The bariolage with which the capriccio opens actually begins earlier at measure 146. The point where the texture changes, at the downbeat of measure 162, marks the Golden Section of the segment between measure 162 and the end of the capriccio at measure 171. There is one other change of texture between measures 162 and 171, however, and that is where the arpeggiation begins at measure 166, which is the negative Golden Section of the latter segment. Whatever Bach's impetus for adding the ripieno, how he treats it reinforces the proportions already inherent in the structure of the solo voice: in both BWV 146 and 1052 the ripieno enters at measure 162 and then changes texture at measure 166, as seen in Example B.9.

13. See Chap. 2 n. 3.

Ex. B.9. BWV 146/1: Texture changes in the capriccio

* Lacking winds, BWV 1052 creates this antiphonal effect between continuo and upper strings.
** BWV 1052 provides written-out arpeggiations incorporating acciacatura-like dissonances. However, the chords given in BWV 146/1, when transposed up an octave to the original register, are typical of arpeggiated triple-stops in virtuosic violin writing. The ripieno accompaniment is similar in texture to that of BWV 1052/1, but differences in voicing and even harmony (m. 168, beat 3) suggest they do not derive from a common source; that is, these arpeggiations would likely have been unaccompanied originally.

It is all the more interesting, then, that the changes made in BWV 1052 to the capriccio of the third movement seem calculated to produce proportions similar to those of the first movement. The alteration of the end of the third-movement capriccio makes it twenty-four measures long, rather than sixteen measures in BWV 1052a or thirty-one measures in BWV 188. As a result of this new length, the change of texture at measure 265 falls at the Golden Section of the entire capriccio, and the entry of the full ripieno at this point underscores the proportion, exactly as in the first movement (Ex. B.7a).

But the capriccios are not the only pair of musical features creating a sense of correlation between the outer movements. There are four other pairs of events shared in remarkably similar form between the two outer movements, and these five events occur in the same order in both. The first of these, shown in Example B.10, is the pair of bariolage passages occurring at measure 62 of the first movement and measure 84 of the third.

Ex. B.10

a. BWV 1052R/1, mm. 62–75

Solo violin (reconstructed*)

* Reconstructed violin line drawn from my forthcoming edition (PRB Productions). I cite a reconstructed violin line rather than the any of the surviving keyboard sources because an important part of the correlation between this passage and mm. 84–106 in the third movement is its use of the open strings of a violin. For consistency, and because it represents what can be ascertained of the earliest form of the concerto, I will cite the reconstructed violin version in the following examples. I do so with the understanding that the musical features I am seeking to illustrate are amply evident in the keyboard sources from which the putative violin original is reconstructed.

Ex. B.10 (cont.)

b. BWV 1052R/3, mm. 84–106

Solo violin
(reconstructed)

* See BWV 1052a and the autograph of BWV 1052 prior to alteration.

Each passage makes extensive use of the violin's open strings before the initial idea appears transposed up a fifth. In the first movement, this transposition brings the local tonal center to the relatively distant key of E minor, which the parallel passage in the third movement notably makes a point of reaching, if only briefly, with still another upward fifth transposition (having initially begun in D minor, whereas the passage in the first movement began in A minor).

The second pair of events (Ex. B.11) begins at measure 95 in the first movement and measure 130 in the third.

Ex. B.11

a. BWV 1052R/1, mm. 95–103

b. BWV 1052R/3, mm. 130–43

Both passages are in G minor and consist of repetitions of gestural "cells" comprising steady sixteenth notes that are of two beats' duration in the first movement and three in the third. In each episode, the harmony changes after every two iterations of the gestural cell, unfolding a nearly identical chord progression in both passages.

The third correspondence (Ex. B.12), beginning at measure 113 in the first movement and 187 in the third, is a pair of events in D minor consisting of a stepwise melodic descent from scale degree $\hat{6}$ over a fifth-based harmonic progression whose harmonic rhythm, once again, moves regularly at the half note in the first movement and at the dotted half in the third.

Ex. B.12

a. BWV 1052R/1, mm. 113–16

* In BWV 1052, the second half of this measure contains E♮s, heightening the similarity with the corresponding section in the third movement.

b. BWV 1052R/3, mm. 187–93

In the first movement, it is immediately followed by a variation of sorts in measures 118–21, where the stepwise descent, now a Phrygian tetrachord, occurs in the bass at the same rate as it did in the treble five measures earlier.

The fourth correspondence is the weakest to the ear but not negligible; it is a large-scale anabasis and catabasis pattern, beginning at measure 135 in the first movement and 193 in the third, in which the anabasis consists of twenty-four beats in each case (6 x 4 in the first movement and 8 x 3 in the third) and the catabasis of sixteen and eighteen beats respectively, accompanied by ripieno figurations of increasing intensity. And of course the fifth pair of corresponding events consists of the two capriccios.

Within individual movements, there is attention to symmetry and balance similar to what characterizes the whole concerto. In the first movement, as noted above, the numerical midpoint is strongly articulated by virtue of being the midpoint of the tonal structure; most musical events occurring on one side of this midpoint have a parallel on the other. In the second movement, the six statements of the ostinato are ordered so as to form a chiasm as shown in Figure B.5. From another perspective, the keys on which these iterations of the ostinato begin form a simple chiasm, shown in Figure B.6.

Fig. B.5. BWV 1052/2: structure of ostinato statements according to texture

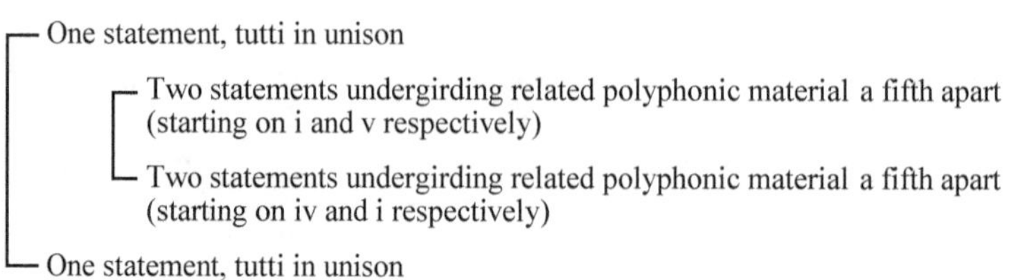

Fig. B.6. BWV 1052/2: structure of ostinato statements according to key

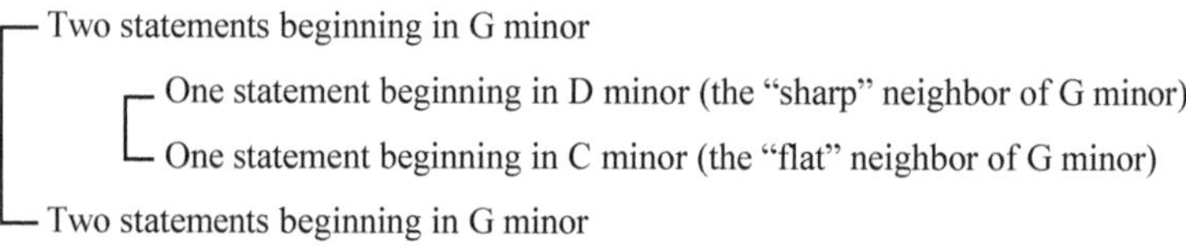

The third movement is a chiastic structure from start to finish, one of the most detailed and elegant in the literature (Fig. B.7).

Fig. B.7. Chiastic structure of BWV 1052/3

A: m. 1: ritornello

B: m. 13: solo episode that is recalled an octave higher in mm. 229–34

C: m. 29: ritornello

D: m. 41: ascending variant of material that opened the first ritornello, beginning in A minor (one flat less than D minor) and modulating back toward D minor

E: m. 45: solo passage introducing and developing a motif (m. 46) that will be reiterated in mm. 116, 118, and 209–11, followed by a major-mode statement of the principal cadential motif

F: m. 55: tutti imitation on the first two measures of the ritornello

m. 61: ritornello with treble and bass inverted

m. 73: deceptive cadence followed by a viola solo elaborating on the ritornello

[omitted—m. 84: solo episode featuring extensive bariolage subsequently transposed at the fifth]

G: m. 113: cadential motif in bass in F

E"/F": m. 114: recollection of material from m. 55 interspersed with the motif introduced at m. 46 and followed (as in mm. 61 and 165) by a ritornello statement, albeit without inversion of treble and bass

[omitted—m. 130: solo episode in G minor]

G: m. 158: cadential motif in bass in B-flat

F': m. 159: tutti imitation on first two measures of the ritornello, corresponding to m. 55

m. 165: ritornello with treble and bass inverted, corresponding to m. 61

m. 177: deceptive cadence followed by a continuo solo, corresponding to the viola solo at m. 73

[omitted—m. 187: solo with ripieno outlining circle-of-fifths progression under the melodic descent $\hat{6}$, $\hat{5}$, $\hat{4}$, $\hat{3}$]

[omitted—m. 193: large-scale anabasis-catabasis pattern with steady harmonic motion at the dotted half note and increasingly intense ripieno accompaniment]

E': m. 209: variant of the motif introduced at m. 45 followed by a major-mode statement of the movement's principal cadential motif

D': m. 213: variant of material that opened the first ritornello, heard in ascending and descending forms, beginning in B-flat major (one flat more than D minor) and modulating toward D minor

C': m. 224: ritornello (interrupted)

B': m. 229: solo episode whose first six measures correspond to mm. 18–23 but an octave higher

[omitted—large capriccio at m. 250 that precedes the final ritornello]

A': reprise of the opening ritornello (*Da capo*)

The only events notably absent from this structure of symmetrical pairing are precisely the five events mentioned above that have strong parallels in the first movement. In other words, the imperfections of the third movement's structure are "redeemed" to create a greater and more comprehensive perfection than if the form had been perfect to begin with.[14]

Although redemption is indeed pervasive as a theological idea in Bach's context, it should not be assumed that such "redemptive" features in Bach's music must have a primarily theological motivation. At the same time, it is most likely that Bach would at least have consciously acknowledged a parallel with theology[15]; and even if, as previously noted, there is insufficient basis to claim that Bach need not necessarily have considered every chiastic structure to have a dimension of Christological representation, what can safely be said is that chiastic structures need not imply a theological program, theme, or "deeper meaning" in the piece within which they occur. At the same time, because such devices as chiasms *may* be used as signifiers, multiple concurrences of potential signifiers in such a way as to coherently parallel a set of related theological ideas can legitimately raise the question of whether these may most plausibly result from the composer's intention rather than mere accident. In the present case, for instance, "redemptive" imagery within a chiastic structure (which can serve as symbol of Christ and/or the cross) is most natural from the standpoint of theological design; and had Bach intended to represent the idea that the cross of Christ effects a redemption that is greater and more perfect than if original sin had never occurred, he could scarcely have used more appropriate or specific means.[16]

If an allusion to the Christian redemptive narrative were intended here, it could lend a further degree of significance to another, smaller "redemptive" compositional decision within the same structural chiasm. When the cadential gesture appears in the full ensemble it is typically accompanied by two repetitions of a figure consisting of an eighth note followed by two sixteenths, occurring on the first and second beats of the measure preceding the cadence (Ex. B.13a). At measure 54, it is feasible for this figure to occur only on the second beat within the essential voice leading that Bach evidently desired (Ex. B.13b). Interestingly, at measure 186, on the other side of

14. Dreyfus describes essentially the same mode of thinking in connection with Bach's compensating for partially unsuccessful compositional operations in parallel passages within a given piece, thereby using the open-endedness resulting from imperfection as a unique opportunity for unification, once again creating a greater perfection than if the original operation had succeeded fully and resulted in a "closed" passage. See Dreyfus, *Bach and the Patterns of Invention*, 19–20.

15. See the second-to-last paragraph of Chap. 2.

16. See Chap. 6 n. 137.

the chiasm, Bach places this rhythm on the first beat alone (Ex. B.13c), such that the rhythm of the two imperfect statements combined would create a perfect iteration.

Ex. B.13

a. First statement of the cadential motif in BWV 1052(R)/3

b. BWV 1052(R)/3, mm. 54–55

c. BWV 1052(R)/3, mm. 186–87, ripieno following BWV 1052

His reason for doing so might well be to "redeem" the first imperfection, since there is no contrapuntal reason that the rhythmic gesture of an eighth and two sixteenth notes should not occur on the second beat of measure 186 as well as the first; indeed, it does in Emanuel Bach's transcription (BWV 1052a). If Sebastian Bach were considering theological applications in connection with these "redemptive" compositional decisions, the present example would appear to be an elegant representation of reconciliation through the cross, which is an important idea in both Colossians and Ephesians.[17]

In the first movement, there is another prominent example of musical interfacing involving chiastic structure that creates a coherent and relevant theological parallel. Given the attention to symmetry and balance evident throughout the concerto, it is likely not accidental that the opening gesture of the concerto is tonally chiastic and the three-note-gesture that follows, while too short to be technically chiastic, is likewise symmetrcial (Ex. B.14).

Ex. B.14. Melodic symmetry in the headmotif of BWV 1052/1

But as atypical as the degree of symmetry found throughout the concerto is, still more striking and anomalous are several elements throughout the work that suggest the idea of singularity. Chief among these are the substantial unaccompanied capriccios found in both outer movements, together with the unusual occurrence of several small cadenzas,[18] which suggest instrumental singularity: one *solo* voice. Melodic singularity figures prominently in the concerto by virtue of extensive use of monophony. The latter accounts for the entirety of the opening and closing statements of both the first-movement ritornello and the second-movement ostinato as well as the first measure of the third-movement ritornello, which remains monophonic in most of its reiterations throughout the movement. (Might it be more than coincidence that these intimations of singularity occur in a work whose key signature contains a single flat?)

Interestingly, the tonally chiastic gesture that opens the concerto is also monophonic; that is, it unites the prominent ideas of chiasm and singularity. This, too, would be a most natural pairing for a composer thinking theologically,[19] as many theological ideas and statements prominent within Bach's tradition center on the singularity or "*solo*-ness" of Christ as

17. See Col 1:20; Eph 2:14–16.

18. Movement 1, mm. 109–12; movement 2, m. 74.

19. That Bach would have understood melodic chiasm (not merely larger-scale structural chiasm) as a potential Christological referent is evident from the chiastic subject of the concluding fugue of the *Actus Tragicus* (discussed in Chap. 2), whose composition in Mühlhausen (and therefore in 1707–1708) predates Bach's 1713 encounter with Vivaldi's Op. 3 that must have preceded the composition of the D-minor concerto in its earliest form.

Lord and savior through the cross. These include Luther's *theologia crucis*, expressed succinctly in the assertion that "the cross alone [*CRUX sola*] is our theology,"[20] as well as the already-noted lines "Quoniam tu solus Sanctus, tu solus Dominus, tu solus Altissimus, Jesu Christe"[21] from the Latin Gloria preserved in the Lutheran tradition.[22] Later, conscious adherents of Lutheran and Reformed theology would find the phrase *solus Christus* to be a satisfying summation of a substantial aspect of distinctive Reformation thought. Historically, Luther's emphasis on the cross of Christ alone was directed against the variously manifested idea that the cross is potent but not solely sufficient for salvation, requiring supplementation, for example, in the form of human good works. By contrast, Luther and other Reformers argue repeatedly and emphatically that human good works are an effect of salvation and not to be confused with its cause, which is the perfect sufficiency of Christ through his finished work on the cross. It might therefore not be accidental that the "*X* alone" imagery that opens the D-minor concerto occurs within a ritornello of six measures, recalling the historical associations of the number 6 with perfection and completeness.[23]

To the extent that Christological representation is intended in any of the compositional decisions cited above, it could lend a theological dimension to a structural feature of the Adagio that fascinatingly recurs, albeit with slightly different trappings, in the Adagio of the first Brandenburg concerto (which I explore shortly). The structural feature in question is the previously noted tonal disjunction at the end of the second of six statements of the Adagio's pervasive ostinato, which coincides with striking melodic disjunction in each voice of the ensemble (as seen in Ex. B.6). Since this tonal and melodic rift occurs after two of six statements of the ostinato, it can be understood as representatively cutting off one-third of the movement's "perfect" sixfold structure. Within the world of concepts in which Bach operated, the idea of cutting off one-third—especially one-third of a symbolically perfect entity—suggests nothing more strongly than the passion of Christ; and in light of the strong plausibility of Christological elements elsewhere in the concerto, it is appropriate to consider the possibility of signification in the present case.

In the biblical accounts of Jesus' crucifixion, only one of his seven statements from the cross is recorded in more than one gospel, and that is

20. *WA* 5:176; see 1 Cor 1:23, 2:2.

21. "For you alone are holy, you alone are Lord, you alone are most high, Jesus Christ." In Christian theology, the exaltation of Christ is closely tied to his redeeming work on the cross; see Phil 2:8–9; Matt 28:18; John 10:17; Acts 2:31–33.

22. See also John 14:6; Acts 4:12; Gal 6:14; 1 Tim 2:5.

23. See Chap. 4.

"Eli, eli, lama sabachthani?" which the gospels of Matthew and Mark cite and immediately follow with the translation "My God, my God, why have you forsaken me?"[24] Jesus' question is a direct reference to the opening line of Psalm 22 (אלי אלי למה עזבתני), whose verb is *asav* (עזב) or "forsake." Curiously, Jesus' statement "Eli, eli lama sabachthani" implies not *asav* but *zabach* (זבח), meaning "sacrifice." Jesus' statement, as recorded, might more literally be translated, "My God, my God, why have you made a sacrifice of me?" It seems the gospel writers chose to translate the phrase with the Greek word *enkatelipes* (ἐγκατέλιπες), which means "forsaken," in order to more clearly establish the correlation to Psalm 22. But this raises the theological question of how exactly Jesus' cry is to be understood. Luther's understanding appears quite clear. In his translation of the Bible he changes "sabachthani" (σαβαχθάνι) in the passion accounts of both Matthew and Mark to "asabthani," connecting it to the verb *asav* in order to agree with Psalm 22. In other words, Luther clearly hears Jesus' cry as expressing the imponderable rejection of God by God as Jesus, God the Son, is "cut off out of the land of the living."[25] Had Bach intended the cutting-off of one-third of the movement's "perfect" sixfold structure to represent the cutting-off of one of three persons of the Godhead as Christ died on the cross, he could scarcely have placed a more piercingly dissonant sonority at the very point of this cutting-off than the unprepared minor-ninth chord that appears there. And if Bach had intended to represent the sole foundation of his faith, it is at least an appropriate coincidence that this cutting-off is framed in the bass, the foundation of the musical texture, by the notes *g–A*, that is, in French nomenclature *sol–la*.[26]

If indeed the structure of the Adagio were designed to symbolize the cutting-off of Christ on the cross, it might not be accidental that this imagery occurs in the middlemost of three movements, the outer two of which exhibit an uncommon degree of correlation that creates a sense of symmetry among the three movements. In other words, if the tonal scheme of the second movement should indeed represent the passion of Christ, then this depiction of this most central event in Christian (and especially Lutheran)

24. Matt 27:46; Mark 15:34.

25. Isa 53:8 (in the LB, "aus dem Lande der Lebendigen weggerissen"). Luther, in keeping with historic Christianity, understands the entire chapter as a direct prophesy of Christ. For instance, he titles a lecture on this chapter "De Christi passione et glorificatione" ("On Christ's passion and glorification"). *WA* 25:325–39.

26. Christ is several times likened to a foundation or cornerstone in Biblical literature (see Acts 4:11; Eph 2:20; 1 Pet 2:6; also Matt 7:24 and Luke 6:48). The connection of "*sol-la*" (sola) with Christ the cornerstone at the moment of the gesture recalling the "cutting off" of Christ is an association that is very likely accidental to the compositional process but nonetheless one Bach might conceivably have recognized.

theology would lie at the heart of the symmetrical schema of the concerto as a whole, just as in traditional literary practice the conceptual heart of the message being conveyed through chiastic structure is placed at the heart of the structural symmetry. An especially relevant literary example is the opening of the Gospel of John, whose structure in the original Greek is retained in Luther's German translation, shown in Figure B.8.[27]

Fig. B.8. Structure of John 1:1–2 as preserved in Luther's translation

A (unspoken—i.e. before "dem Anfang" ["the beginning"]: **Gott** [God])

B **Jm anfang**

C war das **Wort/**

D vnd das **wort**

E war bey **Gott/**

E' vnd **Gott** war

D' das **Wort.**

C' **Das selbige** war

B' **im anfang**

A' bey **Gott.**

The essence of this opening statement is the striking claim of the divinity of the Word who "became flesh and tabernacled among us," and it is precisely this that lies at the heart of the chiastic structure. And of course the final fugue of the *Actus Tragicus* demonstrates Bach's awareness of this practice, as he sets the text "durch Jesum Christum, Amen" so that the first syllable of "Christum"—where the letter *X* would occur in Greek—falls at the midpoint of the fugue subject's melodic chiasm (see Ex. 2.2).

In any case, the tonal cutting-off of one-third of the movement seems likely to have had some significance in Bach's mind, as it is reproduced in its essentials in the second movement of the first Brandenburg concerto (BWV 1046), a movement with which the Adagio of the D-minor concerto shares

27. Johannes (John) 1:1–2, LB. "In the beginning was the Word [*Logos*, λόγος], and the Word was with God, and God [nominative] was the Word [subject]. The same was in the beginning with God."

not only a tempo designation and time signature of $\frac{3}{4}$[28] but also a textural profile that makes extensive use of repeated eighth notes under slurs, which lends to each a sighing or sobbing quality.[29]

Brandenburg Concerto No. 1 in F Major, BWV 1046: II. Adagio

The Adagio of the first Brandenburg concerto consists of three cycles of similar material (mm. 1–11, 12–22, 23–33), each comprising eight measures of thematic dialogue in imitation between oboe 1 and piccolo violin followed by three measures in which the texture is turned upside down as the bass takes up the theme while the upper strings serve an accompanimental role. These three cycles of eleven (8 + 3) measures are followed by a short coda that concludes the movement. After the first of the three eleven-measure cycles, there is a striking modulation. What sounds like an A♭ in the bass is reinterpreted as a G#, and what in modern formulation would be understood by the ear as vii$^{\circ}{}^{4}_{\#2}$ in C minor becomes vii°7 in A minor. The startling tonal break resulting from this enharmonic respelling[30] comes, as in BWV 1052, after exactly one-third of the essential structure of the movement.

If this could be understood as the cutting-off of one third, as in BWV 1052, it is not the only feature of the movement that suggests such an idea. The concerto as a whole is scored for three choirs of instruments—horns, double reeds, and strings. In the second movement, however, one of these choirs, the horns, falls silent. Although this in itself is not particularly remarkable—brass instruments are commonly omitted from slow movements of concertos in which they are present—it is noteworthy that the autograph of BWV 1046,[31] unlike in the earlier version of the concerto (BWV

28. If Trinitarian symbolism were intended, the use of triple meter might itself have symbolic overtones.

29. Bach frequently uses such articulation in setting texts connected with lamentation or weeping. Examples include the opening chorus of "Weinen, Klagen, Sorgen, Zagen" ("Weeping, lamentation, trouble, apprehension"), which would later be adapted as the "Crucifixus" of the B-Minor Mass, as well as the final chorus of the St. Matthew Passion, "Wir setzen uns mit Tränen nieder" ("We sit down in tears").

30. Here I must make a clear distinction between two uses of the word *enharmonic*. Thus far, I have used it, according to Heinichen's practice, to refer to the "flats" end of the tonal spectrum. By "enharmonic respelling," however, I am referring to something fundamentally different: changing the actual or implied spelling of one pitch into another that would be played by the same note on a keyboard (in the present case, for instance, changing *G#* into *A♭*).

31. *D-B Am. B. 78.*

1046a/1071) as it survives in the 1760 copy by Christian Friedrich Penzel,[32] emphasizes the silence of the horns by including staves for them but leaving those staves empty.

The striking inclusion of these blank staves seems quite intentional, and since they serve no musical purpose, it could be that Bach intended them to have an extramusical meaning.[33] Had Bach intended to signify the passion of Christ, as the foregoing parallels with BWV 1052 might suggest, then the inclusion of blank staves for the horns could be more than simply a representative cutting-off of one-third; it could be understood as a theological statement on the fundamental integrity of the Trinity even in the face of the death of Christ. Just as the three choirs of instruments remain consistently represented on the page even when one is silent, so the Trinity remains intact even in the death of Christ on the cross; at no point does the Trinity become a dyad.[34]

Here it may perhaps be useful to take a step back and reflect on methodology. Such detailed theological correlations as what I have described above can, in isolation, legitimately raise the question of whether they may be coincidental and therefore mere interpolation. And certainly, as a matter of general principle, there is a degree of correspondence that can be attributed to coincidence. But if prominent musical features concur in unusual ways to create a rich parallel with a particular extramusical idea, it is reasonable to consider whether representing that idea may have been the intention of the composer.

There are three such concurring features that I wish to explore in connection with the possibility of Christological representation in the tonal break at measure 12. Together with the correlations already discussed, they contribute to a degree of parallel between unusual compositional features and a theology of the passion that, I propose, is less convincingly attributed to coincidence than to design. The first of these is the noteworthy treatment of the lamenting tetrachord, which is present in both the principal

32. *D-B Mus. ms. Bach P 1061.*

33. Michael Marissen makes a similar claim regarding the blank staves for the two violas da gamba in the second movement of the sixth Brandenburg concerto: "the conventionally privileged gambas would not merely be absent from the score; they would be, as it were, conspicuously absent." Marissen, *The Social and Religious Designs*, 132.

34. Luther regards the being of all three persons of the Trinity as essential to the very nature of the Godhead, stating that "each person [of the Trinity] represents the fullness of divinity, as if there were no other; and yet it is true that no person is alone divinity, as though the others were not" ("Ut quaelibet persona sit ipsa tota divinitas, ac si nulla esset alia. Et tamen verum est, Nullam personam esse solam, quasi alia non sit, divinitatem"). Doctoral disputation of Georg Major and Johannes Faber, theses IX and X, in *WA* 39 II:287.

theme and the accompanying bass line at the beginning of the movement (Ex. B.15).

Ex. B.15. The descending tetrachord in melody and bass in BWV 1046/2, mm. 1–8

* The piccolo violin is originally notated a minor third lower to accommodate its tuning a minor third above the violin proper.

What is interesting, though, is that, despite the similarity among the movement's three eight-measure thematic segments, it is only in the first—the one demarcated by the tonal break—that the tetrachord is especially prominent. In fact, the corresponding parts of the second and third sections are modified such that the descending tetrachord is substantially evaded, as if to emphasize the intentionality of the lamenting tetrachord within the section demarcated by the enharmonic rift and thus to emphasize the association of sorrow and woe with the "cut off" third.

Parenthetically, enharmonic respelling itself, which creates the tonal rift by which the sorrowing one-third of the movement is "cut off," has strong associations with anguish and sorrow. In Bach's day, enharmonic spelling was a rarely used device, and outside the genre of the keyboard fantasia[35] (which increasingly sought to generate its accustomed sense of spontaneity and surprise by pushing beyond the established extremes of key[36] and norms of modulation) it most commonly occurs in the context of vocal or programmatic music, in which it almost invariably fulfills a definite expressive or illustrative purpose, most commonly conveying extremes of suffering or woe.[37]

This topic would properly require a separate study, but several notable examples may briefly be cited. Within the works of Bach, the first recitative of Cantata 48,[38] dating from 1723, contains an enharmonic respelling in the vocal line precisely when the text, speaking of "pain" and "wretchedness" ("O Schmerz, o Elend . . .") reaches a high point of intensity on the word *Gift* ("poison") at measure 10.[39]

35. Examples from Bach's oeuvre that feature enharmonic reinterpretation include the "Chromatic" Fantasia and Fugue (BWV 903) and the "Great" G-minor Fantasia and Fugue for organ (BWV 542).

36. As late as 1711, Heinichen defines the scope of usable keys as being between B major ("extremum chromaticum") and B♭ minor ("extremum enharmonicum"). See my Chap. 3 n. 82. As observed in n. 30 of the present appendix, this terminology describes something entirely different from the "enharmonic respelling" that I am currently discussing.

37. A notable exception by Bach himself is the end of the first recitative of Cantata 121, where an enharmonic respelling that turns the tonality of the recitative from F# minor to C major (i.e., a tritone away) accompanies a description of the wonder of Christ's becoming incarnate in order to turn sinful man back to himself. Chafe notes that this association with transformation appears to be a common theme among Bach's few uses of enharmonic respelling in his vocal works. Chafe, *J. S. Bach's Johannine Theology*, 188.

38. The opening text of the cantata comes from Rom 7:24: "Ich elender Mensch, wer wird mich erlösen vom Leibe dieses Todes!" ("Wretched man that I am, who shall save me from the body of this death!")

39. The full text of the recitative is: "O Schmerz, o Elend, so mich trifft,/ Indem der Sünden Gift/ Bei mir in Brust und Adern wütet:/ Die Welt wird mir ein Siech- und Sterbehaus,/ Der Leib muß seine Plagen/ Bis zu dem Grabe mit sich tragen./ Allein die Seele fühlet den stärksten Gift,/ Damit sie angestecket;/Drum, wenn der Schmerz den Leib des Todes trifft,/ Wenn ihr der Kreuzkelch bitter schmecket,/ So treibt er ihr

A second striking example is from the Mass in B Minor, in the dissonant and eerily unstable Adagio that introduces the text "Et expecto resurrectionem mortuorum." In the midst of this passage, which evokes not the longed-for resurrection but rather the death-ravaged state in which we long for it, there is a moment at which soprano 1 is heard alone, confessing the hope of resurrection. After one measure, the arrival note, *c"*, is transformed into *b#'*, suggesting the hope of transformation amid the present reality of sorrow and death.

Although not strictly a texted composition, Bach's early[40] organ setting of the chorale "Durch Adams Fall" (BWV 637) necessarily recalls the chorale's text. In Bach's serpentine setting, a deceptive respelling of D# to E♭ occurs in the pedals precisely at the moment where the first stanza of text describes Eve being catastrophically deceived by the serpent (m. 10 into 11).[41]

A final example from Bach, an enharmonic respelling with a single intermediary tone between the equivalent pitches, is found in the chorale "Wenn ich einmal soll scheiden" ("When I one day must depart") from the St. Matthew Passion. At the beginning of the word *allerbängsten*, describing the utmost pains of death from which Jesus is entreated to deliver the soul, what had previously sounded as a *d#* in the bass two notes prior reappears as an *e♭*.

Outside the Bach oeuvre, two notable examples of enharmonic respellings, both associated with sorrow, occur in the recitative "Thy rebuke hath broken his heart" from Handel's *Messiah*[42] and in the musical depiction of the tears of the village boy ("Il pianto del villanello") in the first movement of "Summer" from Vivaldi's "Four Seasons."[43]

Returning to the Adagio of the first Brandenburg concerto, a second musical consideration relating to the possibility of Christological symbolism in the tonal break at measure 12 is the interval that frames the break,

---

ein brünstig Seufzen aus." ("O pain, O wretchedness that afflicts me/ on account of the poison of sin/ raging in my breast:/ the world becomes to me a house of plague and death:/ the body must carry her ailments/ with her even to the grave./ [But] the soul alone feels the strongest poison,/ with which she is infected/ so that, when the pain comes to the body of death,/ when she tastes the bitter cup of the cross/ it drives out from her a burning sigh.")

40. See Stinson, "The Compositional History of Bach's *Orgelbüchlein* Reconsidered," 54.

41. "Darein die Schlang Eva bezwang . . ."

42. M. 6.

43. Mm. 122–23.

namely, the minor third from C to A.[44] The fact that the corresponding tonal rift in BWV 1052 is articulated by the same interval, moving from a C-minor chord in measure 27 to an A-dominant minor-9 chord at measure 28, suggests the interval itself might have had some significance to Bach in the context of the tonal rift. Had Christological symbolism been on Bach's mind, it is plausible (given its recurrence in both concertos) that the interval of a minor third or *kleine terz* could obliquely refer to the idea that one person of the Trinity—namely, Christ—has become "small" (*klein*) in the sense of submitting himself to the will of the Father,[45] assuming a mere human frame, taking on the role of a servant,[46] and submitting himself even to death.[47] The analogy is not far removed from Werckmeister's 1687 allegorical interpretations of the harmonic series cited in Chapter 1. In one of these interpretations he differentiates the thirds by quality, likening the major third to the sun and the minor third to the moon.[48] In another he likens the fourth, fifth, and sixth partials of the series to the Trinity because they form a triad, three sonorities in one.[49] A similar line of reasoning might also underlie Luther's considering the solmization syllables *re*, *mi*, *fa* to represent the Trinity[50]; whereas *re* to *mi* is a whole tone, *fa* is only a semitone above *mi*, possibly representing the person of the Trinity who made himself small, especially as the relationship of *fa* to *re* is a minor third.

Third, to the extent that the tonal break after the first of the movement's three cycles of eleven measures could be understood to parallel the "cutting off" of one person of the triune Godhead, the threefold structure of the movement would itself invite associations with the Trinity. Thus it is interesting that the relationships among the three eleven-measure sections that constitute the movement's essential structure neatly parallel the three definitive aspects of the Trinity that the Lutheran Augsburg Confession sees fit to address and defend in its very first article:[51] that God is one in his

44. That is, the chord that is enharmonically reinterpreted sounds at first as though it should function in C minor but actually functions in A minor.

45. Matt 26:39; John 6:38.

46. Matt 20:28; John 13:4–16.

47. John 10:17–18; Phil 2:6–8.

48. Werckmeister, *Musicae Mathematicae*, 143 (appendix, chap. 2). See my Table 1.1 (day/octave IV).

49. Ibid., 147 (appendix, chap. 5). See my Table 1.2 (octave III). On Joachim Burmeister's expression of the same idea in 1599, see my Chap. 6 n. 24.

50. *WA TR*, no. 815; see Leaver, *Luther's Liturgical Music*, 98–99.

51. "Erstlich wird einträchtiglich gelehrt und gehalten . . . , daß ein einig göttlich Wesen sei, welches gennant wird und warhaftiglich ist Gott, und sind doch drei Personen in demselben einigen göttlichen Wesen, gleich gewaltig, gleich ewig . . ." ("Firstly

triunity, that he is three in his unity, and that the three persons of the Godhead are coequal. As a student of theology, Bach would certainly have been keenly aware of the importance of this threefold formulation of Trinitarian belief in articulating the orthodox position against the heresies of tritheism, Monarchianism, and Arianism respectively.

Specifically, the fact that all three essential units of the Adagio's structure are of the same musical "nature" (consisting of eight measures in which the opening theme is elaborated in imitation between oboe 1 and piccolo violin followed by three measures in which the theme appears in the bass) parallels the belief in the essential unity of the triune God, in contrast to the tritheist position holding that there are three distinct divinities. Second, although these three sections of the Adagio share a common musical "nature," they are nonetheless not identical (nor, for that matter, mere transpositions of each other), which parallels the belief that Father, Son, and Holy Spirit, though unified in essence, are indeed distinct persons. This is in contrast to the Monarchian teaching that Father, Son, and Holy Spirit are not three persons but rather three forms that the one divinity assumes at different times. And finally, the fact that all three musical sections are of equal size—an unusual eleven measures in length—parallels the belief that Father, Son, and Holy Spirit are coequal in greatness ("gleich gewaltig"), in contrast to the Arian position that the Son is inferior to the Father.

Beyond the "triune" structure of the movement and the tonal rift that cuts off one-third of the structure from the rest, there is another element of the musical fabric that contains striking and unusual musical imagery uncannily paralleling Christian theology. In all three of the eleven-measure sections, the theme is presented in imitative dialogue between oboe 1 and piccolo violin, recalling overtly Christological imagery in Cantata 182 and other works, to which I return shortly. This theme subsequently appears "in the depths"—in the bass line—for an unusual three measures, by virtue of which the structure of the entire ensemble becomes inverted; the lowly bass, which has been providing the plainest of accompaniments, is now "exalted" by being given the melody, while the soloistic upper voices are humbled to providing scant accompaniment. Parallel to this, Christ's spending three days "in the depths of the earth"[52] is the archetype of the motif of inversion that permeates the writings of the New Testament.

---

it will be held and taught with one accord that there is one divine Being, who is called and verily is God, and there are three persons in this same unified divine Being, equally great, equally eternal . . .") It is noteworthy that Bach personally owned, or would come to own, August Pfeiffer's detailed commentary on the Augsburg Confession, *Der wohlbewährte Evangelische Aug-Apfel.*

52. Matt 12:40. The importance of the three days is underscored by the connection

Because the force of this parallel derives considerably from the premise that the theme of the movement has Christ-focused theological associations, I now turn my attention to describing these theological associations in greater detail. In his vocal music, Bach sometimes represents the dual-natured Christ by distributing essentially the same material between a wind instrument and a violin, either by imitation, as in the first Brandenburg concerto, or by unison. Perhaps the most compelling example is the sinfonia to the Palm Sunday cantata "Himmelskönig, sei willkommen," BWV 182 (1714), from whose first moments it is clear that Bach is creating a sound-picture. The steady, plodding pizzicatos of the strings evoke the steady clicking of the donkey's hooves as Jesus rides into Jerusalem. Sitting atop these pizzicatos, as it were, is a regal theme in dotted rhythms, fitting for the heavenly king (*Himmelskönig*) who rides on the trotting donkey. However, this single kingly rider is represented not by one instrumental line but by two, recorder and violin, in imitative dialogue.[53] A second striking example is the opening chorus of "Herr Christ, der ein'ge Gottessohn" ("Lord Christ, the only Son of God"), BWV 96, which describes Christ as the Morningstar whose brilliance outshines other stars.[54] Shining out above the typical festive texture of SATB choir, strings, oboes, and continuo is a piccolo flute line in running sixteenths that is to be doubled at the octave by a piccolo violin. A third example is the soprano aria "Mein gläubiges Herze" ("My faithful heart") from the Whit Monday cantata "Also hat Gott die Welt geliebt," BWV 68, which, despite its association with Pentecost, focuses notably on Christ's incarnation. In this aria, only an obbligato piccolo cello and basso continuo accompany the solo soprano; but after the soprano concludes with the words "dein Jesus ist da!" ("your Jesus is here!"), a violin and oboe suddenly enter and, for a striking one-third of the movement, engage in an imitative instrumental sonatina with the piccolo cello, whose contrasting lower register and association with the "faithful heart" invite the passage to be heard as depicting the union of the believer with Christ.

In all of these cases, the choice of violin and a wind instrument in connection with the dual-natured Christ appears not to be arbitrary. As noted in connection with the B-minor solo violin partia, Bach would certainly

---

with Jonah's spending three days and three nights in the belly of the fish.

53. A similar representation of the dual-natured Christ could possibly be intended in the first statement of the imitative head motif of the duet "Et in unum Dominum Jesum Christum" from the B-Minor Mass, in which the two oboes play in unison for the only time in the movement, jointly leading the two-part imitation (together with violin 1) whose following voice consists of violin 2 alone.

54. "Er ist der Morgensterne, sein'n Glanz streckt er so ferne vor andern Sternen klar."

have been familiar with the profound relationship between the concepts of "wind," "breath," and "spirit" in Biblical literature, as the three are expressed by a single word in both Hebrew and Greek: *ruach* (רוח) in Hebrew, *pneuma* (πνεῦμα) in Greek. It seems scarcely accidental, then, that the instrumental ensemble accompanying the "Et in Spiritum sanctum" from the Mass in B Minor, the only movement of Bach's only setting of the Nicene Creed to pertain directly to the Holy Spirit, is scored for two oboes d'amore and continuo. In other words, the only instruments that Bach explicitly specifies are wind instruments.[55]

Nor does Bach's incorporation of an obbligato flute in the "Domine Deus" of the B-Minor Mass seem haphazard. A duet for soprano and tenor, it sets three segments of text:

> "Domine Deus, Rex coelestis, Deus Pater omnipotens,"
>
> "Domine Fili unigenite Jesu Christe,"
>
> "Domine Deus, Agnus Dei, Filius Patris."

The movement is divided into two portions at exactly the Golden Section,[56] that is, after fifty-nine measures out of the duet's total of ninety-five. Only in the second, shorter segment do the voices sing the same text, and then only the third portion of the text ("Domine Deus, Aguns Dei, Filius Patris"). In the first and larger portion of the aria, the first two segments of text are distributed between the two solo voices in such a way that both are always heard simultaneously, emphasizing the unity of Father and Son within the Godhead. But to a Trinitarian such as Bach, no representation of the Godhead would be complete without a reference to the Holy Spirit; however, as the portion of the text set in this duet makes no mention of the Holy Spirit, Bach would have needed to find other means of reference if he were so inclined. That is why Bach's use of an obbligato flute to supplement the usual core of ripieno strings is interesting; as a "wind/breath" instrument, the flute functions most naturally as a trope for the idea of "spirit"—or, on the basis of John 3:8[57] and 20:22,[58] as a possible trope for the Holy Spirit.[59]

55. Parenthetically, then, the ideal makeup of the continuo for this aria must certainly be bassoon and organ, both of both of which produce their tone by wind.

56. See Chap. 2 n. 3.

57. "'The wind blows where it wishes and you hear the sound of it, but do not know where it comes from and where it is going; so is everyone who is born of the Spirit.'"

58. "He breathed on them and said to them, 'Receive the Holy Spirit.'"

59. Olearius's biblical commentary, which Bach owned, notes that the word for "wind" in John 3:8 is *pneuma* and that it is also used of the Holy Spirit ("welches Wort vom Heiligen Geist . . . auch gebrauchet wird"). Olearius, *Biblische Erklärung* 5:618.

Finally, it is interesting that, independent of this linguistic association, Eric Chafe has concluded that in at least two vocal works of Bach's, Cantatas 12 and 21, an obbligato oboe likely serves as "an instrumental symbol of the soul," that is, a spiritual entity.[60]

It seems entirely plausible, then, that Bach likely considered wind instruments as a possible symbol of the idea of "spirit." But it is equally clear that this idea can encompass a range from the human soul to the Holy Spirit. In the case of Cantata 182, the significance seems to be to represent the divine nature of Christ as God, who is Spirit,[61] while the violin would implicitly correspond to his human nature. And even though the mere fact of being a nonwind instrument would qualify the violin to complete the imagery of the dual nature of Christ, there are indeed associations of the violin with the human within the sacred music of Bach, though these are admittedly less concrete than the associations of wind instruments with spirit. For example, in the St. Matthew Passion, the two arias with violin obbligato are the beloved "Erbarme dich" and the fiery "Gebt mir meinen Jesum wieder," each a particularly strong expression of emotion whose humanity is amplified through the use of the first person. In the Mass in B Minor, the one aria featuring an obbligato violin is the "Laudamus te,"[62] which explicitly expresses the (human) confessors' adoration of God, making similar use of the first person. The piccolo violin seems to have similar associations with humanity, receiving its only solo among the surviving Bach cantatas in a single movement of "Wachet Auf," BWV 140, where it provides a florid obbligato line above a poignant duet between soprano and bass, representing the soul and Christ. The soprano's longing question, "Wenn kömmst du, mein Heil?" ("When will you come, my Lord?") is answered only by "Ich komme, dein Teil" ("I am coming, as your portion"), poignantly and elegantly expressing the longing of broken humanity in a world where we see only "in a mirror dimly"[63] and rest solely in the hope of God's faithfulness.

Interestingly, the piccolo violin has an association that is still earthier. In his autobiographical sketch published by Mattheson in 1740, Telemann associates the piccolo violin with dance music played in the rural taverns of Poland.[64] That Bach had this association in mind while composing the first Brandenburg concerto seems likely since the Poloinesse of the fourth

60. Chafe, *Tears into Wine*, 514.

61. John 4:24; see also 2 Cor 3:17.

62. The obbligato instrument of the "Benedictus" is unspecified, but stylistic considerations make it seem more likely intended for flute than violin. See Stauffer, *Bach, The Mass in B Minor*, 161.

63. 1 Cor 13:12.

64. Telemann, "Telemann," 360.

movement—one of only three Polish dances in the surviving works of Bach[65]—not only omits a part for the piccolo violin but contains explicit instructions that the piccolo violin should remain silent and not double the first violins ("Violino piccolo tacet"), even while gratuitously inserting the word "Tutti" as an afterthought before the designation "Violini è Viole," as the penmanship of the autograph indicates. In other words, it is so deeply ironic that one of the only three explicitly Polish dances to be found within Bach's entire oeuvre should occur in the one concerto that featues a piccolo violin, and that the piccolo violin should be explicitly and emphatically excluded from this section, that it seems Bach must have intended this irony.[66] But of course, that would mean Bach would have had to be familiar with the association of the piccolo violin with Polish dance music.

In any case, the means by which Bach represents the dual-natured Christ in Cantatas 68, 96, and 182 seem to be grounded in associations evident elsewhere in Bach's sacred output. This raises the question of whether strikingly similar devices in the theme of the Adagio of the first Brandenburg concerto could indicate that Bach intended it to have a dimension of Christological symbolism, especially because the three-measure "entombment" of this potentially Christological theme is accompanied by an inversion of the hierarchies of the entire ensemble, just as the death of Christ is the focal point of the upside-down world of the gospel.

Supporting the viability of such a reading is the fact that the relationship between oboe 1 and piccolo violin, the two voices plausibly representing the dual-natured Christ, is such that it creates further parallels with Christian theology. The "spiritual" oboe is heard at the very beginning of the movement, preceding the "earthly" piccolo violin by four measures. This is by far the longest period in the entire movement between a subject and its imitation, which heightens awareness of the oboe's precedence. Once the piccolo violin enters, however, the two "natures" fully intermingle in the same thematic material; the oboe leads the next imitative statement of the theme, and the piccolo violin leads the third and final one. At no point, however, do the two "natures" become synonymous by doubling each other and losing their distinct timbral identity. Similarly, according to historic Christian theology, Christ existed from the beginning as God,[67] who

65. The other two are from the B-minor Ouverture, BWV 1067, and the sixth "French" suite in E major, BWV 817.

66. Marissen connects this exclusion with subversion of the typical role of Konzertmeister-soloist throughout the concerto, in keeping with representations of hierarchical inversion found throughout the Brandenburg concertos. Marissen, *The Social and Religious Designs*, 34–35.

67. John 1:1–2.

is Spirit,[68] prior to assuming flesh. In his incarnation, however, Jesus has become fully man in addition to being fully God, and his two natures are distinct yet equal expressions of the same Person.[69]

If this Christological interpretation of the movement's theme is accurate, then it is notable that the three-measure "entombment" of this theme at the end of each eleven-measure section accords independently with the deeper structural imagery suggesting the "cutting off" of Christ. It would then seem that the movement is decidedly passion-themed. In this case, it is interesting to consider some possible implications of the six-measure coda that concludes the movement.

Immediately following the conclusion of the last of the three eleven-measure sections, there is a virtuosic but agonized "cry" from the first oboe in the form of a short cadenza over a dissonant diminished-7 chord. To the extent that this movement is experienced as a representation of the passion of Christ, this final "cry" from the oboe (a wind instrument) could represent the cry with which Jesus gives up his spirit (again, with overtones of "wind"),[70] as this cry can be understood as not only agonized but also virtuosic, representing the accomplishment of his triumph over sin, death, and the powers of evil in the most paradoxical way imaginable.[71] Rambach describes that on the cross "the Prince of Life would attack death in its own camp, defeat it, triumph over it and swallow it up in victory,"[72] emphasizing that God's sovereignty not merely negates the devices of evil but turns them against themselves to serve His purposes,[73] just as the horror of the cross becomes the very means of redemption that makes death incapable of anything but speeding the believer into the victory of Christ and glorified eternal life. As Rambach again writes, "For those that believe on him and suffer for his name, he has transformed gallows, wheel, and raven stone [i.e., devices of execution] into a bed of honor and a ladder on which one ascends to the throne of glory."[74]

68. See this appendix, n. 61.

69. The Athanasian Creed states, "[He is] altogether one, not by the mixing of his natures, but as a unified person" ("Unus omnino, non confusione substantiae, sed unitate personae").

70. See Matt 27:50; Mark 15:37; Luke 23:46; John 19:30.

71. See John 19:30; 1 Cor 15:20–23, 56–57; Col 2:15.

72. *BLC*, 947–48. See 1 Cor 15:54.

73. "Diese Probe soll denen, die an JEsum glauben, zur Versicherung dienen, daß ihnen alle Dinge zum Besten mitwircken müssen, und daß auch die Anschläge ihrer Feinde zur Beforderung des Rathes GOttes ausschlagen werden." *BLC*, 1000. See Gen 50:20; Rom 8:28; CB 2:560 (on v. 11).

74. "Er hat denen, die an ihn glauben und um seines Namens willen leiden, Galgen,

Interpreting the oboe's "cry" as the virtuosic victory cry of the crucified Christ would provide a sensible context for the striking and unusual cadence that immediately follows. At the downbeat of measure 36, the point where the cadence falls, only the bass completes the expected cadential gesture; all other voices suddenly fall silent. This measure begins a descending Phrygian tetrachord descent in the bass, which, interestingly, is countered by ascending motion in the upper voices, concluding on a bright A-major chord, at which point the *piano* indicated at the beginning of the Phrygian progression yields to *forte*. The most natural association would seem to be the hope and eventual breaking forth of resurrection light,[75] whose viability in the context of the following movement I return to shortly.

First, however, I must observe that the function of this "Phrygian codetta" that concludes the movement has a similar function to that which concludes the Grave of the A-minor solo violin sonata. In connection with the latter, I mentioned that Phrygian codettas often feel like an afterthought appended to the movement. This is not only because they are frequently unrelated motivically to the remainder of the movement but also because they tend to pull the harmony away from the tonal center of the movement and toward V. But the Phrygian codetta that concludes the Adagio of the first Brandenburg concerto is exceptional in both respects. We have already observed that the theme of the movement is built on the descending tetrachord in both treble and bass (see Ex. B.15), so the tetrachordal descent in the bass that concludes the Adagio actually rounds out the entire movement with motivic unification, as in the Grave of the A-minor violin sonata. More strikingly, the concluding Phrygian descent does not pull the movement away from its tonal root because, despite the harmony's functioning as if in D minor, the governing scale of the movement is best understood not as modern D minor but rather as transposed Phrygian (A—A),[76] which is most unusual in Bach's concerted writing. That is, far from pulling away from the movement's tonal center, the final Phrygian cadence is actually what brings tonal (or, more precisely, modal) unity to the entire structure.

From a listener's perspective, however, because the tetrachord that begins the movement is in the treble rather than the bass, it is easy for the

Rad und Raben-Stein in ein Bette der Ehren und in eine Leiter verwandelt, auf welcher man auf den Thron der Herrlichkeit steiget." *BLC*, 951. See Rom 8:38–39; 1 Cor 15:54–55; Phil 1:21; Rev 3:21.

75. See, for instance, the aria "Auf, Gläubige" from Cantata 134 for Easter Tuesday, which speaks of the "glorious, renewed light" ("herrlich verneuetes Licht") of Jesus' resurrection.

76. Note that the harmony with which the movement begins is A major, not D minor.

connection with the final codetta to go undetected at first; and because of the modern harmonic language suggesting the functional tonality of D minor (especially in view of the cadence on D minor at m. 36), it is easy to feel the movement to be in D minor rather than A-Phrygian. Therefore my experience as a listener has been to hear the Phrygian codetta of the Adagio in the familiar way—as if it were an essentially unrelated appendix pulling the movement away from tonal unity—and then to realize with some surprise that the movement has been structured from the beginning such that the Phrygian descent to A major is necessary in order to bring unity, resolution, and coherence to the whole, both modally and motivically. And I must wonder if this surprise might not indeed have been on Bach's mind to some degree, since to whatever extent the lamenting tetrachord of the final cadence can be connected with the passion associations pervading the movement, such a surprise is in fact none other than that inherent within the Christ story. Just as the final lamenting tetrachord initially feels like an ultimate digression from the tonal design of the movement, so the passion of Christ seems like a catastrophic end to the Messianic narrative; and indeed the gospels uniformly indicate that the disciples initially thought it was so.[77] But in hindsight it is understood, according to the New Testament, that the death of Christ is neither a catastrophe nor an afterthought that merely makes the best of a bad situation—God's sovereignty is thwarted neither in Eden nor on the cross—but rather that the death of Christ for the redemption of the world was God's sovereign design planned and foretold from the beginning.[78] It might perhaps not be accidental, then, that the coda of the Adagio—from the oboe's "cry" to the final A-major chord—is a "perfect" six measures.

I conclude by considering the second movement of the first Brandenburg concerto in the context of the entire concerto. Marissen has observed that the first movement of the concerto evinces a curious progression in its treatment of the horns.[79] At the beginning of the movement, they are entirely set apart from the rest of the ensemble; their pitches do not always coincide with the harmonies created by the other instruments, and their triplet rhythms clash with the running sixteenth notes that form the rhythmic basis of the remainder of the ensemble. Moreover, their opening motif is a quotation from a contemporary Saxon hunting call,[80] reinforcing the

77. See Mark 14:50, John 20:19, John 21:3 (in light of Matt 4:20, Mark 1:18), etc.

78. Acts 2:23. See Chap. 6 n. 137.

79. Marissen, *The Social and Religious Designs*, 22–35. The remainder of the paragraph is a summary of Marissen's observations.

80. Fitzpatrick, *The Horn and Horn-Playing*, 20.

horns' already-strong association with the privileged aristocracy (to whom the expensive luxuries of the hunt exclusively belonged) and further setting them apart from the lower social statuses evoked by the other instruments in the ensemble.[81] As the movement progresses, however, the horns gradually become assimilated into the texture of the rest of the ensemble, even going so far as to engage in chains of suspensions and resolutions that are derived from high Renaissance counterpoint but are most atypical of horn writing (mm. 36–37, 65–66). In short, the first movement of the concerto represents a progression by which the symbol of aristocracy moves from being set apart from the rest of the ensemble to intermingling with them fully, even forsaking its own accustomed idiom in the process.

Marissen views this gesture as symbolic but interprets it socially, referring it to the Lutheran belief that the hierarchies of this world are without ultimate significance.[82] But I wonder whether a still closer correspondence to the musical progression Marissen describes might be found in Christianity's *reason* for believing that the hierarchies of this world are without ultimate significance, namely, that the patterns of this world have been turned upside down when its Lord and maker descended from the glories of heaven to mingle among lowly humanity, forsaking the status he was accustomed to in order to assume the form of man.[83] Indeed, Marissen interprets the use of the horn in the "Quoniam tu solus Sanctus" from the Mass in B Minor as representing "God's entry into the world as a human being in the form of Christ the king,"[84] even though the text of the "Quoniam" explicitly speaks only of Christ's lordship, not his incarnation.[85] If the first movement of the first Brandenburg concerto is read similarly in terms of the incarnation of Christ, the second movement with its proposed allusions to the passion of Christ would follow naturally as the next episode of the story.

The third movement contains imagery that is essentially the inverse of that of the first movement. The piccolo violin, the most diminutive member of the ensemble, having been nearly inconspicuous in the first movement

81. See Marissen, *The Social and Religious Designs*, 26.

82. Ibid., 115.

83. Without doubt, the presence of a contemporary hunting call lends credence to a social interpretation. But if reading the social overtones as having deeper allegorical significance were to yield a still closer correspondence to the total content of the concerto, it would be in keeping both with the allegorical orientation of musical thought in Bach's culture (see Chap. 1) and with the typological sensibilities he would have acquired from Christian theology.

84. Ibid., 23.

85. The full text of the movement is "Quoniam tu solus Sanctus, tu solus Dominus, tu solus Altissimus, Jesu Christe . . ." ("For you alone are the Holy One, you alone are Lord, you alone are Most High, Jesus Christ . . .").

and an equal partner with the first oboe in the second movement, becomes "exalted" to a position of dominance in the third movement in terms of both its prominence within the texture and the virtuosity of its passage-work, which is unmatched by any other instrument in this movement and contains a good deal of double, triple, and quadruple-stopping.

The progression of the first three movements, therefore, bears a striking resemblance to the Christ story as encapsulated in Philippians 2:5–9:

> "Christ Jesus . . . although He existed in the form of God, did not regard equality with God a thing to be grasped, but emptied Himself, taking the form of a bond-servant, *and* being made in the likeness of men. Being found in appearance as a man, He humbled Himself by becoming obedient to the point of death, even death on a cross. For this reason also, God highly exalted Him, and bestowed on Him the name which is above every name. . ."

The fourth and final movement is also compatible with this progression. Consisting of a Menuet alternating with three trios, it is a "perfect" seven-part chiastic structure (Fig. B.9).

Fig. B.9. Chiastic structure of BWV 1046/4

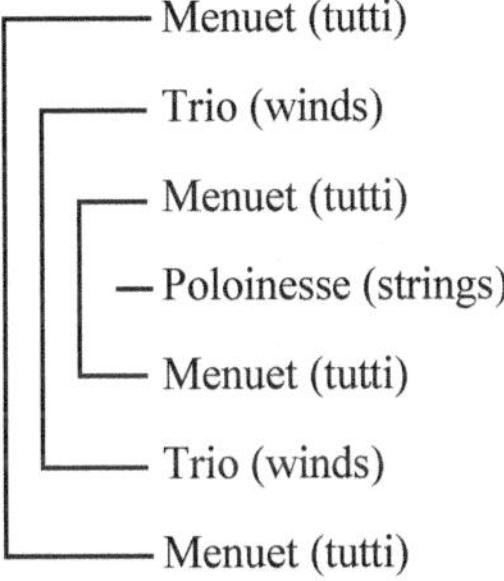

At the heart of this chiasm is the Poloinesse that exemplifies ironic inversion by explicitly excluding the piccolo violin, which not only silences the concertmaster-soloist while the rest of the strings play but also excludes the one instrument of the ensemble with particularly strong Polish associations from the only polonaise in Bach's surviving concerto output.[86] Coming on the heels of the first three movements, therefore, this final Menuet and

86. Marissen, *The Social and Religious Designs*, 32–34.

trios could serve as an elegant symbol of the upside-down kingdom[87] of the crucified, risen, and exalted Christ (*X*), which is aptly represented by the number 7—a symbol of perfection and rest—not only because of the divine perfection of Christ's kingdom[88] but also because the blessedness of heaven entails entering into the rest of Christ himself, whose redeeming work stands decisively finished; and therefore, writes the author of Hebrews, "there remains a Sabbath rest for the people of God. For the one who has entered His rest has himself also rested from his works, as God did from his."[89]

87. Matt 19:30; 20:16.

88. 1 Cor 13:10. On associations of the number 7 with perfection and completeness, see Chap. 2 n. 6. Werckmeister connects the number 7 not merely with completeness but with the depths of the wisdom of the "sevenfold" God (Rev 1:4; 5:6), whose mysteries remain hidden from us—recalling the language used in 1 John 3:2 in connection with the coming of the kingdom of God: "deßen Geheimniß sind uns noch verborgen/ Denn wer kan die Tieffe der Gottheit ergründen/ da er in seinem Gaben siebenfalt gennet wird/ wie insonderheit in Apocalypsi kan gelesen werden." Werckmeister, *Musicalische Paradoxal-Discourse*, 96.

89. Heb 4:9–10. See Chap. 3 nn. 69 and 70.

Bibliography

Agricola, Johann Friedrich, and Carl Philipp Emanuel Bach. "(. . .) der im Orgelspielen Weltberühmte HochEdle Herr Johann Sebastian Bach, Königlich-Pohlnischer und Churfürstlich Sächsischer Hofcompositeur, und Musikdirector in Leipzig." Obituary for J. S. Bach. *Musikalische Bibliothek* 4 (1754) 158–73.

Ahle, Johann Georg. *Musicalisches Frühlings-Gespräche*. Mühlhausen, 1695. Facsimile edition in Johann Georg Ahle, *Schriften zur Musik*. Edited by Markus Rathey. Hildesheim: Olms, 2007.

Althaus, Paul. *The Theology of Martin Luther*. Translated by Robert C. Schultz. Philadelphia: Fortress, 1966.

Arndt, Johann. *Der ganze Psalter Davids, des H. Königs und Propheten, in 462 Predigten außgelegt und erklärt*. . . . 3 vols. in 1. Franckfurt: Sunner & Börlin, 1701.

———. *Gecreutzigter und wieder auferstandener Christus, Das ist: Geistreiche und erbauliche Paßions- und Oster-Predigten*. Nördlingen: Mundbach, 1740.

———. *Wahres Christenthum*. Magdeburg: Francke, 1619.

Augustine. *The City of God against the Pagans*. Translated by R. W. Dyson. New York: Cambridge University Press, 1998.

Aulén, Gustaf. *Christus Victor: An Historical Study of the Three Main Types of the Idea of Atonement*. Translated by A. G. Hebert. 1931. Reprinted, Eugene, OR: Wipf & Stock, 2003.

Bach, Carl Philipp Emanuel. *Versuch über die wahre Art das Clavier zu Spielen*. Vol. 2. Berlin: Winter, 1762.

Bach-Dokumente. Supplement to *Johann Sebastian Bach: Neue Ausgabe Sämtliche Werke*. 7 vols. Kassel: Bärenreiter, 1963–2008.

Bacon, Francis. *The Advancement of Learning*. Edited by William Aldis Wright. New York: Macmillan, 1885.

Barnett, Gregory. *Bolognese Instrumental Music, 1660–1710: Spiritual Comfort, Courtly Delight, and Commercial Triumph*. Burlington, VT: Ashgate, 2008.

Bartel, Dietrich. *Musica Poetica: Musical-Rhetorical Figures in German Baroque Music*. Lincoln: University of Nebraska Press, 1997.

Ben-Horin, Michal. "The Secular and Its Dissonances in Modern Jewish Literature." In *Secularism in Question: Jews and Judaism in Modern Times*, edited by Ari Joskowicz and Ethan B. Katz, 115–41. Philadelphia: University of Pennsylvania Press, 2015.

Bernhard, Christoph. *Tractatus Compositionis Augmentatus; Ausführlicher Bericht vom Gebrauche der Con- und Dissonantien*. In *Die Kompositionslehre Heinrich Schützens in der Fassung seines Schülers Chr. Bernhard*. Joseph M. Müller-Blattau, ed. 2nd ed. Kassel, Bärenreiter, 1963.

Boethius, Anicius Torquatus Severinus. *De Institutione Musica*. In *De Institutione Arithmetica, Libri Duo; De Institutione Musica, Libri Quinque*. Edited by Gottfried Friedlein. Leipzig: Teubner, 1867.

Boyden, David. *The History of Violin Playing from Its Origins to 1761 and Its Relationship to the Violin and Violin Music*. New York: Oxford University Press, 2002.

Breig, Werner. "Bachs Violinkonzert d-Moll. Studien zu seiner Gestalt und seiner Entstehungsgeschichte." *Bach-Jahrbuch* 62 (January 1976) 7–34.

Bugenhagen, Johan. *Eine Christliche Predigt über der Leich und begrebnis des Ehrwirdigen D. Martini Luthers*. Wittemberg: Rhau, 1546.

Burkholder, Peter, Donald Jay Grout, and Claude V. Palisca. *A History of Western Music*. 9th ed. New York: Norton, 2014.

Burmeister, Joachim. *Hypomnematum musicae poeticae*. Rostock: Myliandri, 1599.

———. *Musical Poetics*. Translated, with introduction and notes by Benito V. Rivera. Music Theory Translation Series. New Haven: Yale University Press, 1993.

Burtius Nicolaus. *Musices opusculum*. Bologna: Ugo Ruggieri, 1487. Facsimile edition. Bibliotheca musica Bononiensis II/4. Bologna: Forni, 1969.

Buszin, Walter E. "Luther on Music." *Musical Quarterly* 32 (1946) 80–97.

Butt, John. "Bach's Metaphysics of Music." In *The Cambridge Companion to Bach*, edited by John Butt, 46–59. New York: Cambridge University Press, 1997.

Buttstett, Johann Heinrich. *Ut, Mi, Sol,/Re, Fa, La,/ Tota Musica et Harmonia Æterna, Oder Neu-eröffnetes, altes, wahres, eintziges, und ewiges Fundamentum Musices, entgegen gesetzt Dem neu-eröffneten Orchestre . . . .* Erfurt: Werthern, 1716.

Calov, Abraham, ed. *Die Heilige Bibel nach S. Herrn D. Martini Lutheri*. 6 vols. Wittenberg: Schrödtern, 1681–82.

Chafe, Eric. "Allegorical Music: The 'Symbolism' of Tonality in the Bach Canons." *Journal of Musicology* 3 (1984) 340–62.

———. *Analyzing Bach Cantatas*. New York: Oxford University Press, 2000.

———. *J. S. Bach's Johannine Theology: The St. John Passion and the Cantatas for Spring 1725*. New York: Oxford University Press, 2014.

———. *Tears into Wine: J. S. Bach's Cantata 21 in Its Musical and Theological Contexts*. New York: Oxford University Press, 2015.

———. *Tonal Allegory in the Vocal Music of J. S. Bach*. Berkeley: University of California Press, 1991.

Clement, Albert. *Der dritte Teil der Clavier-Übung von Johann Sebastian Bach. Musik—Text—Theologie*. Middelburg: AlmaRes, 1999.

Concordia Triglotta. St. Louis: Concordia, 1921.

Cox, Howard H. *The Calov Bible of J. S. Bach*. Studies in Musicology 92. Ann Arbor: UMI Research Press, 1985.

Cunningham, Andrew, and Ole Peter Grell. *The Four Horsemen of the Apocalypse: Religion, War, Famine and Death in Reformation Europe*. Cambridge: Cambridge University Press, 2000.

Cypess, Rebecca. *Curious and Modern Inventions: Instrumental Music as Discovery in Galileo's Italy*. Chicago: University of Chicago Press, 2016.

Dadelsen, Georg von. Preface to *J. S. Bach: Suiten, Sonaten, Capriccios und Variationen*. iv–v. Munich: Henle, 1975.

Dahlhaus, Carl. "Die Termini Dur und Moll." *Archiv für Musikwissenschaft* 12 (1955) 280–96.

Darmstadt, Gerhart. "Andante und Mystik: Zur Symbolik des Weges in der Barockmusik." *Symbolon, Jahrbuch für Symbolforschung* N.S. 12 (1995) 43–104.

Davidson, Lyle. "The Structure of Lassus' Motets a2 (1577)." *Sonus* 2/2 (1982) 71–90.

Dell'Antonio, Andrew. *Syntax, Form, and Genre in Sonatas and Canzonas 1621–1635*. Lucca: Libreria Musicale Italiana, 1997.

Dentler, Hans-Eberhard. *L'Arte della fuga di Johann Sebastian Bach: un'opera pitagorica e la sua realizzazione*. Milan: Skira, 2000.

Dieterich, Conrad. *Ulmische Orgel Predigt*. Ulm: Meder, 1624.

Dornenburg, John. "Andante: What's the Rush?" *Early Music America* 12/3 (2006) 56, 54.

Dreyfus, Laurence. *Bach and the Patterns of Invention*. Cambridge: Harvard University Press, 1998.

Dürr, Alfred. *Johann Sebastian Bach's St. John Passion: Genesis, Transmission, and Meaning*. Translated by Alfred Clayton. New York: Oxford University Press, 2002.

Eichberg, Hartwig. "Unechtes unter Johann Sebastian Bachs Klavierwerken." *Bach-Jahrbuch* 61 (1975) 7–49.

Elferen, Isabella van. *Mystical Love in the German Baroque: Theology, Poetry, Music*. Contextual Bach Studies 2. Lanham, MD: Scarecrow, 2009.

Fanselau, Clemens. *Mehrstimmigkeit in J. S. Bachs Werken für Melodieinstrument ohne Begleitung*. Berliner Musik Studien 22. Sinzig: Studio, 2000.

Fitzpatrick, Horace. *The Horn and Horn-Playing and the Austro-Bohemian Tradition from 1630–1830*. New York: Oxford University Press, 1970.

Forkel, Johann Nikolaus. *Ueber Johann Sebastian Bachs Leben, Kunst und Kunstwerke*. Leipzig: Hoffmeister & Kühnel, 1802.

Franconis. *Ars cantus mensurabilis*. Edited by Edmonde de Coussemaker and Friedrich Gennrich. Musikwissenschaftliche Studien-Bibliothek 15/16. Darmstadt: Gennrich, 1957.

Gardiner, John Eliot. *Bach: Music in the Castle of Heaven*. New York: Knopf, 2014.

Geistliche Lieder auffs new gebessert zu Wittemberg. Wittenberg: Klug, 1535. Facs. ed. by Konrad Ameln. Kassel: Bärenreiter, 1954.

Glarean, Heinrich. *Dodecachordon*. Basel: Petri, 1547.

Goehr, Lydia. *The Imaginary Museum of Musical Works: An Essay in the Philosophy of Music*. Oxford: Clarendon, 1992.

Gritsch, Eric W. *Martin Luther's Anti-Semitism: Against His Better Judgment*. Grand Rapids: Eerdmans, 2012.

Guidonis Monachi Aretini (Guido d'Arezzo). *Micrologus ad praestantiores codices mss. exactus*. Rome: Desclée, Lefebvre, 1904.

Heinichen, Johann David. *Neu erfundene und gründliche Anweisung . . . des General-Basses*. Hamburg: Schiller, 1711.

Holborn, Hans L. "Bach and Pietism: The Relationship of the Church Music of Johann Sebastian Bach to Eighteenth-Century Lutheran Orthodoxy and Pietism with Special Reference to the *Saint Matthew Passion*." DMin diss., School of Theology at Claremont, 1976.

Hosler, Bellamy. *Changing Aesthetic Views of Instrumental Music in 18th-Century Germany*. UMI Research Press, 1981.

Ikegami, Ken'ichiro. "Siciliano in der Instrumentalmusik Joseph Haydns und seiner Zeitgenossen." PhD diss., Julius-Maximilians-Universität Würzburg, 2014.

Jambe de Fer, Philibert. *L'Epitome musical*. Lyon, 1556. Facs. ed. by François Lesure. *Annales musicologiques 6*. Neuilly-sur-Seine: Société de musique d'autrefois, 1964.

Johann Sebastian Bach: Neue Ausgabe Sämtliche Werke. 119 vols. Kassel: Bärenreiter, 1954–2007.

Johann Sebastian Bach: Neue Ausgabe Sämtliche Werke. Kritische Berichte. 103 vols. Kassel: Bärenreiter, 1955–2008.

Jordan, Myles. "Realizations: A New Look at Old Music." 2008. http://www.mylesjordancello.com/linernotes.pdf.

Kimbell, John. *The Atonement in Lukan Theology*. Newcastle: Cambridge Scholars, 2014.

Kircher, Athanasius. *Musurgia Universalis*. Rome: Corbelletti, 1650.

Kołakowski, Leszek. *Religion: If There Is No God . . . : On God, the Devil, Sin and Other Worries of the So-Called Philosophy of Religion*. South Bend, IN: St. Augustine's, 2001.

Kuhnau, Johann. Foreword to *Musicalische Vorstellung einiger biblischer Historien*. Leipzig: Tietzen, 1700 and 1710.

Leahy, Anne. "Bach's Prelude, Fugue and Allegro for Lute (BWV 998): A Trinitarian Statement of Faith?" *Journal of the Society for Musicology in Ireland* 1 (2005) 33–51.

Leaver, Robin A. "Bach and Pietism: Similarities Today." *Concordia Theological Quarterly* 55 (1991) 5–22.

———. *Bachs theologische Bibliothek: eine kritische Bibliographie*. Neuhausen-Stuttgart: Hänssler, 1983.

———. *J. S. Bach and Scripture: Glosses from the Calov Bible Commentary*. St. Louis: Concordia, 1985.

———. *Luther's Liturgical Music*. Grand Rapids: Eerdmans, 2007.

Leavis, Ralph. "Zur Frage der Authentizität von Bachs Violinkonzert d-Moll." *Bach-Jahrbuch* 65 (1979) 19–28.

Ledbetter, David. *Bach's Well-Tempered Clavier: The 48 Preludes and Fugues*. New Haven: Yale University Press, 2002.

———. *Unaccompanied Bach: Performing the Solo Works*. New Haven: Yale University Press, 2007.

Lester, Joel. *Bach's Works for Solo Violin: Style, Structure, Performance*. New York: Oxford University Press, 1999.

———. *Between Modes and Keys: German Theory 1592–1802*. Stuyvesant, NY: Pendragon, 1989.

———. "J. S. Bach Teaches Us How to Compose: Four Pattern Preludes of the 'Well-Tempered Clavier.'" *College Music Symposium* 38 (1998) 33–46.

Lindley, Mark, and Ibo Ortgies. "Bach-style Keyboard Tuning." *Early Music* 34 (2006) 613–23.

Lippius, Johannes. *Synopsis musicae novae*. Strasburg: Kieffer, 1612.

Little, Meredith, and Natalie Jenne. *Dance and the Music of J. S. Bach*. Exp. ed. Indianapolis: Indiana University Press, 2009.

Luther, Martin. *D. Martin Luthers Werke: Kritische Gesamtausgabe*. 73 vols. Weimar: Böhlau, 1883–2009.

———. *D. Martin Luthers Werke: Kritische Gesamtausgabe*. Briefwechsel. 18 vols. Weimar: Böhlau, 1930–1985.

———. *D. Martin Luthers Werke: Kritische Gesamtausgabe*. Tischreden. 6 vols. Weimar: Böhlau, 1912–1921.

Marissen, Michael. *The Social and Religious Designs of J. S. Bach's Brandenburg Concertos*. Princeton: Princeton University Press, 1995.

———. "The Theological Character of J. S. Bach's *Musical Offering*." In *Bach Studies* 2, edited by Daniel R. Melamed, 85–106. New York: Cambridge University Press, 1995.

Markham, Michael. "The New Mythologies: Deep Bach, Saint Mahler, and the Death Chaconne." *Los Angeles Review of Books*, Oct. 26, 2013. https://lareviewofbooks.org/essay/the-new-mythologies-deep-bach-saint-mahler-and-the-death-chaconne.

Matthäi, Conrad. *Kurtzer, doch ausführlicher Bericht von den Modis Musicis*. Königsberg: Matthäi, 1652.

Mattheson, Johann. *Das Beschützte Orchestre* . . . . Hamburg: Schiller, 1717.

———. *Das Neu-Eröffnete Orchestre* . . . . Hamburg: Schiller, 1713.

———. *Der Musicalische Patriot*. Hamburg, 1728.

———. *Der Vollkommene Capellmeister*. Hamburg: Herold, 1739.

———. *Grosse General-Baß-Schule*. Hamburg: Kißner, 1731.

———. *Kern Melodischer Wissenschaft*. Hamburg: Herold, 1737.

Mizler, Lorenz Christoph. *Neu eröffnete musikalische Bibliothek*. 4 vols. Leipzig: 1736–1754.

Monelle, Raymond. *The Musical Topic: Hunt, Military and Pastoral*. Musical Meaning and Interpretation. Bloomington: Indiana University Press, 2006.

Montéclair, Michel Pignolet de. *Principes de musique*. Paris, 1736.

Nelson's Dictionary of Christianity. Edited by George Thomas Kurian. Nashville: Nelson, 2005.

Niedt, Friedrich Erhard. *Musicalische Handleitung*. Hamburg: Schiller, 1710.

North, Roger. "Of Composition in Generall." In *Roger North on Music; Being a Selection from His Essays Written during the Years c. 1695–1728*, edited by John Whitridge Wilson, 107–31. London: Novello, 1959.

Olearius, Johann. *Biblische Erklärung*. 5 vols. Leipzig, 1678–1681.

Opitz, Martin. *Buch von der Deutschen Poeterey*. Brieg, 1624.

Ott, Hans. *Secundus tomus novi operis musici*. Nürnberg: Formschneyder, 1538. Facsimile edition. Faksimile Heilbronner Musikschatz 9. Stuttgart: Cornetto, 1996.

Pelikan, Jaroslav. *Bach among the Theologians*. 1986. Reprinted, Eugene, OR: Wipf & Stock, 2003.

Pfeiffer, August. *Der wohlbewährte Evangelische Aug-Apfel, oder Schrifftmässige Erklärung aller Articul der Augspurgischen Confession, als des Evangelischen Glaubens-Bekäntnüsses* . . . Leipzig, 1685.

Poos, Heinrich. "J. S. Bachs Chaconne für Violine solo aus der Partita d-Moll, BWV 1004. Ein hermeneutischer Versuch." *Jahrbuch des Staatlichen Instituts für Musikforschung Preußischer Kulturbesitz* (1993) 151–203.

Quantz, Johann Joachim. *Versuch einer Anweisung, die Flöte traversiere zu spielen*. Berlin: Voss, 1752.

Rambach, Johann Jacob. *Betrachtung über das ganze Leiden Christi*. Jena: Hartung, 1730.

Rampe, Siegbert. "Virtuoses, Pädagogisches, Publiziertes: Die Klaviermusik. Allgemeines zur Klaviermusik; Suiten und Klavierübung." In *Bach-Handbuch*, edited by Konrad Küster, 715–87. Kassel: Bärenreiter, 1999.

Randwijck, Rutger J. C. van. "Music in Context: Four Case Studies." PhD diss., Universiteit Utrecht, 2008.

Riederer, Johann Friedrich. *Gründliche Untersuchung der Zahl Sieben*. Franckfurth: Tauber, 1719.

Rosand, Ellen. "The Descending Tetrachord: An Emblem of Lament." *Musical Quarterly* 65 (1979) 346–59.

Ruf, Wolfgang. "Polyphonie in Bachs Sonaten für Violine solo." In *Das Wohltemperierte Klavier I. Tradition, Entstehung, Funktion, Analyse*, edited by Siegbert Rampe, 219–33. Musikwissenschaftliche Studien 38. Munich: Katzbichler, 2002.

Sachs, Klaus-Jürgen. "Aspekte der numerischen und tonartlichen Disposition instrumentalmusikalischer Zyklen des ausgehenden 17. und beginnenden 18. Jahrhunderts." *Archiv für Musikwissenschaft* 41 (1984) 237–56.

Sackmann, Dominik. "Warum komponierte Bach die Sonaten und Partiten für Violine solo BWV 1001–1006?" Paper, Projekt 2005: Johann Sebastian Bach, Sonaten und Partiten für Violine solo from Theater Winterthur, Wintherthur, May 27, 2005. http://www.theaterforum.ch/uploads/media/Vortrag_Dominik_Sackmann.pdf

Schiltz, Katelijne. *Music and Riddle Culture in the Renaissance*. New York: Cambridge University Press, 2015.

Schlagel, Stephanie. "The *Liber selectarum cantionum* and the 'German Josquin Renaissance.'" *The Journal of Musicology* 19 (2002) 564–615.

Schröder, Jaap. *Bach's Solo Violin Works*. New Haven: Yale University Press, 2007.

Schuldiges Lob Gottes, Oder: Geistreiches Gesang-Buch . . . . Weimar: Mumbach, 1713.

Schulenberg, David. *The Keyboard Music of J. S. Bach*. 2nd ed. New York: Routledge, 2007.

Seiffert, Max. "Die Chorbibliothek der St. Michaelisschule in Lüneburg zu Seb. Bach's Zeit." *Sammelbände der Internationalen Musikgesellschaft* 19/4 (July–Sept. 1908) 593–621.

Smend, Friedrich. "Luther und Bach." *Bach-Studien*, 153–75. Kassel: Bärenreiter, 1969.

Spitta, Philipp. *Johann Sebastian Bach*. 2 vols. 1873, 1880. Reprinted, Leipzig: Breitkopf & Härtel, 1921.

Stauffer, George B. *Bach, The Mass in B Minor: The Great Catholic Mass*. New Haven: Yale University Press, 2003.

Steblin, Rita. *A History of Key Characteristics in the Eighteenth and Early Nineteenth Centuries*. 2nd ed. Rochester: University of Rochester Press, 2002.

Stinson, Russell. *The Bach Manuscripts of Johann Peter Kellner and His Circle: A Case Study in Reception History*. Durham: Duke University Press, 1990.

———. "The Compositional History of Bach's *Orgelbüchlein* Reconsidered." In *Bach Perspectives*, vol. 1, edited by Russell Stinson, 43–78. Lincoln: University of Nebraska Press, 1995.

———. "J. P. Kellner's Copy of Bach's Sonatas and Partitas for Violin Solo." *Early Music* 13/2 (1985) 199–211.

Strunk, Oliver, ed. *Source Readings in Music History*. Rev. ed. Leo Treitler, general ed. New York: Norton, 1998.

Szabó, Zoltán. "Remaining Silhouettes of Lost Bach Manuscripts? Re-evaluating J. P. Kellner's Copy of J. S. Bach's Solo String Compositions." *Understanding Bach* 10 (2015) 71–83.

Tatlow, Ruth. *Bach and the Riddle of the Number Alphabet*. New York: Cambridge University Press, 1991.

———. *Bach's Numbers: Compositional Proportion and Significance*. New York: Cambridge University Press, 2015.

———. "Bach's Parallel Proportions and the Qualities of an Authentic Bachian Collection." *Dortmunder Bach-Forschungen* 8: *Bach oder nicht Bach?* edited by Reinmar Emans and Martin Geck, 135–55. Dortmund: Klangfarben, 2009.

———. "Collections, Bars and Numbers: Analytical Coincidence or Bach's Design?" *Understanding Bach* 2 (2007) 37–58.

———. "The Use and Abuse of Fibonacci Numbers and the Golden Section in Musicology Today." *Understanding Bach* 1 (2006) 69–86.

Telemann, Georg Philipp. "Telemann." In *Grundlage einer Ehren-Pforte*, compiled and edited by Johann Mattheson, 354–69. Hamburg, 1740.

Teutsch Kirche ampt: mit lobgsengen, vn götlichen psalmen . . . . Straßburg: Köpphel, 1525.

Thoene, Helga. *Johann Sebastian Bach: Ciaccona, Tanz oder Tombeau?* Oschersleben: Ziethen, 2003.

———. *Johann Sebastian Bach: Sonata A-Moll, Eine wortlose Passion*. Oschersleben: Ziethen, 2005.

———. *Johann Sebastian Bach: Sonata C-Dur, Lob sey Gott dem Heiligen Geist*. Oschersleben: Ziethen, 2008.

Walther, Johann Gottfried. *Musicalisches Lexicon*. Leipzig: Deer, 1732.

Werckmeister, Andreas. *Musicae Mathematicae Hodegus Curiosus*. Leipzig: Calvisius, 1686.

———. *Musicalische Paradoxal-Discourse*. Quedlingburg: Calvisius, 1707.

Wiesend, Reinhard. "Siciliana: Literarische und musikalische Traditionen." Habilitation diss., Julius-Maximilians-Universität Würzburg, 1986.

Williams, Peter F. "J. S. Bach—Orgelsachverständiger unter dem Einfluss Andreas Werckmeisters?" *Bach-Jahrbuch* 68 (1982) 131–42.

———. "Noch einmal: J. S. Bach—Orgelsachverständiger unter dem Einfluss Andreas Werckmeisters?" *Bach-Jahrbuch* 72 (1986) 123–25.

———. *The Organ Music of J. S. Bach*. 2nd ed. New York: Cambridge University Press, 2003.

Wingren, Gustaf. *Luther on Vocation*. Translated by Carl C. Rasmussen. 1957. Reprinted, Eugene, OR: Wipf & Stock, 2004.

Wolff, Christoph. "Johann Adam Reinken and Johann Sebastian Bach: On the Context of Bach's Early Works." In *J. S. Bach as Organist: His Instruments, Music, and Performance Practices*, edited by George Stauffer and Ernest May, 57–80. Bloomington: Indiana University Press, 1986.

———. *Johann Sebastian Bach: The Learned Musician*. New York: Norton, 2000.

———. "Sicilianos and Organ Recitals: Observations on J. S. Bach's Concertos." In *J. S. Bach's Concerted Instrumental Music, The Concerto*. Bach Perspectives 7, edited by Gregory Butler, 97–114. Champaign: University of Illinois Press, 2008.

Wolff, Christoph, Arthur Mendel, and Hans T. David, eds. *The New Bach Reader: A Life of Johann Sebastian Bach in Letters and Documents*. New York: Norton, 1998.

Wollny, Peter. "Aufzeichnungen zur Generalbaßlehre." *Generalbaß- und Satzlehre, Skizzen, Entwürfe*, edited by Peter Wollny, 1–38. Supplement to *Johann Sebastian Bach: Neue Ausgabe Sämtliche Werke*. Kassel: Bärenreiter, 2011. Translation by Thomas Braatz accessible at http://www.bach-cantatas.com/Articles/GBLehre.pdf.

Wood, A. Skevington. *Captive to the Word. Martin Luther: Doctor of Sacred Scripture.* Toronto: Paternoster, 1969.

Yearsley, David. *Bach and the Meanings of Counterpoint.* New York: Cambridge University Press, 1997.

Zarlino, Gioseffo. *Le Istitutioni Harmoniche.* Venice, 1558.

Zedler, Johann Heinrich. *Großes Vollständiges Universal Lexicon aller Wissenschaften und Künste.* 64 vols. Leipzig, 1731–1754.

Zohn, Steven. *Music for a Mixed Taste: Style, Genre, and Meaning in Telemann's Instrumental Works.* New York: Oxford University Press, 2008.

Index of Bach's Works

Cantatas:

Chorale harmonizations:

Masses, Passions, and Oratorios:

Organ music:

Clavier music:

1. On the instrumentation of BWV 588, cf. Williams, *The Organ Music of J. S. Bach*, 192.

Chamber music:

Orchestral music:

Canons and counterpoint studies:

Subject Index

CPSIA information can be obtained
at www.ICGtesting.com
Printed in the USA
LVHW081412020119
602325LV00025BA/941/P

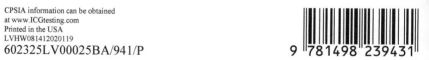

9 781498 239431